Samuel Johnson and the Life of Writing

By the same author

Theory of Prosody in Eighteenth-Century England
Poetic Meter and Poetic Form
The Rhetorical World of Augustan Humanism:
Ethics and Imagery from Swift to Burke
The Great War and Modern Memory
Abroad: British Literary Traveling Between
the Wars
The Boy Scout Handbook and Other Observations
Class: A Guide through the American Status System

EDITOR
English Augustan Poetry
The Ordeal of Alfred M. Hale
Siegfried Sassoon's Long Journey

CO-EDITOR
Eighteenth-Century English Literature

Paul Fussell

Samuel Johnson
and the Life of Writing

W · W · NORTON & COMPANY
New York · London

Published simultaneously in Canada by
Penguin Books Canada Ltd.,
2801 John Street, Markham, Ontario L3R 1B4

First published as a Norton paperback 1986

Library of Congress Catalog Card Number: 76-142087

ISBN 0-393-30258-X

1 2 3 4 5 6 7 8 9 0

To

NORTHROP FRYE

and the memory of

R. P. BLACKMUR

Contents

Preface

A publishing house, we are told, recently received the following postcard from a reader of its *Opera Guide*:

Gentlemen:

The book *Opera Guide* I have received even two copies. I do NOT like it. I did not know it is a translation. Otherwise I would have bought the unspoiled German original.

Who is this mysterious DR. JOHNSON whose dictum you put right in the first line of the Introduction? Dr. Johnson is my dentist and he never had anything to do with that. There is no Literature Guide to which I might refer. HOW FIND OUT WHO THAT FAMOUS DR. JOHNSON IS?[1]

---

1. The notes are on pages 279–284.

Although I have not written exactly a "Literature Guide," I have tried to deal with the question WHO THAT FAMOUS DR. JOHNSON IS.

Not everyone is as innocent as this engaging complainant. Most people who read know something about Johnson, enough at least to summon up images of him asseverating "No, Sir," knocking back endless cups of tea, rambling over the Hebrides, puffing out his breath like a whale, repressing Boswell, standing bareheaded in Uttoxeter Market, and having a frisk with Beauclerk and Langton. And now, thanks to the Johnsonians of Yale, Columbia, Oxford, and Lichfield, our knowledge of the man and his social environment has increased more than anyone fifty years ago could have imagined. But despite prodigies of research and documentation, an interest in Johnson that could be called literary has been wanting. One suspects that for every hundred persons familiar with the classic Johnson anecdotes there is perhaps only one who has actually read the *Rambler* or the *Idler* or even the *Lives of the Poets*. And if the writings are still little read for their own sake, they are almost as little written about as attractive objects of criticism.

Yale's new edition of the writings, the first since the early nineteenth century, is an occasion to perceive that for all his value as conversational goad and wit and for all his attractiveness as a moral and religious hero, Johnson's identity remains stubbornly that of a writer. In some of the vast anecdotal material that has accreted around him we hear of a Mrs. Cotterell who once begged him to introduce her to a famous writer. "Dearest Madam," he said, "you had better let it alone; the best part of every author is in general to be found in his book." Although I have tried to recognize the claims on our attention of his perpetually interesting life story, it is largely to Johnson's book that I have gone, hoping to read there and in its artistic environment home truths literary as well as moral.

I have set myself two tasks. One is to examine Johnson's behavior as a writer and to consider especially his "manner of proceeding" (the phrase is Geoffrey Tillotson's),[2] his special way of covering the necessary pages with the necessary words. My other task has been to set forth some of the conceptions about writing that governed Johnson's achievement, conceptions that we must recover if we are to understand the quality of that achievement. At times these two tasks have drawn me in contrary directions, toward Johnsonian fact, on the one hand, and toward general literary theory, on the other. But anyone who deals with Johnson and his writings gets accustomed early to making contrary motions. I hope that mine will not initially discourage the reader anxious for unambiguous and wholly paraphrasable "views" but may finally persuade him that only through an open embrace of apparent contradictions can we experience the complexity and delight of either life or writing.

I have modernized quotations, reducing them to American norms of spelling, capitalization, and punctuation; but I have retained elisions in poetry (for example, *lab'ring*) for the sake of the original meter. A book quoting so many remarks by Johnson's friends and contemporaries will end up stumbling over its own footnotes if, for example, every one of Boswell's observations is solemnly ticketed and located in the *Life of Johnson*. To avoid tedium I have severely limited documentation and have used notes largely to acknowledge the work of modern interpreters. Readers who want to taste more of the writers I quote may sample some of the books in my list of sources at the end.

I have a debt to the Research Council of Rutgers University, and especially to its Associate Director C. F. Main. It was the Council that made this book possible by relieving me of the more debilitating academic duties during 1965–66 and 1969–70. Professor Main's loyal support of my projects over many years I can never adequately register, let alone acknowledge. Not all American universities constitute happy settings for humanistic research and speculation, and I am grateful for the rare opportunities which Rutgers has provided. I owe much to Professor Richard Poirier, whose kind encouragement of my ventures has always meant much to me. I have profited by talking about Johnson and about general critical matters with my students, especially William Vesterman, Alan Helms, Roderick Townley, Steven Rosen, and William McCarthy. I want to thank Professor Donald J. Greene not only for having written *The Politics of Samuel Johnson*—a book with which any modern interpretation of Johnson must begin—but also for letting me use the manuscript of his valuable "List of the Writings Attributed to Samuel Johnson." I am grateful to my colleague Daniel F. Howard, who has again helped with proofreading and much else. And how can I ever adequately acknowledge the encouragement of Betty, my wife?

I must also thank Professor Joseph Frank and the Committee of the Christian Gauss Seminars in Criticism, of Princeton University, for inviting me to present some of these materials as a Christian Gauss Seminar in 1967. The first part of my dedication acknowledges my recognition that most of what I have said about literature for many years derives from *Anatomy of Criticism*. The second part records my debt, personal as well as intellectual, to Profesor Frank's predecessor as Director of the Gauss Seminars and to the example he set there of what I should like to call creative skepticism.

Rutgers University,   P. F.
July, 1970

Samuel Johnson and the Life of Writing

Chronology of
The Major Writings of Samuel Johnson

Year	Age	
1738	29	*London: A Poem*
1744	35	*An Account of the Life of Mr. Richard Savage*
1747	38	*Prologue Spoken at the Opening of the Theater in Drury Lane*
1749	40	*The Vanity of Human Wishes* *Irene*
1750–52	41–43	*The Rambler*
1753–54	44–45	Contributions to *The Adventurer*
1755	46	*A Dictionary of the English Language*
1758–60	49–51	*The Idler*
1759	50	*The Prince of Abyssinia: A Tale (Rasselas)*
1765	56	Editor, *The Plays of William Shakespeare*
1775	66	*A Journey to the Western Islands of Scotland*
1779–81	70–72	*Prefaces, Biographical and Critical, to the Works of the English Poets*
1783	74	*On the Death of Dr. Robert Levet*

CHAPTER I

"A Life Radically Wretched"

One of the most attractive characters in folklore is the Male Cinderella, the ill-favored, destitute, unpromising boy like Moses, Jesus, Beowulf, or Lincoln, who astonishes the world by turning into a hero. Johnson's life story has always been hard to resist because it incarnates so tidily this familiar and always gratifying action. Indeed, his life—like Keats's or Byron's—is so interesting that for years it has been confused with his literary achievement, and has even become a substitute for his literary meaning. What makes his life so interesting is the unlikeliness of it all. He was an ugly, brilliant, neurotic boy from the English Midlands who somehow got through seventy-five years of pain and misery, becoming in the process one of the most sophisticated and versatile of English writers. Just before his death he looked back and saw his existence as "a life radically wretched." The Latin inscription on his monument, erected at St. Paul's by his friends, ends with a wish that can be translated, "May he receive among the blessed fit requital for his troubles." His troubles began from his first moment, on September 18, 1709.

"I was born almost dead," he reports, "and could not cry for some time." It was soon clear that something was seriously wrong with him: he was deaf in one ear, all but blind in one eye and nearsighted in the other, and spotted with the running sores of scrofula. A visitation of smallpox helped complete the damage. As he says, "I remember my aunt . . . told me . . . that she would not have picked such a poor creature up in the street." Recognizing from the first his remote chance of surviving infancy, his parents had him baptized the day he was born. And two and a half years later, hoping that some sort of magic might be efficacious against his scrofula, his mother took him on the difficult three-day journey to London to be "touched" by Queen Anne. Even as an adult he shared his mother's hopes: for the rest of his life he wore around his neck the gold amulet given him by the Queen on this occasion.

The theater of these early troubles was the small cathedral city of Lichfield, Staffordshire, fifteen miles north of Birmingham. In Johnson's day its population was about 3,000, and the damage left by the Civil Wars fifty years earlier had not yet been entirely repaired. His father was a genteel, debt-ridden, nervous bookseller and stationer who kept a shop in the market place. From him, Johnson said later, he inherited "a vile melancholy . . . which has made me mad all my life, at least not sober." Boswell thus depicts the relation between physical defect, pride, and violence in the boy Johnson:

One day, when the servant who used to be sent to school to conduct him home had not come in time, he set out by himself, though he was then so nearsighted that he was obliged to stoop down on his hands and knees to take a view of the kennel [i.e., the gutter] before he ventured to step over it. His schoolmistress, afraid that he might miss his way, or fall into the kennel, or be run over by a cart, followed him at some distance. He happened to turn about and perceive her.

Feeling her careful attention as an insult to his manliness, he ran back to her in a rage and beat her, as well as his strength would permit.

This "jealous independence of spirit and impetuosity of temper," says Boswell, "never forsook him," making him successively an erratic, willful student, a violently impatient reader, a rapid, impulsive writer, and, as a conversationalist, the terror and delight of London drawing rooms. As Boswell says again, "Everything about his character and manners was forcible and violent": whether eating, drinking, or lovemaking, reading, writing, or arguing, he found moderation all but impossible, and consequently tended to overvalue it as an ideal principle and to urge it often upon others. The key to his character is his impetuosity, impatience, and irrationality. But even to say that may be to go too far. For to try to interpret his behavior by recourse to any consistent pattern would be like dictating rules of conduct to an earthquake or a volcano. There is something seismic about his surprises.

His early education was supervised first by his mother, who inducted him into the principles and imagery of a simplified Anglican Christianity with heavy emphasis on hellfire, and then by one Dame Oliver, a local woman who ran both an infant school and a confectionery shop. It was she who, overseeing his perilous progress home from school, received his blows and kicks. When he was seven, he moved on to study English with a local shoemaker-teacher, Tom Browne, and six months later he entered Lichfield Grammar School, a distinguished institution famous especially for the number of jurists and writers among its graduates. Joseph Addison had once been a student there. "Grammar" meant largely Latin grammar and literature, and, in the higher grades, Greek. By the time Johnson entered, he was already locally renowned for precocity, and he had also already developed his characteristic way with literature—a violent oscillation between total boredom and idleness, on the one hand, and, on the other, a total engagement that left him exhausted and frightened. When the heat was on him, he could rummage under the skin of a book with uncanny concentration, and his memory of what he read was prodigious. As Boswell says, he had "a peculiar facility in seizing at once what was valuable in any book, without submitting to the labor of perusing it from beginning to end." And as James Clifford adds, "It might almost be said that the rapacity with which he dug into a book was only equalled by the speed with which he put it down."[1]

At Lichfield Grammar School, encouraged when necessary by the cane, he mastered Latin and Greek and learned to write Latin and English poems in a great variety of traditional forms. "Originality" was the last thing wanted in these exercises: what was aimed at was perfection in managing inherited subject matter within recognizable forms. He supplemented his school studies by pulling out and leafing through the books in his father's stock. But for all his early fondness for wild, improbable romances, he wasted little time on frivolous books. As he later told Boswell, he read "not voyages and travels, but all literature, Sir, all ancient writers, all manly." Adam Smith once accurately said of him, "Johnson knew more books than any man alive."

Such was the general respect for learning in eighteenth-century Lichfield that Johnson's boyish distinction brought him the genuine admiration of even his schoolfellows, whom he dominated shamelessly. Boswell reports that "in winter . . . he took a pleasure in being drawn upon the ice by a boy barefooted, who pulled him along by a garter fixed round him; no very easy operation, as his size was remarkably large." But those less well acquainted with his mind regarded him as a freak and called him "the great boy," as if he were some drooling natural fool, an impression which his oversized body, his squint, his scars and pock-marks, and his deafness did nothing to dispel. To one observer, he was "the huge, overgrown, misshapen, and probably dirty stripling." He had already acquired his lifetime habit of rocking to and fro while reading or concentrating, and while swaying he hummed, talked to himself, or made clucking noises with his tongue. Nor did he improve in amenity as he aged. When he was sixty-six, a woman meeting him for the first time described him as "more beastly in his dress and person than anything I ever beheld. He feeds nastily and ferociously, and eats quantities most unthankfully."[2]

As a young person he was thus hardly a prepossessing recruit to the ranks of polite literature. But actually, a career in literature was not in his mind at this stage: what he seems to have been drawn to as a youth was either schoolteaching or the law. He was to become a writer by default and by accident, prevented by poverty and ugliness from aspiring to any other life. He finally had to find a profession in which his shocking person could be concealed from his audience.

When he was sixteen he spent some months with his expansive, worldly cousin Cornelius Ford at Pedmore, near Stourbridge, seven miles west of Birmingham. Ford, later to become famous as the convivial parson of Hogarth's print *A Midnight Modern Conversation,* was a man of money, experience, and sophistication. In prolonged talks he managed to suggest to the boy some of the dimensions of the great world winking and glittering outside Lichfield and its environs. Johnson loved it, and almost before he realized how time was passing, the new term at Lichfield had begun, and he was not there. Ford tutored him in Classics, reminisced about the Great he had met—people like Pope and Lord Chesterfield—and introduced him to his neighbor, the elegant George, Lord Lyttelton. When Johnson finally tore himself away it was too late: the Lichfield Grammar School declined to take him back. Ford had him admitted to the Stourbridge School instead, where he proceeded to refine his Latin and Greek and to produce, as school exercises, some impressive poems—translations from Virgil, Horace, and Homer.

As these translations indicate, by the age of seventeen he had already developed one of his poetic signatures, a small thing but one which, like a fingerprint, gives a unique technical identity to his subsequent body of poetry. It is the conjunction in pentameter lines of a multisyllabic and often ostentatiously Latinate adjective with a monosyllabic and usually Anglo-Saxon noun. We first find it in his school exercise rendering Addison's Latin *Battle of the*

Pygmies and Cranes into English heroic couplets. The pygmy
troops, Johnson tells us, overturned the cranes' nests and smashed
the eggs in a frenzy of genocide:

> Whene'er the lab'ring bird with anxious care
> Had formed her nest and placed her burden there,
> Some furious soldier would approach, that bore
> Death in his look, and hands imbrued in gore,
> Who to the ground the shattered building flung
> And crushed the yet *unanimated young.*

This looks forward to the "animated eyes" of the *Epilogue to
Philips' The Distressed Mother*, written a little later; to the "dissipated wealth," "consecrated earth," "counterfeited tear," "undiscovered shore," "persecuting fate," and "Senatorian band" of
London, written twelve years later; to the "sympathetic friend" and
"salutary woe" of the *Drury Lane Prologue*, written twenty-one
years later; and to the "philosophic eye," "luxurious board," "universal charm," "everlasting debt," "military state," "solitary coast,"
and "supplicating voice" of *The Vanity of Human Wishes*, written
twenty-three years later. At the age of fifty-seven he does the same
thing in *The Ant* ("unremitted flight"), and at fifty-nine he is still
doing it in the *Prologue to Goldsmith's Good-natured Man* ("epi-
demic care").

Visible in this tiny dictional and metrical habit is one of Johnson's key psychological actions—the all but simultaneous embrace
of antithetical or distant properties. The same set of mind that
urges him to juxtapose the high-flown and the blunt, the Roman
and the local, encourages him to relish the juxtaposition of tragic
and comic in Shakespeare's "mingled drama," and, as we shall see,
to operate brilliantly as a critic with an instructively inconsistent
equipment.

And it is suggestive of the literary environment in which he is
operating that he develops this dictional technique so early and uses
it for a lifetime. In the eighteenth century a writer does not
"develop" the way we assume nineteenth- and twentieth-century

writers do. Joyce's *Dubliners* is not like *Finnegans Wake* in the way Johnson's earliest work is like his last. The pattern of the literary career conceivable in Johnson's time does not imply development and change—it implies intensification. One's work becomes better as one goes along; it does not become essentially different. The early and late works of Pope, Swift, and Fielding differ much less from each other than the early and late works of Shakespeare, to look in one direction, or Yeats, to look in another. As Clifford has perceived, "By the time [Johnson] was nineteen he could read Latin as easily as when he was an old man, and once he even went so far as to claim that at this age he knew almost as much as he ever did."[3] In "Notes on Camp," Susan Sontag acutely observes that the sense of "instant character"—as distinguished from the sense of the development of character—is "very eighteenth century."[4] So, we may add, is the sense of the instant literary career, whose meaning is similar at seventeen to what it is at seventy. The understanding of the literary career as a static thing arises in part from certain expectations of the audience and in part from the author's assumptions about man and literature and their relation to the accessible past, assumptions which we will be examining in Johnson.

After less than a year at Stourbridge School, Johnson returned to Lichfield, where he helped his father in the bookshop and continued his education on his own, now binding the books, now reading the heart out of them. He did much better at reading than at shopkeeping, and as he bumbled through day after ineffective day, his incapacity for a career in trade became all too clear. But what was to become of him? No one had any idea.

The problem was momentarily solved when he was nineteen: his mother received a small inheritance, and this, together with the promise of some money from a well-to-do young friend, made possible thirteen straitened months as a Commoner at Pembroke College, Oxford. There he continued reading Classics—primarily Greek—and dipped into law; he also spent lots of time playing cricket, sliding on the ice, pub-crawling, and arguing. Already he was rebelling against authority and contesting very aggressively the assertions of both teachers and fellow students. As he said later, "I was miserably poor, and I thought to fight my way by my literature and my wit; so I disregarded all power and all authority."

But while setting out to contest all authority, something happened which seriously complicated his life. Up until his time at Oxford, he could be best described as a lapsed Anglican; he was even, as he once described himself to Boswell, "a lax *talker* against religion." There are stories of his arguing skeptically with his mother about her simple piety. But while at Oxford he underwent something very like a religious conversion, effected by a single reading of William Law's popular devotional book, *A Serious Call to a Devout and Holy Life* (1728). As he later recalled, "While at Oxford, I took up Law's *Serious Call* . . . , expecting to find it a dull book (as such books generally are), and perhaps to laugh at it. But I found Law quite an overmatch for me; and this was the first occasion of my thinking in earnest of religion. . . ." From this time on, Boswell says—and quite correctly without any qualification—"religion was the predominant object of his thoughts." Religion, notice: not literature, writing, or literary judgment. The writing, as we shall see, was undertaken largely as a ritual obligation in a highly self-conscious process of Christian redemption. As Boswell says again: "He habitually endeavored to refer every transaction of his life to the will of the Supreme Being." And at the end of the *Life of Johnson* Boswell yet again hammers away at the truth about Johnson's essential orientation: his piety was "constant, and the ruling principle of all his conduct." But there was no ecstasy in Johnson's new religious awareness: what it brought him instead was torment and wretchedness as he agonized over his idleness and irregularity.

When he had to return to Lichfield in 1729—his last few weeks at Pembroke, his money running out, were humiliating—he was a vigorous, sensual, and emotional youth, but now, thanks to Law's *Serious Call*, also a guilt-ridden one. His violent appetites seemed dangerously at war with his desire to contain them. Strain set in, and he became so melancholic that sometimes he feared he would simply go mad. His compulsive tics and swayings and mutterings became more conspicuous. He even talked of suicide. Forever after he labored under a conviction that he could very easily lose his mind and that his sanity depended almost wholly upon his own self-control.

What was he to do now? He was twenty-three years old, but he had neither academic degree nor preparation for any profession. He seemed destined to clerk forever in his father's shop and to grow old and harmless in Lichfield. When his father died in 1731, this prospect seemed even more likely. He was rescued momentarily by a teaching job at the grammar school at Market Bosworth, in Leicestershire; but this was an unhappy situation, for the job required him to be civil to the main patron of the school, Sir Wolstan Dixie, to live in his nearby stately home and to serve there as a sort of lay chaplain. Sir Wolstan's ignorance and brutality made him an insupportable patron, and Johnson lasted only six months.

The pattern of his life was becoming increasingly clear and depressing: a series of temporary jobs for which he was not fitted, aborted hopes, failure at everything he tried. No wonder his frustration and melancholy grew upon him. He apparently was condemned to act out the universal scenario of pride and poverty which he encapsulated six years later in a line in *London*:

> Slow rises worth, by poverty depressed.

His friends were almost as worried about his prospects as he was. One of them, Edmund Hector, a fellow student at Lichfield Grammar School, invited him to Birmingham. Here for some months Johnson enjoyed a livelier social life than Lichfield offered—in these days he drank very freely, although he was proud to assert that no one ever *saw* him drunk—and he fell into some minor literary projects handed him by Hector and his friends, who perceived that if he was to avoid hopeless neurosis his mind had to be kept full and his hands busy.

At Hector's suggestion he set to work on an abridged translation from the French of a book by a Portuguese Jesuit—Father Jerome Lobo's *Voyage to Abyssinia*, a book he had first encountered at Oxford. The translating was hard going not because he had any trouble with the French but because he hated work: Hector finally got him to finish by telling him that the printer was in danger of starving for want of copy. From bed, where idleness and melancholy had confined him, he managed to dictate the end of the translation to Hector, who carried it to the printer and even read the proofs for Johnson. This exercise earned him six guineas.

His preface to Lobo's book indicates that just as he had already contrived his stylistic signature in poetry, so he had already adopted his essential intellectual stance. He is skeptical of wonders and suspicious of the exotic, but he has learned already how to prevent this skepticism from turning bitter by infusing it with a tincture of ironic humor. As he says in praise of Father Lobo:

The Portuguese traveler, contrary to the general vein of his countrymen, has amused his reader with no romantic absurdities or incredible fictions; whatever he relates, whether true or not, is at least probable.

"Whether true or not"—"at least probable": the sense of this opposition, humorous as it is here, will become essential to Johnson's whole literary activity later on as he engages with one received literary genre after another and adapts the "true" impulse generated inside himself to the recognized rhetorical requirements of the kind of writing he is doing. He goes on:

[Father Lobo] appears, by his modest and unaffected narration, to have described things as he saw them, to have copied nature from the life, and to have consulted his senses, not his imagination.

Unlike other writers of travel books, a genre long known for dramatic exaggeration and even outright lies, Lobo

meets with no basilisks that destroy with their eyes, his crocodiles devour their prey without tears, and his cataracts fall from the rocks without deafening the neighboring inhabitants.

Excited now by the opportunity to expose absolutism and dogmatism, Johnson warms to his work, delivering a series of ironic negatives:

The reader will here find no regions cursed with irremediable barrenness, or blessed with spontaneous fecundity; no perpetual gloom, or unceasing sunshine; nor are the nations here described either devoid of all sense of humanity, or consummate in all private and social virtues. Here are no Hottentots without religion, polity, or articulate language; no Chinese perfectly polite, and completely skilled in all sciences.

Actually, the reader will discover in Lobo's book

what will always be discovered by a diligent and impartial inquirer, that wherever human nature is to be found, there is a mixture of vice and virtue, a contest of passion and reason. . . .

And it is this "mixture" of vice and virtue, of defect and merit, the inert and the lively, that years later Johnson is going to notice and discriminate in the writings that pass under his critical eye. His treatment of them will be as little absolute and reductive as he indicates Lobo's treatment of Abyssinian institutions has been. This is not to say that Johnson's work on this translation taught him a method: rather, the work provided an opportunity to sketch out the method which was his by instinct all along and which would prove to preside over his literary actions until the end.

Hector knew people and introduced Johnson to the minor Birmingham gentry. One of the people he met was a sprightly forty-six-year-old widow, Elizabeth Porter. He married her in July, 1735, when he was twenty-six. About her character, value, and even appearance posterity has puzzled itself. Johnson, who was impatient with both fools and fakes, loved her deeply, and although their marriage had its strains, he admired her intelligence and respected her person and her memory. On the other hand, Boswell, motivated perhaps by envy, carefully gives us Garrick's description of her as "very fat, with a bosom of more than ordinary protuberance [what's wrong with that?], with swelled cheeks of a florid red, produced by thick painting, and increased by the liberal use of cordials; flaring and fantastic in her dress, and affected both in her speech and her general behavior." Whatever she was like, it would hardly have seemed that she had the best of the bargain: it appeared to her family that a deformed, twitching, unstable, and argumentative small-town boy was no great catch as a husband. No one had any idea that Johnson was going to be famous. So far, he appeared to be an unattractive, excitable youth embarrassingly learned beyond his station and distinguished mainly by not having any profession or, indeed, any means for supporting his new wife. He must have struck the respectable Porter family as something very close to a modern drop-out or hippie. Mrs. Porter's eldest son was so appalled by her marriage to Johnson that he contrived never to see her again.

Johnson and "Tetty," as he called her, were to have no children, but one fruit of their union was the almost six hundred pounds she brought him. Not that he married primarily for money: the money was a useful attendant of a relation which all observers agree was—at least in its early stages—passionate and eminently satisfactory. With the money he at last had a chance to do something for which he conceived his talents appropriate. Not to write, it should be noted, but to start a school of his own. At Edial, near Lichfield, he rented a large brick house and established there what Donald Greene has called "perhaps the most unsuccessful private school in the history of education."[5] Johnson was not a good teacher: he was too eccentric and took the work too seriously. The school attracted very few pupils, no more than eight, and probably only four or five, among whom were David Garrick and his younger brother, George. Garrick later entertained London parties with unkind but very funny mimicry of the newly-wedded Johnson's "tumultuous" gestures and manners as revealed to the boys through the nuptial keyhole. As it became increasingly clear that the school at Edial was going to follow Johnson's other ventures into the limbo of failure, he thought of reviving his fortunes by writing a five-act play. This was the standard avenue to instant, flashy success in his day: it was the equivalent of producing a best-selling novel in ours. In his accustomed environment of bankruptcy and disaster, he buckled down to writing a blank-verse tragedy called *Irene* (pronounced I-reen-ie). It was supposed to be a vivid drama all about a fifteenth-century Turkish sultan and a Greek slave girl and their predicaments of love and honor. But he found the writing hard and slow, and he got only three acts written at Edial while his school was in the process of failing. Even these three acts seemed to turn out frigid and unaffecting. Everything he touched appeared to be turning out ill, and apparently he was going to be as bad at original writing as he had been at shopkeeping and schoolmastering. And now Tetty's money was all spent.

In the eighteenth century, when clever young men arrived at an impasse like this, some joined the Army or hanged themselves; others emigrated to the Americas; and a few went to London, especially to Grub Street, where they spent their lives writing rubbish or doing anonymous journeywork for publishers while hoping to write something noteworthy on their own. Johnson chose Grub Street.

He did not actually live on the Street; rather, he fell into the world designated by its name, as in our time a young man becomes part of Wall Street or Madison Avenue without necessarily working at either address. Grub Street was a real street in the Moorfields district of London. It had been the haunt of hack writers and fly-by-night publishers since at least the middle of the seventeenth century. In Johnson's day the ground floors were occupied by printers and booksellers (that is, publishers), while authors and their families lived above in conditions like those depicted in Hogarth's *The Distressed Poet.*

The whole operation was, curiously, a by-blow of improvements in transportation. As John Wain has observed,

Literature, in the form in which we know it [that is, "consumer" literature], cannot get started without good roads and an effective transport system. The eighteenth century was the first epoch in which the ordinary citizen of the country, no matter where he lived, could deploy his purchasing power to the benefit of publishers and authors. The appeal to the public, which enables the writer to bypass court and *chapelle*, is not possible unless the public can be got at.[6]

Improved roads thus made possible the national circulation of journalistic products, whose manufactory was Grub Street. The Street's reputation for knavery, venality, and sheer bad writing became so egregious that in 1829 a group of its householders petitioned to have its name changed, *causa pudoris*, to "Milton Street." The change was made in 1830, and Milton Street it remains to this day.

Visiting Milton Street now in the expectation of finding anything interesting is a depressing experience, although it might be instructive to anyone who imagines that something of his own world will persist for at least a couple of centuries. The street is no more than three hundred yards long, bleak and deserted: on one side is an uninviting twentieth-century pub and the dead face of a late-nineteenth-century warehouse; on the other, a row of recent mock-Bauhaus office buildings of unrelieved banality. No plaque commemorates Grub Street and the thousands of indigent writers who once peopled it: the only sign visible is on one of the office buildings, and it reads, "Scientific Control Systems, Ltd."

But despite the disappearance of Grub Street, the thing it represents has not only persisted—it has flourished, as George Gissing made clear to Victorian readers in *New Grub Street* (1891) or as a glance at any current popular magazine will confirm for us. Wherever journalistic articles are rapidly and ignorantly written to be consumed and forgotten (they must be forgotten to make room in the reader's mind for next week's similar articles), there is Grub Street. I have a modern example before me: *The [London] Sunday Times Magazine* for March 8, 1970. The format, with its chic color reproductions and general atmosphere of knowingness, is not eighteenth century, but the prose is sheer Grub Street. Johnson himself would easily recognize as such a piece on Thomas

Chatterton. It is full of grotesquely bad, pretentious writing ("The enduring sadness of Chatterton is the sad waste of him"), impertinent generalization ("His brilliance was squandered in times when hypocrisy was king"), illiterate use of technical terms ("In this cheap hack work he had practically forgotten the saga of poems attributed to Rowley"), naïve grammar ("nothing but mystery or morality plays were known then"), incoherence ("It is impossible to explain the process by which the character of Rowley ... became printed over his own: there are elements in it of psychic visitation, of a split personality born of an uncomfortable time in class"), mad confusion ("At the same time he was cultivating his most injurious patron, a principal cause of his suicide, the paltry William Barrett. This was less of a surgeon than a male nurse"), bizarre critical opinions ("[Horace] Walpole was a dreadful man, a self-preening fastidious trifler, scratching with long fingernails and spiteful sayings at art and letters"), and misquotation (Johnson: "It is marvellous that [actually *wonderful how*] the whelp has written such things").

Like its modern counterpart, the eighteenth-century Grub Street world was a production and consumption milieu in which one was expected to write irresponsibly and badly. Johnson's distinction is that he never did. Although he was of this world, he always transcended it. He used the conventions and mechanisms of Grub Street—writing rapidly, writing to order, writing in a standard genre—to generate literature, happily defined by Ezra Pound as "news that *stays* news."[7]

Johnson's entry into Grub Street was distinctly a last resort, undertaken only after every other means of earning a living had blown up in his face. The only thing he knew he could do successfully, even if painfully, was to earn a bit of money by translating from the French, as he had done with Lobo's *Voyage to Abyssinia.* He hoped he might also make a tiny income translating from Latin. It was with this unexciting sense of himself as a prospective ill-paid translator that in March, 1737, he left Tetty temporarily behind and set off with Garrick on the 120 miles to London. He carried with him the three acts of *Irene*, and there was always the hope that once he found some paying literary work he could press forward with his play, get it performed, and call Tetty to London to share with him a scene of something like worldly success. That would be a novelty for both of them.

He was not going to London entirely cold. Six years before, the London publisher and entrepreneur Edward Cave had founded a new journalistic venture, the monthly *Gentleman's Magazine*. Johnson had been impressed by the numbers he had seen in Lichfield and Birmingham and had written Cave, indicating his willingness to contribute to the poetry section, as well as to submit "short literary dissertations in Latin or English, [and] critical remarks on authors ancient or modern." Cave's response to this ambitious and slightly naïve inquiry is not known.

Johnson had, at any rate, a target before him: he knew of a London publisher from whom he could solicit work. Upon arrival he took a cheap room and began frequenting the taverns and coffee houses where literary gossip could be picked up. He tried to apply himself to *Irene*, but the play proved as hard to finish in London as in Lichfield. He wrote Cave again, this time suggesting a translation from the French of Father Paul Sarpi's *History of the Council of Trent*. Although this project finally aborted, Cave did see him and gave him some assurance of future work. The prospects were brightening: Tetty joined him and he managed to write the last two acts of *Irene*. But no one seemed interested in producing it, and in 1738, at the age of twenty-nine, he began working for Cave as a hack. For the next six years he earned a frugal living by supplying the *Gentleman's Magazine* with poems, brief biographies of learned men, reviews, and essays. Some months half the magazine consisted of his pieces. All these were anonymous: his name was not to appear on a title page until *The Vanity of Human Wishes*, twelve years later.

Anonymity was required especially for his most important work for Cave, his monthly reports of the debates in Parliament, a strictly illegal undertaking thinly disguised by the title "Debates in the Senate of Magna Lilliputia." If all this anonymous journalism brought in only a trickle of money, it did have some advantages: Johnson learned from it how to express convincingly views not his own and how to wear numerous literary masks. He was also learning how to write plausibly in a variety of received literary forms.

Readers of the *Gentleman's Magazine* were also reading Alexander Pope in the late 1730's, and Pope was creating a sensation by his "imitations" of the satires of Horace. His practice was to bring Horace up to date by writing in the Horatian style about the corruptions of modern England, especially those which could be imputed to the Whig Prime Minister, Sir Robert Walpole. Perceiving that the public was accustomed to this subject and this technique, Johnson tried it himself. He chose Juvenal's *Third Satire* as his model and produced 263 lines of heroic couplet, Pope's fashionable verse form, in which he deplored political corruption, the high crime rate, and the luxury of contemporary London, which he affected to find nauseating. Actually, Johnson adored London and was exhilarated no end by its racy surface, enormities included. What he was doing in *London: A Poem* was turning a penny and bidding for reputation by providing readers with something familiar and yet just slightly novel. His "real" relation to the views of which *London* is constructed is perhaps best illuminated by Donald Greene's remark: "Satire is a *genre*, and if you are going to write satire, you must find something to satirize. Since satire was fashionable in the eighteenth century, every budding poet, whatever his politics, wrote satire and found the state of England deplorable."[8] Johnson sold *London* to the publisher Robert Dodsley for ten guineas. Many readers thought the unknown poet of *London* even more impressive than Pope, and during Johnson's lifetime *London* remained his most popular poem. After 1738 it was possible for him to overcome some of his depression and think of himself as an actual professional writer. The curtain was beginning to lift, although there were still years of darkness ahead.

No producer was showing any interest in *Irene*, and Johnson survived by doing more and more anonymous work for Cave: he became finally the virtual assistant editor of the magazine. But his constitutional indolence and neurotic impulsiveness made the work anything but pleasurable, and what he earned was not enough to elevate him and Tetty very far above poverty. Their small pleasures were found in the taverns and in conversation with the swarm of tacky journalists, small poets, threadbare playwrights, and unemployed scholars they were thrown among.

Of this group of attractive failures certainly the most compelling was the sensationally improvident Richard Savage, an impulsive, masochistic poet who said that he was really the illegitimate son of the Countess of Macclesfield by the Earl Rivers and thus, like Huck Finn's King and Dauphin, an aristocrat scandalously deprived of his identity and perquisites. Although many were skeptical, Johnson believed his story. They became intimate friends. Savage's long acquaintance with misery and frustration endeared him to Johnson as a fellow-sufferer, and his conversation, rich with anecdotes of the literary and social Great, delighted the Johnson who was himself becoming a distinguished practitioner of the art of talk. There are so many stories of Johnson's impulsive night rambles with Savage that we must suspect that about this time he and Tetty had had some sort of falling-out and were, for a time, not living together.

It was while under the influence of Savage that he tried another avenue to quick literary success. He had done well working in Pope's vein. He now turned to imitating the popular ironical essays of Swift. He brought out in 1739 two pamphlets designed, like *London*, to appeal to those who disapproved of Walpole's administration: he titled them *Marmor Norfolciense* (that is, the stone found in Norfolk) and *A Complete Vindication of the Licensers of the Stage.* Thanks to the convention of anonymous authorship, *Marmor Norfolciense* can operate in that world of tongue-in-cheek literary fraud so attractive to an audience that was relishing exercises in outrageous plausibility like Swift's *Gulliver's Travels* and *A Modest Proposal.* Johnson's pamphlet details circumstantially the discovery of an ancient stone near Lynn, Norfolk—Walpole's county—carved with an ancient Latin inscription predicting a host of future miseries and horrors for England. The "author" goes on to print a verse translation of this inscription (Johnson is finally functioning as a translator from the Latin, even if the Latin is his own) and to offer a solemn, mock-pedantic commentary, which innocently exposes all the scandals of the Walpole administration and predicts England's ruin if Walpole is continued in office. The pamphlet ends with a satire of a different but equally Swiftian sort, a straightfaced "proposal" for the establishment of an academic Society of Commentators, consisting of argumentative lawyers and assertive Army officers, who will devote themselves to further explication of the inscription. It is all a bit strained and not quite funny enough.

The same is true of *A Complete Vindication of the Licensers of the Stage.* Here the speaker, using many of Swift's well-known mannerisms, ironically defends the theatrical licensing act of 1737. Although Johnson's deployment of Swift's weapons is fairly crude, a careless reader might just have imagined that Swift was the author and have told his friends to buy copies. Such sales, rather than any very profound objection to the current administration, would seem to have been Johnson's main motive. But neither pamphlet was such a success that Johnson was tempted to continue in the Swiftian mode, although *Marmor Norfolciense* generated some partisan stir—Pope was one of the many in the Opposition who liked it—and may even have got the printer into trouble. As a writer, Johnson had missed again. *London* had succeeded, but nothing else had.

With an entirely characteristic impulsiveness, he now chucked the whole thing. He left his writing ambitions as well as Tetty in London and retreated for six months to Lichfield, where he knew a moderately affectionate local audience was to be found. The measure of his despair about his writing career is his soliciting now a new teaching job in Leicestershire. He knew by this time that he was an appalling teacher, and yet he was apparently convinced that even teaching would be preferable to a life of the sort of writing he had done so far. For this new teaching job he needed an academic degree. A friend tried to get Swift to pressure Trinity College, Dublin, into awarding Johnson, as the author of *London*, an honorary degree of Master of Arts. But nothing came of it. Despite the flash success of *London*, the old pattern of frustration seemed to be taking over again. A mortgage on the Lichfield house enabled him to remit twenty pounds to Tetty, and encouraged by this temporary stay against disaster, he returned to London, rejoined Cave's stable of writers, and continued trying to get *Irene* produced. He was not to return to Lichfield for twenty years.

During the early 1740's—he was now in his early thirties—he continued writing for Cave but also branched out into a great variety of other literary projects to supplement his income. Typical is his work for his old Lichfield school friend Dr. Robert James, for whose *Medicinal Dictionary* he wrote a prospectus, a dedication (in James's voice), and some of the actual articles. Another job of work was a Preface to the Harleian Catalog, a list of the books in the library of the late Earl of Oxford. But the greatest literary opportunity of these years occurred in 1743 with Savage's death in debtor's prison, an event which called forth, early the next year, Johnson's sensational 180-page anonymous book, *An Account of the Life of Mr. Richard Savage*.

But projects like these, even executed with such brilliance as the *Life of Savage*, constituted only a temporary bulwark against bankruptcy. What was wanted was a sizable literary job extending over several years. At one time Johnson kept a list of such large projects, and doubtless he discussed many of them with publishers. On his list these ideas appear: a "History of Criticism . . . from Aristotle to the Present Age" (this presumably would have been a book like George Saintsbury's *History of Literary Criticism* or W. K. Wimsatt and Cleanth Brooks's *Literary Criticism: A Short History*); new editions of Chaucer and of Fairfax's translation of Tasso; editions of Oldham or of Roscommon or of Claudian;

"Lives of the Philosophers, written with a polite air, in such a manner as may divert as well as instruct"; "History of the Heathen Mythology, with an explication of the Fables, both allegorical and historical; with references to the poets"—here he apparently had in mind something like Douglas Bush's famous mid-twentieth-century volume, *Mythology and the Renaissance Tradition in English Poetry*; a collection of important letters, arranged, apparently, by subject; a new translation of Cicero; a "History of the Revival of Learning in Europe," an anticipation of such later interpretations of the Renaissance as Burckhardt's *The Civilization of the Renaissance in Italy* or Pater's *Studies in the History of the Renaissance*; a collection (presumably a dictionary) of proverbs; a dictionary of ancient history and myth, which would have resembled a modern reference work like Sir Paul Harvey's *Oxford Companion to Classical Literature*; a handbook to literature, "containing the history of learning, directions for editions, commentaries, etc."; "Lives of Illustrious Persons, as well of the active as the learned, in imitation of Plutarch"; a new translation of Plutarch's *Lives*; and a "Poetical Dictionary of the English Tongue," doubtless planned as a poet's handbook like Edward Bysshe's *The Art of English Poetry* with rhyming dictionary and prosodic instructions.

In addition, at one time or another he thought of writing biographies of Alfred the Great, Francis Bacon, and Oliver Cromwell; and of his friends Garrick and Goldsmith. He projected a biographical dictionary and a collection of the lives of the painters; a play on the instructively ironic career of Charles XII of Sweden; a translation of Boethius; a new edition of Richard Hooker's *The Laws of Ecclesiastical Polity*; a new edition of Politian; a work provisionally titled "The History of Memory," designed perhaps as an inquiry, starting from Lockean assumptions, into the operations of memory in the making of poetry, myth, and history; a military dictionary defining "the terms of war and navigation"; a history of warfare; an anthology of prayers, introduced by a critical discourse on prayer as a literary form; and "a small book of precepts and directions for piety." Speaking of Johnson's arrangements for publishing *The Vanity of Human Wishes*, Boswell says: "It will be observed that he reserves to himself the right of printing one edition of this satire, which was his practice upon occasion of the sale of all his writings, it being his fixed intention to publish at some period, for his own profit, a complete collection of all his works."

These were his "schemes." Not one of them was realized. It is not hard to imagine the amount of guilt generated by all these unaccomplished plans and aborted "fixed intentions," nor to appreciate how much shame must have arisen from Johnson's suspicion that all these projects might actually have been completed with a little more assiduity in early rising.

If all these ambitious projects failed to fructify, one of Johnson's even more taxing ones did appeal to a publisher, and in 1746, at the age of thirty-seven, he signed with Dodsley and a group of other publishers a contract for an English dictionary. He hoped to finish it in three years. His fee was £1,575. This was a flat, one-time fee, not an advance on royalties: the convention in Johnson's time was for a publisher simply to buy a work outright. Once the fee was paid, the deal was over, regardless of the number of copies ultimately sold. Considering the sums of ten and fifteen guineas he had earned on earlier writings, £1,575 was princely remuneration. Even though the work took nine years, and even though he had to hire six assistants—they cost twenty-three shillings a week—to help with the copying and filing of thousands of paper slips, the earnings from the *Dictionary* were the first substantial return literature had given him. From now on the most straitened days of poverty were behind him. But it had taken him half his life to begin making an adequate living out of writing.

Busy as he was now with the *Dictionary*, in the next three years he found time and motive to write two of his best poems, the *Prologue Spoken at the Opening of the Theater in Drury Lane* and *The Vanity of Human Wishes*, based on Juvenal's Tenth Satire. The *Prologue* was written as an act of friendship for Garrick, but *The Vanity of Human Wishes*, recognized today not only as

Johnson's greatest poem but also as the greatest poem of his age, brought him fifteen guineas. The contract for the *Dictionary* had apparently changed his literary luck: he was writing better than ever before, and writing now in a style no longer Pope's or Swift's. Finally even the star-crossed *Irene* got produced—in 1749 Garrick presented it at Drury Lane, where it ran for nine nights, yielding the author three nights' receipts. Furthermore, his name as a writer was now attractive enough to appear openly, on title pages and in advertisements. "Samuel Johnson" was beginning to mean something.

The late 1740's constitute a notable moment in his compositional as well as his public career. He is now moving away from the inherited tones of the Augustans to disclose his own: the road is now clear that will lead to the *Rambler, Rasselas,* and finally, *The Lives of the Poets.* With *Irene* produced and out of the way, he is free to exploit his most credible literary role, that of the moralist and the ethical and psychological theorist. And with practice in the role goes mastery of the method, which we see pre-eminently in the *Rambler.* The method betokens an eloquent seriousness, but it is a seriousness that is never hostile to wit and even comedy.

Thus in his writing career everything was improving. But the radical private and domestic troubles which had begun at his birth were not. Tetty, who was to die three years later, was now, according to Dr. Robert Levet, "always drunk," and we hear as well of her addiction to opium. For some time she had been withholding her favors from her eminently needy husband. None of this improved Johnson's physical or psychological state: his tics and convulsive gestures persisted, he added asthma to his long list of infirmities, and his conviction of failure and guilt took even deeper root in his heart.

"In 1750," says Boswell with some sonority, "he came forth in the character for which he was eminently qualified, a majestic teacher of moral and religious wisdom." Boswell is referring to the *Rambler,* the twice-weekly essay-periodical of which Johnson produced 208 numbers from March 20, 1750, to March 14, 1752.

Boswell's own personal need for the sort of moral stiffening provided by the *Rambler* makes it easy for him to overlook the many other "characters" which Johnson could make his own with almost equal ease and apparent authenticity: those of satiric poet, ironic biographer, prologue writer, lexicographer, and later, oriental-tale narrator, scholarly editor and commentator, travel-book author, and writer of other people's legal briefs and lectures, sermons, dedications, prefaces, and advertisements.

While at work on the *Rambler*, earning two guineas a number, he was also deep in the work for the *Dictionary*, and one of his tasks for that project doubtless colored the matter and mode of the *Rambler*. He was reading all seventeenth-century English literature, or all he could lay his hands on, searching in moralists and historians for the quotations he needed to exemplify definitions of words. From this reading derives a large part of the *Rambler*'s distinctly old-fashioned—indeed, seventeenth-century—moral seriousness. Like any professional writer, Johnson is seldom engaged in only one literary project at once, and one project tinctures another in ways that have not always been understood. Despite its seriousness the *Rambler* was, or rather became, popular: by the time of Johnson's death, it had gone into ten collected editions, and as Boswell says, "Its [final] sale has far exceeded that of any periodical papers since the reign of Queen Anne." That is, its reception was second only to the *Spectator*'s.

Three days after he stopped writing the *Rambler,* Tetty died, an old woman of sixty-three. Her death gave him augmented cause for self-torment. He recorded this prayer a year after her death:

O Lord, who givest the grace of repentance, and hearest the prayers of the penitent, grant that by true contrition I may obtain forgiveness for all the sins committed and of all duties neglected in my union with the wife whom thou hast taken from me: for the neglect of joint devotion, patient exhortation, and mild instruction. And O Lord, who canst change evil to good, grant that the loss of my wife may so mortify all inordinate affections in me that I may henceforth please thee by holiness of life.

But his "inordinate affections" were not so cooled that, a year later, he was not seeking another wife. He never found one. Twenty-six years later, as an old man of sixty-nine, he wrote in his diary: "Poor Tetty, whatever were our faults and failings, we loved each other."

Two years' experience of writing two *Ramblers* a week had made work in the short essay form second nature to him, and it must have been with a satisfying sense of continuing to do what he knew he could do well that during 1753 and 1754 he contributed twenty-nine essays on morality and the ambiguities of the human condition to John Hawkesworth's twice-weekly periodical *The Adventurer.* The *Dictionary* was almost finished, and Lord Chesterfield's belated public support of it drew from Johnson his distinguished letter of scornful independence which has been taken to mark the end of private literary patronage. Henceforth writers would turn for support to publishers rather than to noblemen. With the publication of the *Dictionary* in two immense folio volumes in 1755, "the world," as Boswell says, "contemplated with wonder so stupendous a work achieved by one man, while other countries had thought such undertakings fit only for whole academies." And this astonishing work had not only been achieved by one man: it had been finished, as Johnson proudly asserts in his Preface, "with little assistance of the learned, and without any patronage of the Great; not in the soft obscurities of retirement, or under the shelter of academic bowers, but amidst inconvenience and distraction, in sickness and in sorrow...." The dual achievement of the *Rambler* and the *Dictionary* persuaded Oxford that he might have an honorary degree of Master of Arts, and the degree was granted in time for the letters A.M. to appear after his name on the title page of the *Dictionary.* If the degree had come fifteen years before, it might have got him a teaching job. Now it was only an honor.

He had long since spent his earnings from the *Dictionary,* and a new literary job was required. He found one on the monthly *Literary Magazine, or Universal Review,* which he both contributed to and helped edit for over a year. Arthur Murphy gives a winning picture of him during this time:

He resigned himself to indolence, took no exercise, rose about two, and then received the visits of his friends. Authors long since forgotten waited on him as their oracle, and he gave responses in the chair of criticism. He listened to the complaints, the schemes, and the hopes and fears of a crowd of inferior writers. . . . His house was filled with a succession of visitors until four or five in the evening. During the whole time he presided at his tea-table.

But if he spent his afternoons this way, he somehow found time to do considerable reviewing for the *Literary Magazine*, and one of his reviews, of Soame Jenyns's fatuous, optimistic book *A Free Inquiry into the Nature and Origin of Evil*, has become a classic. It projects unforgettably Johnson's sympathy with actual, frail human persons in all their pathetic inconsistency and frustration. It constitutes an implicit defense of the sad "authors long since forgotten" and the messy "crowd of inferior writers" against pert and ignorant devisers of geometric "systems" for rationalizing human experience. Human beings and the "problem" they represent are not, Johnson insists, to be understood in the study: "Life must be seen before it can be known."

He knew well his own constitutional indolence and his profound dislike of writing, and yet he knew from his experience with the *Dictionary* that he could force himself to finish a large project, even if he finished it late. In 1756 he undertook another: an eight-volume edition of Shakespeare with preface, notes, and commentary. He promised subscribers that the work would be out by Christmas, 1757. Actually, it was eight years in appearing, and he had long since spent all the income from it. Just as while working on the *Dictionary* he had devised the *Rambler* as a distraction from the rigors of scholarship—and also, perhaps, as an additional masochistic torment—so with the Shakespeare project: this time the similar device was the *Idler*, a set of 104 essays contributed once a week to a newspaper called *The Universal Chronicle*. These ran from April 15, 1758, to April 5, 1760.

Once he told Sir John Hawkins: "My inducement to [work] is not love or desire of fame, but the want of money, which is the only motive to writing that I know of." Faced with a severe want of money in January, 1759, when his ninety-year-old mother died, with funeral expenses and debts to be paid, he sat down and wrote rapidly, as usual, an astringent moral fable in the form of an oriental tale. He titled it *The Prince of Abyssinia.* It is better known by the name of its ingenuous anti-hero, *Rasselas.* He earned a hundred pounds from it, and Dodsley gave him a bonus of twenty-five more when a second edition was called for.

Despite his frequent assertions in conversation that money was his sole motive for writing—assertions which we shall see are very largely disingenuous—he had actually been producing a great body of writing for nothing since the 1740's. He had been secretly writing prefaces and dedications—he was a master of both forms— for his less gifted friends and acquaintances. Some fifty of these have been identified, ranging from the preface and dedication to William Payne's *The Game of Draughts* (1756) and the preface to John Payne's strictly utilitarian *New Tables of Interest* (1758) all the way to the dedications to such major works as Charles Burney's *General History of Music* (1776) and Sir Joshua Reynolds's *Seven Discourses* (1778), addressed respectively to the Queen and the King. If friendship solicited, or even simple need, he forgot money entirely and simply wrote free what his suppliants required. Thus he wrote many sermons for friends, and if a promising poem came to his hands in manuscript, he was happy to supply lines for nothing. He contributed to both Goldsmith's *The Traveler* and Crabbe's *The Village,* and donated a verse prologue to Goldsmith's play *The Good-natured Man.* His main gratuitous contribution, the secret writing for Robert Chambers of his Oxford law lectures—there were sixty lectures in all, constituting a large book—was undertaken purely out of motives of friendship and pity. If Johnson had charged for this outpouring of free prefaces, dedications, sermons, poetic passages, and law lectures, he could have been, if not rich, at least very comfortable. When we hear him asserting that "no man but a blockhead ever wrote except for money," we would do well to bear in mind what he once also told Boswell: "Nobody at times talks more laxly than I do."

One interesting thing about his preface-writing for others is this: he knew how to write a preface so well that it was not even necessary for him to read the book he was writing about. For example, he never did read Richard Rolt's *Dictionary of Trade and Commerce*, for which he provided a preface in 1756. If one knows the possible *kinds* of books, one needn't know every individual book. Boswell reports:

I asked him whether he knew much of Rolt and of his work. 'Sir,' said he, 'I never saw the man, and never read the book. The booksellers wanted a preface to a Dictionary of Trade and Commerce. I knew very well what such a Dictionary should be, and I wrote a preface accordingly.'

When George III came to the throne in 1760, Johnson was fifty-one and well known as "Dictionary Johnson." The King's predecessor had been a byword of philistinism ("Dunce the Second reigns like Dunce the First," Pope had written), and the new King, a youth of twenty-two and the first of the Hanoverians to be educated in England, wanted to signal a change of climate— and also, perhaps, to buy off a writer who had indicated in *London* his formidable potential for embarrassing an administration. Accordingly, in 1762 the King granted Johnson a lifetime pension of £300 a year. Worried that some party writing would be demanded in return and perhaps nervous about an earlier definition of *Pensioner* in the *Dictionary*—"a slave of state hired by a stipend to obey his master"—Johnson required assurance that, as Lord Bute told him emphatically, "It is not given for anything you are to do, but for what you have done." Bute was presumably thinking of both the *Rambler* and the *Dictionary*.

His money worries finally over, Johnson now had leisure to stretch his legs and enjoy the sort of comfortable, middle-class social diversion provided by Boswell, who met him in 1763; by Sir Joshua

Reynolds, who organized The Club in 1764; and by Mr. and Mrs. Henry Thrale of Southwark and Streatham, who met him in 1765 and on whose premises Johnson delighted to express his playfulness, his fondness for children, and his devotion to copious dining. The Male Cinderella had metamorphosed himself into "Dr." Johnson (Trinity College, Dublin, gave him the LL.D. just before his edition of Shakespeare appeared in 1765), and the years following these heady events of the early 1760's give us the Johnson familiar through Boswell's portraiture: relatively secure psychologically, authoritative, dogmatic, dominating, received in private audience by a respectful George III. But if the face he displayed in public was that of the magisterial "Dr." Johnson, in private he was insecure, self-distrustful and self-tormenting, taxing himself repeatedly in his prayers and private memoranda with idleness, failure, and wickedness. Early in 1766 his melancholy grew so severe that he feared he might go violently insane, and he secretly deposited with Mrs. Thrale a padlock for her to use should physical restraint become necessary.[9] All the worldly honors and comforts that came to him in late middle age were a very thin disguise laid over the frustrated, failure-prone "great boy" from Lichfield.

Although he was persuaded that his pension required no political writing from him, he did gratify Lord North's ministry, as well as his friend Henry Thrale, a Tory M.P., by doing some anonymously during the early 1770's. In a pamphlet called *The False Alarm* (1770), he argued that the House of Commons had the right to bar the obstreperous John Wilkes from his seat; and in *Taxation No Tyranny* (1775), he argued the right of the mother country to exact revenues from its American colonies. What he is doing in these pamphlets is behaving like a lawyer: he is finding, organizing, and articulating the most persuasive arguments on behalf of certain positions. To imagine that either pamphlet is a wholly sincere expression of his own deepest convictions would be as naïve as to imagine that Johnson, the wild enthusiast for London, is personally committed to an assertion like this, spoken by "Indignant Thales" in *London:*

> London! the needy villain's gen'ral home,
> The common shore of Paris and of Rome.

Or an estimate like this:

> Scarce can our fields, such crowds at Tyburn die,
> With hemp the gallows and the fleet supply.

In 1773, when he was sixty-four and a mass of infirmities, Boswell persuaded him to take a tour of the Scottish Highlands and the primitive Hebridean islands. The fruit of this arduous three months of hill-climbing and horseback-riding was his travel book *A Journey to the Western Islands of Scotland,* published in 1775. During that same year he was made Doctor of Laws again, this time by Oxford. It is pleasant to note that he never did refer to himself as Doctor, leaving it entirely to others to bestow honors upon him.

His final large literary project was his ten-volume *Prefaces, Biographical and Critical, to the Works of the English Poets,* of which four volumes appeared in 1779 and six in 1781. He had long been meditating a series of critical Lives of post-Restoration poets. During his famous interview with George III in 1767, the King, Boswell says, "expressed a desire to have the literary biography of this country ably executed, and proposed to Dr. Johnson to undertake it. Johnson signified his readiness to comply with His Majesty's wishes." But typically it was not His Majesty's wishes but professional importunity that finally got the project started. Ten years later, a group of thirty-six London publishers approached Johnson and invited him to furnish—for the sum of £300—prefaces to selections from fifty-two poets, most of them chosen by the consortium rather than by the preface-writer: hence the inclusion of popular nonentities like Edmund Smith, Lord Lyttelton, and Christopher Pitt, the Edith Sitwells of their day. It is in *The Lives of the Poets,* as these *Prefaces* have come to be known, that Johnson performs his most distinguished criticism—mature, sensitive, entirely honest and thus fruitfully inconsistent, the yield of a long lifetime spent in the closest proximity to actual literature; not an exposition of literary theory but rather an exploration of a more embarrassing, problematic matter: the nature of literature as a constructed product, and its effect upon those who use it.

After the publication of the first four volumes of these *Prefaces* he wrote in his Diary:

I am now to review the last year, and find little but dismal vacuity, neither business nor pleasure; much intended and little done. My health is much broken; my nights afford me little rest. I have tried opium, but its help is counterbalanced with great disturbance; it prevents the spasms, but it hinders sleep. O God, have mercy on me.

It was not to be expected that the "great Cham of literature," as Tobias Smollett called him, could go on much longer. Because of his lifetime terror of extinction and his torments about the likelihood of his own damnation, the story of his last days, when he was suffering from acute dropsy and emphysema, makes unhappy reading. He hoped that his unremitting prayers for mercy would be granted, but at the same time he was not convinced that he was not going to be "sent to Hell . . . and punished everlastingly." He suffered a stroke in June, 1783, when he was seventy-three, and his account of it in a letter to Mrs. Thrale is highly characteristic in its irony ("I . . . began to plan schemes of life"); in its fear that his mind, the best part of him, might have been damaged; and in its recourse to a literary test of his continuing adequacy:

On Monday the 16th I sat for my picture, and walked a considerable way with little inconvenience. In the afternoon and evening I felt myself light and easy, and began to plan schemes of life. Thus I went to bed, and in a short time waked and sat up as has long been my custom, when I felt a confusion and indistinctness in my head which lasted I suppose about half a minute; I was alarmed and prayed God that however he might afflict my body he would spare my understanding. This prayer, that I might try the integrity of my faculties, I made in Latin verse. The lines were not very good, but I knew them not to be very good. I made them easily, and concluded myself to be unimpaired in my faculties.

His Latin prayer on this occasion begs God to spare his mind, "the only faculty with which I may hope to please Thee." A year and a half later, after a terrible struggle ("I will be conquered; I will not capitulate"), he was dead. He was not taken back to Lichfield to be buried. He was buried in Westminster Abbey near Chaucer and Spenser. The life radically wretched had ended with his reception into the institution of literature.

The Club which his friend Reynolds organized in 1764 met regularly to converse with him. Over the years it included practically everyone of high intelligence and achievement in England. Among the members were Edmund Burke, Oliver Goldsmith, Richard Brinsley Sheridan, David Garrick, Thomas Warton, Adam Smith, Thomas Percy, Edward Gibbon, Charles Burney, Joseph Warton, Edmond Malone, and Reynolds. That is to say, it consisted of the most eloquent political writer of the day, the two best playwrights, the best actor, a distinguished literary historian, the most impressive economist, the best literary antiquarian, the most distinguished historian, the foremost musicologist, an able poet and literary commentator, one of the most devoted of literary scholars and editors, and a distinguished painter and theorist of art. To find these people's equivalents in a later time we would go to names like these: Winston Churchill, Samuel Beckett and Harold Pinter, Laurence Olivier, D. Nichol Smith, John Kenneth Galbraith, Ezra Pound, A. J. P. Taylor, Sir George Grove, Louis MacNeice, R. W. Chapman, and Ben Nicholson. If we can imagine all these sinking their differences and finding the time to assemble weekly or fortnightly for years to listen to a man each one recognizes as his intellectual superior, we will have an idea of what the "poor creature" from Lichfield finally made of himself.

CHAPTER 2

The Facts of Writing
and the
Johnsonian Senses of Literature

If we are to understand everything that Johnson's literary performance has to tell us, we must pause for a moment here to consider
some of the facts of writing. Like "the facts of life," they may seem
at first glance a little startling; but also like those other facts, once
we're in on the secret we wonder how we could have been so
innocent before.

What constitutes literature? Simply this: the decision of an
audience that a piece of writing is "literary." An act of what observers will consent to consider literature can take place only when
an individual talent engages and, as it were, fills in the shape of a
pre-existing form that a particular audience is willing to regard as
belonging to the world of literature. This is the only reason why
lecture notes, say, no matter how brilliantly conceived and finely

executed, are not regarded as literary. This is the only reason why an "outline" is conceived to be pre-literary rather than literary: no matter how much genuine literary distinction it can show (unity, coherence, emphasis, precision of texture), it can never be a work of literature simply because its form is *infra dig*. The same is true of letters to the editor, notes to the milkman, theatrical program-notes, the discourses on phonograph-record sleeves, and the inscriptions authors are pleased to write in presentation copies of their books. William Faulkner's Nobel Prize utterance was widely regarded as literary by some people because it took the form of a genre—the short oration or "address," as in *The Gettysburg Address*—to which such people consent to attach literary value. If it had appeared as a letter to the editor, its value would have been seriously diminished.

To perceive that Joyce's *Ulysses* belongs to the genre "novel," most people would have to have in hand more than a single section. Considered by itself, the language of the Sirens episode is so *outré* that, as Stuart Gilbert reports, "when it was sent by the author from Switzerland to England during the First World War, the Censor held it up, suspecting that it was written in some secret code. Two English writers (it is said) examined the work and came to the conclusion that it was not 'code' but literature of some eccentric kind."[1] And in the opposite way, a detective play currently popular in London works and finally delights only because the audience makes the assumption that a theatrical program is what it appears to be, that it has always the same degree of validity and trustworthiness as genre. It is an assumption about the conventional status of a written document that provides the spring for the play. And as John Sparrow reminds us, a problem we solve only by knowing about genre is this: how do we in fact distinguish between an "inscription" in a public place that is designed to be merely a notice ("George Washington lived here") and one that asks us to attend to its literary quality ("Their Name Liveth Forevermore")?[2]

Like other sorts of public notices, what literature is at any historical moment depends wholly on conventions which appear and depart, wax and wane, fructify or deaden. The making of literature is a matter of the engagement of a vulnerable self with a fairly rigid coded medium so tough that it bends and alters only under the most rigorous pressure, pressure which only the rarest spirits among writers can exert. The idea of the "coded medium" is a modern way of conceiving of a relatively fixed literary genre. *This coded medium comes inevitably from outside the writer*: otherwise it fails to transmit signals recognizable to the observer. Which is another way of saying what Northrop Frye has said: "The *forms* of literature can no more exist outside literature than the forms of sonata and fugue and rondo can exist outside music."[3] The medium is a public property which is not inside the writer.

When a young person today decides that he must perform in the role of writer, his eye fixed on all the romantic emoluments which modern folklore attaches to that role, the first thing he does—most often without realizing it—is to settle on a genre which will satisfy both his sense of social appropriateness and his audience's presumed sense of what literature is. Nine times out of ten he will select either the short or the long autobiographical fiction as the most suitable arena for the exercise and exhibition of his own powers: the archetype he imitates is Joyce's *A Portrait of the Artist as a Young Man*. The tenth time he will select the short, intense, quasi-confessional lyric poem: here Baudelaire as refracted in early Eliot is likely to be the model. The literary beginner of our own time has in effect these two essential choices only, although as his literary career proceeds a third genre may offer itself: the Absurd play, or Camp melodrama, stiff with the residue of Expressionism and Dada. It takes a mature and experienced sensibility which has long since passed through these stages to do what Norman Mailer has done, to appropriate a genre not considered literary—the news story, the "report," the eyewitness account—and make it serve literary purposes. But most writers are not mature and experienced, and it is thus largely within the three genres I have indicated—

autobiographical fiction, confessional lyric, and Absurd play—that the contemporary so-called "creative" imagination harbors,

>   feeding
> A little life with dried tubers.

Add to these three genres the last recourses of the middle-aged literary intelligence in exhaustion—the review, the critical essay, and the critical book—and you have what amounts to a complete catalog of the forms within which it is possible today to imagine serious literary purpose showing itself. The point we will find emerging is ironic: for all its illusion of a new freedom and amplitude, modern writing actually takes place in a vastly shrunken, impoverished, and dis-peopled genre world, even if it is a world where the genres are as rigid as they always have been. To begin a literary career today with, say, a poetic satire, or a long narrative poem, or a sermon, or a straightfaced ironic essay, or a travel book would be to begin no literary career at all. These would be taken as exercises in either high antiquarianism or low journalism, never as exhibitions of "creativity." The fact is that no matter what one's ambitions of freedom, one writes essentially what other people are writing. The fact is that genuine creativity shows itself not in the invention of forms or modes but in the accuracy with which distinct public forms of all kinds are recognized and the appropriateness with which they are exploited.

This is why I want to offer Johnson as a prime example of "the writer." His own life of writing took place in the midst of a heady profusion and variety of genres. Indeed, to think of what an open, "free" literary world would be like, a world where the available forms are almost numberless and infinitely variegated, is to imagine oneself in something like Johnson's literary circumstances. During his long career he exercised himself, often anonymously, in more of the various literary "kinds" than perhaps any other writer has ever done. Consider: he worked in tragedy, biography, the periodical essay, the oriental tale, the travel book, the political tract, the critical essay, and the book review; in the oration, the sermon, the letter, the prayer, the dedication, the preface, the legal brief, and the petition to royalty; in the poetic satire, the Horatian ode, the elegy, the theatrical prologue and epilogue, the song, the Anacreontic lyric, the epigram, and the epitaph. He was a master even of the advertisement, the political handbill, and the medical prescription. Few friends who needed anything written were ever turned away, so long as what they wanted was in a genre in which Johnson felt comfortable. The only consequential contemporary categories to which he never turned his hand were the novel, stage comedy, the Pindaric ode, and the pastoral. He felt no attraction to the first two, he distrusted the third, and he scorned the last. The novel carried implications of sexual looseness, stage comedy implications of sheer levity: knowing himself intimately, he could not imagine himself as the author of either. The Pindaric ode he distrusted as a vehicle likely to unleash at least the appearance of passion, which, given his make-up, was all too likely to surface anyhow. And working in pastoral would mean allying oneself to the tradition of *Lycidas*, which might imply that one was willing to mingle Christian con-clusions with pagan images, thus suggesting, perhaps, that they were of approximately equal validity and use.

If it is true that he could not write everything, it is also true that no other writer of his time wrote in so many forms. One reason he was able to do this is that he was working before the widespread belief that writing is necessarily a self-expressive act verging on confession. By scrutinizing his intercourse with genres we can thus recover, I think, something like an orthodox literary sense of the relation between a writer's individual uniqueness and the objective sameness that characterizes the world of genres. And as I focus from time to time on Johnson's way with genres, I am going to be suggesting that his way is really the way of all writers, despite their often colorful statements to the contrary.

In his own time Johnson's reputation was firmly that of a writer. It was only later, after the dramaturgy of Boswell and

Macaulay, that he turned into the folklore image which still prevents an open access to the writings. With the air of enunciating a commonplace, the author of Johnson's obituary in the *Gentleman's Magazine* called him "the pride of English literature"; Thomas Tyers testified that "he was born for nothing but to write"; and three years after his death George Horne, Bishop of Norwich, observed: "The little stories of his oddities and infirmities in common life will, after a while, be overlooked and forgotten; but his writings will live forever, still more and more studied and admired." But when Boswell and Macaulay had finished with him, he was turned into a combination of Mr. Punch, John Bull, and a sort of Lord North of criticism, with overtones of creepy, half-sane religious superstition and brutal literary "prejudices." As Donald Greene has acutely perceived, the arch-snob James Boswell colored the image of the actual Johnson and offered it as a totem of reaction, "Toryism," and sentimental Jacobitism, largely as a buttress for his own insecure sense of personal sufficiency. What Boswell required was that Johnson seem to validate a world in which a Laird of Auchinleck would have a necessary, rightful place. Hence his worshipful terms for Johnson, terms which have done so much both to frighten readers from his works and to make them misread what they encounter there. To Boswell he is "that literary monarch," "the mighty sage," "the great intellectual light," and, of course, "my illustrious friend."

Macaulay's denigration of Johnson—like Boswell's encomiums, ironically—has had the effect of relieving most people from any obligation to consult the writings. As Macaulay says:

His conversation appears to have been quite equal to his writings in matter, and far superior to them in manner. . . . As soon as he took his pen in his hand to write for the public, his style became systematically vicious. . . . When he wrote for publication, he did his sentences out of English into Johnsonese. . . . His whole code of criticism rested on pure assumption. . . . The characteristic peculiarity of his intellect was the union of great powers with low prejudices.[4]

These canards sent abroad by Macaulay—largely, we now see, for Whig political purposes—still operate powerfully as critical home truths. Michael Joyce, whom no one could convict of a want of essential intelligence, can write in 1955:

The truth is that no man has reached such high eminence in the world of English letters with so little *specific* talent for literature as Johnson. . . . At its best his writing is as masterly as his talk, but it was curiously uneven: he never achieved that complete control of his medium which is the hallmark of the finished artist. . . .[5]

And even the enlightened Mona Wilson, editor of the Nonesuch *Johnson*, feels obliged to recommend him this way:

He is often dull: unless you know him [she has in mind Boswell's *Life*] much of his writing is dead as well as dull.

But by way of palliation she goes on:

Many of his pages were written for bread [notice the assumption that the best writing is necessarily and self-evidently free expression freely undertaken], many in sorrow and despair, all of them in the torture of a melancholy which he may hold off for a time but never dispels.

After this virtual equation of literary value with the self-expression of cheerful materials, she concludes:

It would be a weary if not impossible task to read the whole of Johnson's writing without the support of a personal sympathy.[6]

J. W. M. Thompson feels plenty of that personal sympathy, but even he returns to the old theme: "One needs, of course, a sense of duty to read through all the 208 *Ramblers* from start to finish today."[7]

Persuaded by the testimony of such witnesses, it is little wonder that readers today turn from the writings to embrace a fictive substitute named "Dr." Johnson and to support a quasi-religious cult which detaches him almost entirely from literary theory and shifts him over (I almost wrote Him) into personal and Anglican folklore. Sometimes the folklore veneration approaches actual canonization, with Lichfield serving as the Fatima of the cult. There today at the Birthplace, guided by the curator (a young Chinese devotee from Hong Kong), the faithful are invited to venerate such relics as "Dr. Johnson's silver bib-holder" and "the saucer which was used every morning by Dr. Johnson, on which his breakfast roll was placed."

Venerators and close readers—the two establish the polarities of the Johnsonian "double tradition" noticed by Bertrand Bronson:[8] the tradition, on the one hand, of "Doctor Johnson," the folklore *domine* and Tory projected in Boswell's *Life*, and the tradition, on the other hand, of Samuel Johnson, writer, poet, critic, and foremost literary intelligence of his day. Even if we are sophisticated well above bib-holders and saucers, the way we read him will seem to depend in large part on which of the two traditions has had the greater effect on us. Donald Greene observes:

It is apparent that there has . . . existed a 'double tradition' of Johnson the writer—two quite contradictory ways of reading the words on a Johnsonian page. The one sees it as exuberant with concrete and vivid imagery; the other finds only a drear waste of 'abstraction' and inflated, pompous verbosity. The one sees Johnson the critic as highly concerned to promote the use of effective imagery as an indispensable quality of the highest poetry; the other finds him suspicious, even fearful of it.[9]

Learning to read Johnson requires first a look at what literature seemed to him to be.

Imlac declares to Rasselas: "Inconsistencies cannot both be right; but, imputed to man, they may both be true." Johnson was always hospitable to inconsistencies so long as they constituted an honest registration of empirical actuality. The honesty is what matters. Boswell was fascinated with Johnson's massive inconsistencies, and it is the theme of those inconsistencies that provides him with his fully-orchestrated conclusion to the *Life of Johnson*, a book which is really a series of variations on Boswell's point that "Man is, in general, made up of contradictory qualities." Johnson's tendency

toward inconsistency is perhaps most clearly apparent in his unremitting condemnation of moral backsliding on principle ("Never
accustom your mind to mingle virtue and vice") which accompanies—to Boswell's frequent astonishment—a genuine fellow-
feeling with actual backsliders like Richard Savage, Topham
Beauclerk, Henry Thrale, and Boswell himself. As Bronson has
said, "Philosophy was too narrow a room for his humanity: he
could not look upon a metaphysical system, no matter how pretty
the structure, as a desirable exchange for the rich irrelevancies and
contradictions by which men live."[10]

Johnson's sense of literature derives from a central contradiction
that we would not be surprised to meet if we had not simplified
him out of all recognition. This contradiction is one between the
social sense that literature is a mere rhetorical artifice akin to legal
advocacy, and the religious sense that for the literarily gifted the
production of literature and the living of the life of writing are
very like a Christian sacrament. The opposition is between a cunning knowingness and an almost unbelievable innocence. The
important thing is that both senses are fully developed in Johnson
and that both senses are likely to operate at almost the same time.
We should explore first the side of this polarity where literature
appears as a social, argumentative, and (merely) affective function.

The impact of the law and of lawyers upon Johnson's literary
sensibility has never been emphasized enough. His boyish introduction to learning took place in the legal atmosphere of the Lichfield
Grammar School, proud of its record of producing lawyers and
justices. A boy attending such a school would never have been
allowed to forget what he was there for. As an adult he selected
London lodgings very near the Inns of Court, and the bulk of his
middle-class friends were lawyers. It is no accident that his two
main biographers, Boswell and Sir John Hawkins, were lawyer and
judge respectively: as legally trained professionals, both were drawn
to a mind which so ably could conceive of literature in terms they
too could understand, namely, as quasi-legal argument. At the age
of thirty-two Johnson spent three whole years writing legal argu-

ment as he unlawfully—the contradiction is pleasant and instructive—wrote for *The Gentleman's Magazine* the accounts of the parliamentary debates. We remember the very many times Boswell solicited his advice on specific cases and points of law, and we remember the many brilliant legal briefs Johnson wrote for Boswell as a result. His experience of the law was both theoretical and practical. William Bowles reports: "At one period of his life he used to frequent the office of a Justice of the Peace, under the idea that much of real life is to be learned at such places."[11]

But his deepest immersion in the legal occurred late in his fifties. The great jurist Sir William Blackstone had vacated the Vinerian chair at Oxford. One of Johnson's friends, Judge Robert Chambers, was elected in 1766 to succeed Blackstone in the professorship. Chambers was only twenty-nine, and he was neither a gifted writer nor an impressive legal intelligence. For the next two years Johnson secretly assisted him by quietly writing the Vinerian law lectures for him. The sixty lectures comprise some 1600 pages. Johnson's seriousness about all this, his sense that even though he may be embarking on a rhetorical enterprise not too different from a literary fraud substantial public benefits may emerge, can perhaps be inferred from a prayer "Before the Study of Law," which he recorded in 1765, a year before he knew he would be writing for Chambers:

Almighty God, the giver of wisdom, without whose help resolutions are vain, without whose blessing study is ineffectual, enable me, if it be thy will, to attain such knowledge as may qualify me to direct the doubtful, and instruct the ignorant, to prevent wrongs, and terminate contentions; and grant that I may use that knowledge which I shall attain to thy glory and my own salvation, for Jesus Christ's sake. Amen.

It was only his premature departure from Oxford, enforced by poverty, that kept him from the systematic professional training that would have made him a lawyer instead of a writer. There is no doubt that he would have preferred the law. At one point we find him scribbling in some rough notes what we would call a rationalization of the life of writing compared with the life of legal advocacy:

If write well, not less innocent or laudable than prescribing—pleading —judging. . . . If ill, fails with less hazard to the public than others. The prescriber—pleader—judge hurt others.[12]

But despite such attempts to persuade himself that he had done just as well to become a writer, he never stilled in himself the old legal fervor. When he was almost seventy Sir William Scott said to him: "What a pity it is, Sir, that you did not follow the profession of the law. You might have been Lord Chancellor of Great Britain, and attained to the dignity of the Peerage. . . ." Boswell continues his report of the incident: "Johnson, upon this, seemed much agitated; and in an angry tone exclaimed, 'Why will you vex me by suggesting this, when it is too late?' " We can appreciate the weight of Johnson's contribution to Anglo-Saxon jurisprudence in the Chambers lectures by remembering that he was competing with Blackstone, whose Vinerian lectures became his *Commentaries on the Laws of England*.

It would be a mistake to imagine that in his leanings toward the law Johnson is behaving very idiosyncratically. He is only one among countless eighteenth-century writers who were bred to the law only to deviate into literature. Indeed, this was a convention of behavior almost as inviolable in the eighteenth century as the current convention that a respectable lyric poet must teach in a college and that a Beat poet must not. All this legal study and attendance at the Inns of Court by bright young men throughout the eighteenth century could not help stimulate a bent for argument and rhetoric, as well as a feeling that carefully uttered things—poems, for example—must be carefully uttered in a way that one has been taught. All this legal consciousness could not help stimulate skill in the management of images and ideas less for their own delightful sake than as elements in a process of advocacy. From this proximity of the law to literature stems the very eighteenth-century idea that the act of literature is necessarily an act of argument, that the writer, even when he assumes the role of poet, is most comparable to a barrister arguing a case. Like the barrister, the poet is skilled more in selecting and arranging objective points with an eye to their impact on the audience, a jury of readers, than in exposing his personal singularity or unlocking his heart in public. What the advocate actually thinks about the case in hand is irrelevant: what he says about it publicly determines his failure or success.

From this legal, rhetorical, and affective conception of writing emerge many of Johnson's most impressive literary perceptions. When in his legal mood he is deeply suspicious of any conception of literature which would—naïvely and preposterously, in his view—associate the literary act with the impulse toward uncoded self-expression. One of the most delightful moments in the *Life of Pope*, for example, is his dogged refusal to admit that the private, personal letter is anything but a formal and objective literary genre whose conventions are such that, given the depravity of human nature, almost anything *but* the actual truth about the writer can be disclosed in it. "Of [Pope's] social qualities," he writes,

if an estimate be made from his letters, an opinion too favorable cannot easily be formed; they exhibit a perpetual and unclouded effulgence of general benevolence and particular fondness.

But actually, he continues,

Very few can boast of hearts which they dare lay open to themselves, and of which, by whatever accident exposed, they do not shun a distinct and continued view; and certainly what we hide from ourselves we do not show to our friends.

The conclusion is inescapable: the personal letter is exactly the *least* sincere and natural of all the genres:

There is, indeed, no transaction which offers stronger temptations to fallacy and sophistication than epistolary intercourse.

Which is to say that, paradoxically, there is no literary kind, not even the pastoral or the epitaph or the masque, whose conventions and rhetorical environment remove it further from "nature" or the artless than the personal letter. So much for appearances.

Again, writing to Mrs. Thrale in 1777, Johnson takes pains to explode the common myth that a genre like the letter, because it uses the conventions of sincerity and openness, is thus a vehicle of genuine self-disclosure. With the sort of sardonic irony possible only to those whose sense of genre is exquisitely developed, he tells Mrs. Thrale:

In a man's letters, you know, Madam, his soul lies naked; his letters are only the mirror of his breast; whatever passes within him is shown undisguised in its natural process. Nothing is inverted, nothing distorted. You see systems in their elements, you discover actions in their motives.

And he goes on to stigmatize this plausible proposition as a "great truth sounded by the knowing to the ignorant, and so echoed by the ignorant to the knowing." Is he thinking perhaps of Henry Fielding, who had written in his Preface to Sarah Fielding's *Familiar Letters on David Simple* (1747):

Those writings which are called letters may be divided into four classes. Under the first class may be ranged those letters, as well ancient as modern, which have been written by men who have filled up the principal characters on the stage of life upon great and memorable occasions. These have been always esteemed as the most valuable parts of history, as they are not only the most authentic memorials of facts, but as they serve greatly to illustrate the true character of the writer, and do in a manner introduce the person himself to our acquaintance.

Cant, Johnson would say. The Bishop of St. Asaph is another who has not thought about the matter enough. He once said to Johnson that "it appeared from Horace's writings that he was a cheerful, contented man. JOHNSON. 'We have no reason to believe that, my Lord. Are we to think Pope was happy, because he says so in his writings? We see in his writings what he wished the state of his mind to appear.' "

But the letter is only one of the genres whose operation makes "self-expression" either a ridiculous image or a dangerous and ultimately self-destructive illusion. The poem is another. As Johnson observes in the *Life of Pope*, "Poets do not always express their own thoughts." He illustrates this principle in the *Life of Thomson*:

Savage, who lived much with Thomson, once told me he heard a lady remarking that she could gather from his works three parts of his character, that he was 'a great lover, a great swimmer, and rigorously abstinent'; but, said Savage, he knows not any love but that of the sex; he was perhaps never in cold water in his life; and he indulges himself in all the luxury that comes within his reach.

Again, Johnson instructs Lord Monboddo, who, like Thomson's "lady," also entertains simplistic and sentimental notions about literary composition:

It does not always follow. . .that a man who has written a good poem on an art has practiced it. Philip Miller told me that in [John] Philips' *Cider: A Poem* all the precepts were just, and indeed better than in books written for the purpose of instructing, yet Philips had never made cider.

Clearly "making" books is an operation by itself.

What all this shows is that Johnson fully understands that the relation between poet and poem is not the relation between penitent and confessor: it is rather the relation between barrister and client. Regardless of his personal adhesions, the barrister is to collect, arrange, and express appropriately—which means convincingly— all the materials he can find which favor his client's position. As Johnson puts it when talking about the epitaph as a genre,

The writer of an epitaph is not to be considered as saying nothing but what is strictly true. Allowance must be made for some degree of exaggerated praise. In lapidary inscriptions a man is not upon oath.

Nor is he any more "'upon oath" in his temporary engagement
with any other genre. No friend of idleness, Johnson at least would
understand what Blake is getting at with "soft deceit" in

> Soft deceit and idleness,
> These are beauty's sweetest dress.

A good way to get a feeling for Johnson's rhetorical and legal
sense of literature is to attend closely to the recorded activity of
his mind on one given day of his life. The day I choose is Sunday,
August 15, 1773: he and Boswell are starting to tour the Hebrides,
and on August 15 they are in Edinburgh. Boswell spends the day
introducing his "illustrious friend" to various Scottish intellectuals,
and during the long day the talk weaves in and out of numerous
topics. But it returns constantly to two: the law and literature. In
the morning, as Boswell reports,

> We talked of the practice of the law. Sir William Forbes said he
> thought an honest lawyer should never undertake a cause [case] which
> he was satisfied was not a just one. 'Sir,' said Mr. Johnson, 'a lawyer
> has no business with the justice or injustice of the cause which he
> undertakes. . . . The justice or injustice of the cause is to be decided
> by the judge. . . . Lawyers [like poets, we may observe] are a class of
> the community who, by study and experience, have acquired the art
> and power of arranging evidence and of applying to the points at
> issue what the law has settled.'

To this Boswell listens admiringly, and he comments: "This was
sound practical doctrine, and rationally repressed a too-refined
scrupulosity of conscience."

After this conversation in the morning, Johnson and his Scottish
admirers attend a sermon, thus undergoing another experience
of literature employed in the service less of "sincerity" than of
advocacy. The sermon over, conversation turns to James Beattie's
Essay on Truth (1770), an attack on the skepticism of Hume,
and now Johnson chooses to image the philosophic dialogue
between Beattie and Hume as adversary proceedings. As he says:
"Treating your adversary with respect is giving him an advantage

to which he is not entitled. The greatest part of men cannot judge of reasoning, and are impressed by character; so that if you allow your adversary a respectable character, they will think that though you differ from him, you may be in the wrong."

Johnson next receives the historian William Robertson, who arrives after dinner for wine and conversation. The talk turns now to matters of eloquence and literature, and yet the legal theme persists as a sort of ground bass. Edmund Burke, says Johnson, in his literary character has "great variety of knowledge, store of imagery, copiousness of language." According to Boswell's account of the conversation, just forty seconds later Johnson is moved to say that "he believed Burke was intended for the law, but either had not money enough to follow it or had not diligence enough." This leads to talk about general powers of mind. As Boswell reports,

Robertson said one had more judgment, another more imagination. JOHNSON. 'No, Sir; it is only one man has more mind than another. He may direct it differently; he may by accident see the success of one kind of study and take a desire to excel in it. I am persuaded that had Sir Isaac Newton applied to poetry, he would have made a very fine epic poem. I could as easily apply to law as to tragic poetry.' BOSWELL. 'Yet, Sir, you *did* apply to tragic poetry, not to law.' JOHNSON. 'Because, Sir, I had not money to study law.'

Of this virtual equation of advocacy with the arts of epic and tragedy—notice the suggestive word *made*—Jean Hagstrum has rightly said:

In this lively interchange of opinion Johnson denies any special position to literature and removes from it the mystification that has often surrounded it. He relates it to the law, to mathematics, and to other coördinate disciplines. The assumption is that literature . . . is an austere and rigorous mental pursuit.[13]

This long day of conversation associating law, eloquence, intellectual characteristics, the choice of careers, epic, and tragedy ends with Johnson's memorable expression of good-natured contempt for Garrick's flamboyant style in tragic acting. It is a remark emphasizing artistic awareness and control that suitably brings this day to a close. Boswell says, "When I asked him, 'Would not you, Sir, start as Mr. Garrick does if you saw a ghost?' he answered, 'I hope not. If I did, I should frighten the ghost.'"

Making the proper *effect* on the audience is thus what literature is for. Johnson's concern about the affective operations of works of art regardless of the personal intention or actual state of mind of those who "make" them is reflected even in his non-literary moments. Fanny Burney reports a conversation between Johnson and Henry Thrale on the not very momentous matter of Johnson's ambition to buy for his fireplace a jack, that is, a conspicuous clockwork engine for turning a roasting spit mechanically:

JOHNSON. 'I have some thoughts (with a profound gravity) of buying a jack, because I think a jack is some credit to a house.'
MR. THRALE. 'Well, but you'll have a spit too?'
JOHNSON. 'No, Sir, no; that would be superfluous; for we shall never use it; if a jack is seen, a spit will be presumed!'

We could hardly find a more memorable formula for Johnson's shrewd rhetorical sense of literature: "If a jack is seen, a spit will be presumed." Which is to say that if emotion in a poem is seen, a common reader will naturally presume a cause of emotion in the writer of the poem, and that is all to the good. But a more sophisticated reader will know that actually there is no necessary cause of emotion in the writer: what is "in" him at the moment of writing is simply a mastery of techniques for imposing an illusion by the known means appropriate to the genre in which he is working. Actual emotion would be "superfluous," an encumbrance and a waste of time.

This acute awareness of necessary artifice constitutes one of the poles of Johnson's sense of literature. We must now consider the other pole, which we will find him embracing no less seriously. Our text now is his *Life of Milton*, especially the passage embodying the well-known denigration of *Lycidas*. And when considering

Johnson on *Lycidas*, we must remember that his depreciation of that poem occurs within a context of critical praise of Milton's epic achievement so lavish and enthusiastic that it seems hardly to belong to the familiar Johnson at all. He concludes the *Life of Milton* and his appraisal of *Paradise Lost* in these terms: "[*Paradise Lost*] is not the greatest of heroic poems, only because it is not the first." That is, it is second only to the *Iliad*: it is superior to all others, including the *Odyssey*, the *Aeneid*, and the epics of the Italian Renaissance. This is a remarkable flux of enthusiasm from Johnson, the man who was constantly reminding his friends that nothing damaged an object or person so severely as excessive praise. We should always be mindful of this warm conclusion of the *Life of Milton* when we encounter his earlier scorn for Milton's republicanism, his "Turkish contempt of females," and his performance in pastoral elegy.

Johnson begins his critical scrutiny of *Lycidas* this way:

> One of the poems on which much praise has been bestowed ["much praise" of anything always triggers Johnson's skeptical contrariness] is *Lycidas*, of which the diction is harsh, the rhymes uncertain, and the numbers unpleasing.

So far Johnson's critical action has taken place well within the boundaries ordained by his sense of literature as rhetoric. Milton's language in *Lycidas* is too rare and remote ("harsh") to operate upon the normal reader. The rhymes occur unpredictably, with the result that the reader, naturally expecting rhyming at established, predictable intervals, is frustrated as he reads. And the versification likewise distresses the reader accustomed to the milder metrical surprises customary in Augustan poetry. Johnson maintains his affective focus through the next sentence:

> What beauty there is we must therefore seek in the sentiments and images.

We notice that Johnson's eye is still on that part of the process of literary transmission where rhetoric presides; that is, on the relation, necessarily social as well as artistic, between speaker and audience.

But with the next sentence everything changes. We are suddenly whisked out of the world of rhetoric altogether and thrust into quite another critical atmosphere. Sophistication suddenly yields to what must strike us as an almost unbelievable naïveté. For now Johnson attacks on the premise that a poem ought to embody the actual personal emotion of its contriver, presumably—and this is always an embarrassment to theories of self-expression—at the exact moment when the composition was begun:

[*Lycidas*] is not to be considered as the effusion of real passion; for passion runs not after remote allusions and obscure opinions.

Having shifted the critical focus without warning, he goes on now to talk not about the effect of the work on the apprehender but about a totally different subject, the authenticity of the "passion" which, we are asked to assume with Johnson, gave rise to the poetic artifact in the first place:

Passion plucks no berries from the myrtle and ivy, nor calls upon Arethuse and Mincius, nor tells of 'rough satyrs and fauns with cloven heel.'

What Johnson assumes here—and in a way which he would be quick to reprehend when in his "rhetorical" mood—is that actual passion was actually felt by the maker of the poem, and that this undeniable passion has leaked away or been invalidated by having been encoded injudiciously. Assuming that actual grief ought really to be present in the writer—that is, that the man and the poet are identical—he goes on to assert: "Where there is leisure for fiction there is little grief."

The premises underlying such formulations are close to the premises of Method acting, and in his rhetorical moments Johnson is quite ready to equate the actor with the writer or rhetor. When he is in his rhetorical posture he naturally feels nothing but disdain

for the assumptions made by the eighteenth-century equivalent of
the Method actor. As Boswell writes:

> Johnson . . . had thought more upon the subject of acting than
> might be generally supposed. Talking of it one day to Mr. [John
> Philip] Kemble, he said, 'Are you, Sir, one of those enthusiasts who
> believe yourself transformed into the very character you represent?'
> Upon Mr. Kemble's answering that he never felt so strong a per-
> suasion himself: 'To be sure not, Sir (said Johnson) ; the thing is
> impossible. And if Garrick really believed himself to be that monster
> Richard the Third, he deserved to be hanged every time he per-
> formed it.'

But what Johnson demands of the Milton of *Lycidas* is very like
what he condemns in theatrical "enthusiasts"; he really expects
Milton on this occasion to have behaved like a Method actor, to
have felt real grief and to have embodied it in some presumably
non-literary code.

On another, more important, occasion, Johnson likewise indicates
that he will have no truck with the assumptions ultimately underlying theories of literary "sincerity." The occasion is the *Preface to
Shakespeare*, where he advances hard-headed empirical arguments
against the unities of time and place in the drama:

> The truth is that the spectators are always in their senses, and know,
> from the first act to the last, that the stage is only a stage, and that
> the players are only players. They come to hear a certain number of
> lines recited with just gesture and elegant modulation. . . . Where is
> the absurdity of allowing that space to represent first Athens, and then
> Sicily, which was always known to be neither Sicily nor Athens, but
> a modern theater?

But what he requires of *Lycidas* is that it cease being a poem, that
is, a confessed theater of artifice, and become instead an actual
utterance of instinctive grief, like a cry or a sob. In his other mood,
he knows, of course, much better than this: when, for example, he
wants to lament the death of Dr. Robert Levet, he betakes himself to the artificial mechanisms of stanza form and poetic diction,

and he uses a meter deriving from previous poems rather than from the pulses of his heart. Likewise in his Prayers, where he stays as close as he can to convention so that he will have something meaningful to say. But with *Lycidas* he chooses to forget that a poem is only a poem, and that by definition the poet is a contriver of effects, not an experiencer of emotion. He chooses to forget that the reader of a poem, very like the spectator in the theater, comes to the poem to be given "a certain number of lines" contrived "with just gesture and elegant modulation."

After his inquiry into the validity of the grief felt by the man Milton before or perhaps during the composition of *Lycidas* (or maybe even during one of its revisions—which one?), an inquiry which strikes us as so un-shrewd as to embarrass any critic, he proceeds, oscillating now between his polar senses of literature as self-expression and actual record, on the one hand, and, on the other, of literature as rhetoric and necessary artifice:

In this poem, there is no nature, for there is no truth.

This means two things at once: it means that considered as an act of self-expression the poem is too grossly a lie because we know that the grief it pretends to register was not felt by the author; and at the same time it means that the poem, considered as a piece of rhetoric, employs a code which strikes the reader as too "remote" from the artistically familiar to stimulate a conventional, and thus a literary or even "stock," response. Johnson's statement means these two things at once, but the simultaneousness of the meanings does not make them any more compatible. And he continues:

There is no art, for there is nothing new.

He has now stepped wholly back into the critical world of rhetorical analysis, deploring the exhaustion of a genre. It is his powerful sense of the exhaustion of the genre of pastoral elegy that urges him to his next lively, perpetually delightful statement:

Its form is that of a pastoral, easy, vulgar, and therefore disgusting; whatever images it can supply are long ago exhausted——

But as he goes on, he swings toward the other pole, momentarily abandoning objective questions of genre-exhaustion to probe again the matter of sincerity:

——and its inherent improbability always forces dissatisfaction on the mind.

The antithetic critical emphases, now on rhetoric, now on sincerity, interweave as Johnson proceeds, but we feel that what the interweaving produces is not of one texture: it is rather like a fabric made by weaving together the inorganic and the organic, steel filaments with silk:

When Cowley tells of Hervey that they studied together, it is easy *to suppose* how much *he must miss* the companion of his labors and the partner of his discoveries; but what image of tenderness *can be excited by* these lines!

> We drove afield, and both together heard
> What time the grey fly winds her sultry horn,
> Batt'ning our flocks with the fresh dews of night.

We know that they never drove afield, and that they had no flocks to batten; and though it be allowed that *the representation* may be allegorical, the true meaning is so uncertain and remote that *it is never sought* because *it cannot be known* when it is found [my emphases].

After another paragraph devoted to condemning "mythological imagery, such as a college easily supplies," Johnson implicitly discloses what has been troubling him all along: the poem, taken either as "expression" or artifact, can easily embolden impiety because it mingles pagan with Christian myth as if they are of equal efficacy:

This poem has yet a grosser fault. With these trifling fictions [that is, 'the puerilities of obsolete mythology'] are mingled the most awful and sacred truths, such as ought never to be polluted with such irreverent combinations. The shepherd . . . is now a feeder of sheep, and afterwards an ecclesiastical pastor, a superintendent of a Christian flock. Such equivocations are always unskillful; but here they are indecent, and at least approach to impiety, of which, however, I believe the writer not to have been conscious.

Of course Milton was not conscious of any risk of impiety in the way Johnson was, for Johnson was beleaguered by Freethinkers and aware that he did not have much company in his defense of the shaky Christian fortress against the assaults of critics like Voltaire and Hume. His sensitivity to the tiniest literary threats to orthodoxy is acute. In *Rambler* 140 he censures Milton's reference in *Samson Agonistes* to the patently fictive phoenix as if it were as real as the rest of his materials. And in *Rambler* 168 his objection to the "low" word *dunnest* in *Macbeth* I, v, 48–52 ("an epithet now seldom heard but in the stable") arises not from linguistic snobbery but from the fact that the word occurs only two lines before the word *heaven* used as a metaphor for God: its proximity thus might be thought to lower or trivialize a religious image associated with the obligations of conscience.

We see, then, that it is Johnson's sense of the subtle moral and theological damage *Lycidas* may do *to the reader* that provides the spring for the whole critique. In perceiving that his care is ultimately for the reader, we may say that what finally wins out is his sense that literature is primarily rhetoric. But this sense wins out only after a very dubious battle with a contradictory conception of what writing is.

Any lingering superstition that Johnson can be meaningfully described as, in some way, a "neo-classic" critic ("With him it is all white or black, right or wrong: there exists only one standard, which is the classical, that can win the approval of Samuel Johnson the Dictator"—L. Archer-Hind, 1925)[14] will be evaporated by a close scrutiny of his remarks on *Lycidas*, a poem in which "there is no art, for there is nothing new." It is precisely the neo-classic element in the poem that disgusts him.

To turn to the *Life of Prior* is to see clearly that Johnson is not a neo-classicist but an empiricist. And here again we experience his oscillations between the poles established by the rhetorical and the self-expressive conceptions of writing. He begins the critical part of the *Life of Prior* by stressing Prior's skill in rhetoric, his willingness to exercise himself in a variety of known styles, not all of which, obviously, can "naturally" be his "own," in the sense that a person is conceived to have one style in which he expresses himself most "sincerely." "Prior," Johnson says,

has written with great variety, and his variety has made him popular. He has tried all styles, from the grotesque to the solemn, and has not so failed in any as to incur derision or disgrace.

After thus registering Prior's easy intercourse with a whole world of objective styles, and registering it with a high consciousness of the social contexts of rhetoric ("derision or disgrace"), Johnson focuses on Prior's performance within the various genres. And now of Prior's love poems he astonishes us by saying:

In his amorous effusions he is less happy [than in his Tales]; for they are not dictated by nature or by passion, and have neither gallantry nor tenderness.

Surely what he is saying is that these love poems fail of the illusions of gallantry and tenderness *because* they are not dictated by actual or natural passion. As he points out, the artistic result of this deplorable insincerity is a plethora of neo-classical Venuses and Cupids, darts and quivers, all of which, he says, "is surely despicable." And, he continues, "even when [Prior] tries to act the lover without the help of gods or goddesses, his thoughts are unaffecting or remote." We are to deduce that the thoughts are unaffecting or remote because they issue from a convention rather than a unique, genuine personal occasion. Boswell reports: "Mrs. Thrale disputed with him on the merit of Prior. He attacked him powerfully; said he wrote of love like a man who had never felt it: his love verses were college verses." In the *Life of Hammond* Johnson puts the point a little differently, but no less clearly: "He that courts his mistress with Roman imagery deserves to lose her; for she may with good reason suspect his sincerity." Again, in the

Life of Cowley, he argues that Petrarch's love poems are more valid than Cowley's because Petrarch was really a lover. As he says, "He that professes love ought to feel its power." Here his assumptions about literary sincerity are like those in the *Life of Waller*, where he takes Waller to task for writing panegyrics alike to Charles I, Cromwell, and Charles II in their seasons. It is impossible, says Johnson, to witness behavior like this "without some contempt and indignation."

But while he is implying that certain kinds of writing must be sincere to be valid, he is implying at the same time that there are certain poetic forms in which it is difficult for communication to take place. As we have seen, neo-classic pastoral is one such form. Another is the neo-classic love poem. A third is the religious lyric. Like the love song, it deals with a matter too elemental— or too embarrassing—to be embodied in poetry. As Johnson says in the *Life of Waller*:

Contemplative piety, or the intercourse between God and the human soul, cannot be poetical. Man, admitted to implore the mercy of his Creator, and plead the merits of his Redeemer, is already in a higher state than poetry can confer.

Which is to say that literature is only literature after all. As Maurice Quinlan has perceived, "His general dislike of religious poetry . . . was based on his belief that verse was a too artful and therefore not a sincere means of addressing or praising the Deity."[15] But even here, where Johnson is finding certain poetic forms or rhetorical stances impossible, he is really focusing on the nature of the *passion* which presumably underlies and determines them. That the passion is genuine, even sacred, and not affected for purposes of artistic illusion he has no doubts.

These, then, are the poles defining the Johnsonian senses of literature. On the one hand, literature is akin to legal argument and implies a similar objective process: a canvass of received formulations and devices which will work—that is, persuade—

because they are familiar. On the other hand, literature is what happens when genuine self-expression occurs: it emanates from a motive which shuns the familiar in favor of the unique, the "authentic." It could be argued, I suppose, that Johnson's relation to these poles is something like a coherent suspension (the word *tension* would come in nicely) rather than the contradictory oscillation I have suggested. But the trouble with such a view is that it would risk imposing a system (or, in Johnson's own skeptical term, a "scheme") on a literary sensibility which, for all its appearance of judiciousness, is really madly irrational, unsystematic, impulsive, and untidy. As a critic adrift without the neo-classic certainties, Johnson could be said to have been mad all his life, or at least not sober. Dr. Richard Brocklesby gives an acute interpretation of his predicament:

His religion . . . made his extraordinary talents of mind continually at war with each other, so that in his later days his philosophy seemed to draw his mind one way, and his religion biassed him to the contrary. . . .[16]

This warfare seems to be the cause as it is the analogue of the battle between his two senses of literature—between the "philosophic," indeed worldly, sense that literature ought to be rhetorical, i.e., effective; and the ultimately religious sense that it ought to be, before all else, honest.

Of Johnson's conversation Oliver Goldsmith once said: "There is no arguing with Johnson; for when his pistol misses fire, he knocks you down with the butt end of it." The two Johnsonian senses of literature seem to me as far apart as the business end and the butt end of the pistol. His theory of literature can be said to achieve unity only in the sense that the mind busy at either pole applies to its tasks the same energy and raciness, brings to its inconsistent, pragmatic, empirical but none the less urgent business the same quality of honesty. It is an honesty which refuses to report contradictions as elements in a coherent system. "Inconsistencies cannot both be right; but, imputed to man, they may both be true."

And why shouldn't Johnson be inconsistent? He had no notion that two hundred years after his time he would be an "object of study." He is engaged in a day-by-day struggle to be plausible, intelligent, and faithful to the pressure of the moment, and the schemes and systems of a reason-worshiping world—especially those systems the future has devised for making literature a teachable, memorizable subject—are irrelevant to his activity. Perhaps they are irrelevant to ours.

CHAPTER 3

The Force of Genre

In considering Johnson's vigorous but richly inconsistent approach to literature, we have perceived his implicit unwillingness to decide finally whether literature is essentially an objective function related to a world of fixed literary forms outside the writer and validated by the impact of the work on the reader; or whether literature is essentially a private and internal function validated by its accuracy in registering the state of the writer's convictions or emotions at the moment of composition. When we see him associating writing with legal argument, we see him conceiving of it in one way; when we see him doubting Milton's or Prior's sincerity, we see him conceiving of it in quite another way.

We need now to explore more of the implications of these two views of what writing is. I am first going to consider the theory of genre to which Johnson commits himself when he thinks of literature as analogous to legal argument. Then I want to examine the powerful religious causes of his occasional adherence to the opposite, the "sincere" conception of writing.

The theory of literature I am relying on to shed some light on Johnson's life of writing is simple, empirical, and quite unoriginal. It derives largely from three well-known places: Harry Levin's essay of 1946, "Literature as an Institution";[1] Northrop Frye's speculations, in *Anatomy of Criticism*, about the autotelic world of literary forms; and E. H. Gombrich's demonstration, in *Art and Illusion*, of the indispensability of a "coded" or pre-structured or systematized medium if artistic communication is to take place at all. What I assume is that we recognize a piece of writing as literature only through our prior acceptance of the convention that its genre is literary: otherwise we do not notice it, or we do not notice it artistically. We don't regard our notes to the milkman as in any way literary not because they *are* not, in fact, literary but because we have been trained to regard them as not literary. But we can easily imagine a world quite like ours in which such notes—as well as lecture notes, minutes of meetings, editorials, written political arguments—seem obviously the genres in which "literature" takes place and where it is thus to be looked for, while poems, short stories, novels, and plays are conceived and written so sloppily that they have ceased to engage the attention of the critically sophisticated. Although Johnson cannot quite be said to have lived in such a world, he did inhabit a literary environment whose recognized formal species seemed more numerous and more permanent, and were more likely to assume the form of some kind of workaday prose, than in those artistic environments that have succeeded his. It is this matter of the recognized force of genre in Johnson's literary world that I want to examine.

In writing undertaken under a consciousness of the idea of literary sincerity or self-expression, the writer perforce focuses on himself, or at least on that space between himself and the work he is contriving as a simulacrum of his presumed state of mind. But in writing undertaken under the antithetic consciousness of the force of genre, the writer focuses not on himself but on his audience and on its expectations and probable reactions. These are two different images of what writing is, and they would appear not to sort together. Because we have inherited so much Romantic critical theory, when we scrutinize any earlier writer innocent of the Romantic conception of literature we are very likely to overstress the "private" elements in his writing to the neglect of elements which, with Harry Levin, we can call "institutional." As Levin writes:

Amid the mutations of modern individualism, we may very conceivably have overstressed the private aspects of writing. One convenience of the institutional method is that it gives due credit to the audience, and to the never-ending collaboration between writer and public. It sees no reason to ignore what is relevant in the psychological prepossessions of the craftsman, and it knows that he is ultimately to be rated by the technical resources of his craftsmanship; but it attains its clearest and fullest scope by centering on his craft, upon his social status and his historical function as participant in a skilled calling and a living tradition.[2]

The literary world in which Johnson found himself operating was, in Levin's sense, a consciously institutionalized one, and it is a world superficially so different from ours that sometimes we rub our eyes. But the important point is this: the difference between the two literary worlds is really only superficial, for in our time as in all others genre retains its wonderful power to say what *it* rather than the individual talent would like to say.

We have inherited from Romanticism a critical terminology which persuades us that genres exist—if they can be said to have anything like existence at all—only to be stretched and bent and burst and finally annihilated by the all-powerful unique personality. But sometimes we forget that Romantic critical terminology— terms like *creation, expression, imagination, inspiration*—has no more ultimate validity than that attaching to any similar tools of propaganda. Romantic critical terms are terms of rhetoric, not terms of measurement or description. Their function is to heat up the environment or to make the audience do something. They are as rhetorical as contemporary political terms like *self-determination, freedom,* or *social justice.* If we can put Romantic critical terminology aside for a moment—talking, for example, not of literary "creation" but of "composition" or "construction"—I think we can illuminate not merely Johnson's way with genres but our own less conscious way with them.

In looking at eighteenth-century literature in general we never really get over our surprise that people wrote essentially the same poem over and over again—Horatian ode, Pindaric ode, pseudo-Georgic, topographical poem. This surprises us because we fancy that poets in our time do not do this. But we can easily disabuse ourselves of this notion by taking a look at some of our contemporary genres which are largely unrecognizable only because it seems in no one's interest to recognize them. It is surely not in the poet's interest, for a large part of his stock-in-trade remains—as for his Romantic and late-Romantic predecessors—a reputation for high personal creativeness, "originality," and even gross personal idiosyncrasy. It is humanly too much to ask a poet to repudiate those things in his behavior, work, reputation, and career for which he is specifically noticed and praised. Think of Dylan Thomas.

At the risk of facetiousness we can designate a number of modern poetic genres providing paradigms for contemporary poems which, like those in the eighteenth century, are written over and over again, often without our noticing it. We have, for example, the Lyric of Confession or Self-Accusation, as in Delmore Schwartz's "The Heavy Bear," W. D. Snodgrass's "April Inventory," and more recently Robert Lowell's "Man and Wife." Indeed, Lowell's performances in this genre invite us to devise a subclassification, which we might call The Divorce Meditation. Another standard genre of our time, as conventional as the Prospect Poem was in Johnson's, is The Animal Hymn, practiced by D. H. Lawrence, Marianne Moore, William Carlos Williams, Elizabeth

Bishop, Theodore Roethke, and repeatedly by Robert Bly, whose speciality is those saintly horses rather like Houyhnhnms.

We have The Homecoming Celebration, as in Frost's "Directive," Thomas's "Fern Hill," and Lowell's "Returning." We have the Ironic or Industrial Pastoral, practiced by Williams, Eliot in the "Preludes," Louis MacNeice, and Louis Simpson. We have the Apocalyptic, or Nuclear, Lyric, whose paradigm is hinted in Auden's "September 1, 1939," and one of whose most conspicuous and successful later practitioners has been Lowell, over and over again: a good example is a poem like "Fall, 1961," or his recent "Waking Early Sunday Morning." We have the Italianate Topographical Meditation: examples are Lowell's "Florence," Thomas Kinsella's "O Rome," and Richard Wilbur's "A Baroque Wall-Fountain in the Villa Sciarra." The Death-by-Drowning Elegy retains its popularity, offering now as in Milton's time abundant opportunities for baptism paradoxes: Eliot's "Phlebas the Phoenician," from *The Waste Land*, is the progenitor of Lowell's "In Memory of Arthur Winslow" and William Meredith's "The Wreck of the *Thresher*." The poem we can call The Song of the Foetus, ultimately after Blake, is practiced by MacNeice, Lowell ("Child's Song"), Roethke, Randall Jarrell, and John Berryman. The distinction of Yeats's Crazy Jane songs has resulted in a popular genre handily referred to as The Lady's Lubricious Meditation: such a poem is Auden's "Song for St. Cecilia's Day," or Lowell's "Lady Ralegh's Lament," or Roethke's "Old Lady's Winter Words." We even have The Florida Celebration, practiced by Wallace Stevens, Robert Penn Warren, and Elizabeth Bishop. But perhaps the grandest and most substantial of modern poetic genres is the Lyric Epic, deriving from *Song of Myself* and attaining successive incarnations in *The Bridge*, the *Cantos*, and *Paterson*.

To point to these genres even thus whimsically is not to ridicule them or their practitioners: it is to ridicule a kind of criticism which chooses not to notice the conventionality of contemporary writing but which instead has repeated recourse to the exhausted propaganda slogans of Romantic theory. The actual poets know better than their critics and theorists: they seldom cant about "originality" or "creativeness," spending their time instead writing, often brilliantly, the same conventional kinds of poems again and again. Their actual behavior I would instance, following Frye, as the universal way of writers.

I once heard my friend Geoffrey Hartman speak with some disdain of "the derivative nature of neo-classical verse." But if we inspect any poetry with a close enough attention to its institutional character, we will be forced to wonder why the term *derivative* should continue to carry such a pejorative literary sense. I think we are still capable at times of being hoodwinked by the rhetorical and polemic force of Romantic critical terminology.

A Romantic criticism which programmatically confuses certain meaningful myths of creation with the conditions of actual composition, or which uses the one to "illustrate" the other, seems to me interestingly analogous to that school in modern archeology which bases its operations on a sentimental confusion between the literary and the actual, the artistic and the documentary. This school has been the constant butt of M. I. Finley's pleasant and instructive criticism, which among other things has exposed the "sleight of hand by which Atlantis is dragged from Platonic myth to history."[3] We have all had our laughs over Heinrich Schliemann's conviction, upon uncovering the golden mask at Mycenae, that, as he declared with self-congratulatory orotundity, "I have gazed on the face of Agamemnon."[4] The exhibition of "Juliet's balcony" in Verona can be taken, if we are generous, as tongue-in-cheek. But what are we to think of the naïve literary assumptions underlying Immanuel Velikovsky's *Worlds in Collision*, namely, that literature has a one-to-one relation to actual events? What are we to think of the announced discovery of "Nestor's palace" or of the recent solemn excavations of "King Arthur's Camelot" in Cornwall? All these efforts seem wonderfully expressive of the sort of naïveté about art and its special kinds of validity which is the modern inheritance from Romantic critical propaganda. It is all a little like searching for Spenser's Cave of Error, finding it in the Welsh hills, and then exhibiting it to tourists. For all the sophistication of its technology, contemporary archeology stands in desperate need of an equally sophisticated theory of literature, one recognizing that aspirations toward "documentary" or even accurate annals are only a very recent and thus a unique phenomenon.

We have clearly lost something priceless since the eighteenth century, when no one imagined that writing was not a very sophisticated matter. No one then conceived that the genres did not exist; no one imagined that they were not conventional; and no one fancied that he could write at all without consciously choosing one of them to work in and thus necessarily writing like other people working in that genre. If we are to understand the literary state of things in Johnson's time, we must first disencumber ourselves of Romantic theories of writing, especially theories and images of what a writer is supposed to be like. Far from representing any kind of "spontaneous overflow of powerful feelings," poetry in Johnson's time was thought of as a mode of rhetoric, defined as the art of persuasion or plausibility by means of the selection and disposition of a multitude of traditional techniques of argument. Its nearest "sister art," for all the eighteenth-century chatter about Horace's *ut pictura poesis*, was not painting; nor was its nearest correlative action the act of meditation. Its closest relative was public speaking, as George Campbell explains in *The Philosophy of Rhetoric* (1776):

> Poetry indeed is properly no other than a particular mode or form of certain branches of oratory. . . . The same medium—language—is made use of; the same general rules of composition in narration, description, argumentation are observed; and the same tropes and figures, either for beautifying or invigorating the diction, are employed in both.

This conception of poetry as one of the modes of oratory is a perfectly natural attendant of the education in Latin literature which, until late in the century, was all but universal. Indeed, the only conspicuous poets of the age who did not undergo the

traditional study of the Roman rhetoricians and poets were Chatterton, Burns, and Blake: their susceptibility to the appeal of native
ballad and song styles is the result of their having access to no
other tradition to imitate. All the other eighteenth-century poets
began by studying at school the Roman rhetoricians and oratorical
theorists, especially Quintilian and Cicero. They then proceeded
to apply the devices of Roman argumentation and persuasive
description as they wrote their own Latin school poems. Only
after this careful groundwork did they compose their own poems
in English. Johnson was one who never left his Latin behind,
using it to the end of his life as a decently obscure medium for
registering his more personal delights and sorrows.

All this consciousness of the rhetorical, even the polemic, character of poetry accompanied an awareness of the objective world
of poetic kinds. To most twentieth-century readers a contemporary
poem is a poem: it is hard to sense any determining difference
between, say, the mode of *The Waste Land* and the mode of one
of Pound's *Cantos*. But in Johnson's day the distinctions between
the poetic kinds were still clear and firm, just as they had been
in Roman theory. One began writing a poem with a distinct sense
of the kind of poem one wanted to produce. One then selected
the meter, diction, figures, and structure appropriate to that kind
only, and fit for no other. One wrote, that is, not a "poem," but a
satire, a song, a pastoral, an elegy, an ode, an epitaph, or an
epigram. It is true that the hard-and-fast distinctions between the
poetic kinds seemed to fade as the eighteenth century drew to a
close and as the magisterial ascendancy of Latin learning began
to be challenged. And yet as late as 1799 a critic like Joseph
Robertson could still discriminate the genres and assert the traditional hierarchy of kinds, running from epic at the top, through
stage tragedy and comedy, to pastoral, elegy, "lyric"—that is,
Horatian and Pindaric odes—with satire at the bottom. And Keats's
careful distinction in his own work of the various modes of songs,
odes, epistles, sonnets, tales, Spenserian imitations, and other
precise kinds reveals his proximity to the earlier rhetorical tradi-

tion. So in its odd way does Wordsworth's labored and not very meaningful division of his own poems into new but nonetheless distinct categories like "Poems Founded on the Affections," "Poems of the Fancy," "Poems of the Imagination," and "Poems of Sentiment and Reflection." If the categories are new, the impulse to make them is old. We are a world away: the only arrangement modern poets recognize is the chronological.

In dwelling upon the distinctions between the kinds, eighteenth-century critics usually availed themselves of analogies drawn from the conspicuously inorganic art of architecture. Dryden had found that " 'Tis with a poet, as with a man who designs to build." And more than a half century later, Johnson instinctively compares the playwright to the architect who designs fortresses, just as he readily perceives all the possible parallels between the epic poem and the palace. Besides suggesting the presumed objective existence and the unchanging psychological basis of the genres, these architectural analogues imply that the whole body of poetry constitutes a sort of permanent city of art—like contemporary London, or even like a restored city of Rome—consisting of groups of predominantly public buildings designed for clear and different political, legal, religious, and social purposes. And the city of literature to an eighteenth-century intelligence had all the wonderful solidity and social availability of the actual city of London in which he breathed and had his being, the city whose public

> towers, domes, theaters, and temples

Wordsworth conceived of as constituting a "mighty heart." The metaphor of architecture in which the poetic genres are commonly discussed betokens both the urban and the urbane commitments of those who delight to employ it.

Within this solid world of genres, one way the poet could exhibit his tact was by his initial selection of a poetic kind suited to his individual talents. Johnson thus reveals not his limitations but his strength by declining to write sonnets and composing instead theatrical prologues, satires, elegies, and songs. As a critic of Thomas Gray, Johnson regrets that the author of *Elegy Written in a Country Churchyard* ever so far forgot his natural bent of mind as to attempt Pindaric odes. Having selected the appropriate genre for himself, the poet solicits praise by attending carefully to the technical requirements of his chosen poetic kind. One of the faults Johnson finds in Cowley is that he seems occasionally unaware that each poetic kind requires a different idiom. Cowley, he says, "makes no selection of words. . . . He has given the same diction to the gentle Anacreon and the tempestuous Pindar." Writers are limited creatures, and they can be ruined by undertaking the wrong genre. As Johnson says in *Rambler* 21, "He that happens not to be lulled by praise into supineness may be animated by it to undertakings above his strength, or incited to fancy himself alike qualified for every kind of composition. . . ."

All this concern with rhetorical appropriateness, all this consciousness of the distinctions between categories, might seem to promise only a barren mechanism in writing. But actually, in Johnson's time the universal consciousness of genre was attended by a very English looseness and flexibility, perhaps a result simply of the well-known eccentricity, "humorousness," and empiricism of the English character. It was, after all, the rowdy empiricist Samuel Johnson who demolished the formal neo-classical theory of the unities in the serious drama. In Johnson's time nothing struck foreign observers more forcibly than the English flair for eccentricity. As the astonished Voltaire once wrote back to a friend:

Reason is free here and walks her own way: hypochondriacs [defined by Johnson as those "disordered in the imagination"] especially are welcome. No manner of living appears strange: we have men who walk six miles a day for their health, feed upon roots, never taste flesh, wear a coat in winter thinner than their ladies do in the hottest days.

He sounds like a Bostonian of the 'thirties sending back a startled report on the customs of Hollywood. So delighted with eccentricity were the English of Johnson's time that the prose fiction written for them tends to turn itself into a gallery of oddities: think of Smollett's Captain Obediah Lismahago, Fielding's fur-clad Man of the Hill, and of course Sterne's Uncle Toby. Safe in the hands of a nation of humorists like these—and like Samuel Johnson—even a theory of genre so consciously held was not likely to turn writing rigid or pompous.

The impression of creative eccentricity we get from the eighteenth century—its major works include, after all, *A Tale of a Tub*, the *Dunciad, Tristram Shandy*, and *The Marriage of Heaven and Hell* —derives in part from the number of literary frauds and forgeries committed during Johnson's time. We have James Macpherson's Ossianic poems; Thomas Chatterton's Rowley poems; and the flagrant Shakespeare forgeries of William Ireland, whose palpably fraudulent manuscripts James Boswell himself venerated on his knees. This extraordinary traffic in literary frauds requires an explanation.

Perhaps the most plausible is simply that such frauds were created to satisfy the sentimental lust for literary relics of the Gothick, relics instinct with the sort of "gloomth" cultivated so assiduously and elegantly by Horace Walpole with his antiques at Strawberry Hill. Another cause helping to generate a natural climate of credulity for such stuff is the convention of anonymous publication: we remember that the only major writings to which Johnson ever set his name are *Irene,* the *Dictionary,* and *The Lives of the Poets.* In an environment characterized by anonymous publication, if the author of a work can be anyone, he can as easily be no one—that is, a wholly fictive creature like Gulliver, The Rambler, or Yorick, the gay divine. But another thing to be noticed is this: in a literary milieu dominated by a strong consciousness of genre, together with its corollary, the assumption that a writer is very seldom "upon oath," the line separating the literary "honest" from the literary "fraudulent" is very easily crossed over.

Johnson himself was not unexperienced in the practice of what will strike the rigorous or naïve moralist as literary frauds. His main activity in this line was of course his reports of the debates in Parliament (1741–43), his longest single piece of writing. The reporting of parliamentary debates was illegal, but readers hungered for transcripts of the proceedings. Edward Cave thought of a solution: he sent agents to parliamentary sittings; they brought back reports of the general structure of the day's debate; Johnson, sitting in Cave's office, received the reports, and from them he simply wrote—that is, invented—what the speakers had said. Johnson's success in supplying the speakers with an appropriately noble rhetoric was such that, as M. J. C. Hodgart has said,

The speeches were often reprinted as the works of their supposed authors over the next century or longer. Thus Johnson can be said to have set to his contemporaries the standard of Parliamentary oratory and statesmanship, and to have left to posterity a flattering picture of eighteenth-century attainments in this field.[5]

Ironically, many of Johnson's speeches, contrived out of whole cloth, are still to be found presented as evidence of the eloquence of their putative speakers. If, for example, we turn to Chauncey Goodrich's *Select British Eloquence*, an anthology of speeches still used in university courses in speech and rhetoric, we find orations by Samuel Johnson innocently ascribed to Chesterfield, Pulteney, and Pitt. And Sir Robert Walpole's reputation for eloquence and fire is due in large part to Johnson's skill in finding language for him. We are reminded of the guileless simplicity of archeologists who take fictional literary materials as historical evidence.

Johnson's talent for role-playing appears in his version of a debate in 1741: here, for the sheer literary pleasure of it, he gives all the best arguments and most telling rhetorical techniques to the Whigs. By contrast, the version of the same debate printed by the *London Magazine* is powerfully Tory. Benjamin B. Hoover has pointed to this sort of performance as evidence of Johnson's "naturally forensic nature," and he is right.[6]

We can get a sense of the way Johnson goes about supplying

an appropriate eloquence to British parliamentary debate by comparing different versions of the same speech. In a 1743 address in the Lords about the unhealthiness of the rise in stock prices, Lord Hervey is reported (in one version) to have said: "People cannot employ or dare not trust their money in trade: so they put it in stocks. But this florid look is an unhealthy flushing." Another report of the same utterance goes this way: "Our public credit . . . is so far from being a sign of health, that like the flushings of some diseases it may perhaps be found to be a sign of approaching death." But Johnson knows that a noble Lord addressing a great deliberative body is popularly supposed to talk better than that. He adds a dollop of Cicero, skims off the fat, and comes up with this: "The rise of our stocks, my Lords, is such proof of riches, as dropsical tumors are of health: it shows not the circulation but the stagnation of our money." That, we know, is the way an elevated Augustan statesman is supposed to say it, and we are satisfied.

These debates constitute the only category of his writings which gave Johnson any moral qualms as he approached his death. As John Nichols says:

[Johnson] said that the Parliamentary Debates were the only part of his writings which gave him any compunction: but that at the time he wrote them, he had no conception that he was imposing on the world [he assumed, of course, that his audience was in every way as sophisticated, literarily, as he was], though [the debates] were frequently written from very slender materials, and often from none at all.

A literary action practiced earlier by Swift provided Johnson with a model for another sort of fabrication. When Swift's friend Lady Berkeley grew too warm in admiration of the sentimental *Meditations* of the Honorable Robert Boyle and wearied Swift by making him read them aloud to her, he composed a fatuous *Meditation upon a Broomstick*, inserted the paper into the Boyle volume, and read it to Lady Berkeley with, we are told, "an inflexible gravity of countenance." The burden of Swift's mock-meditation is the finding that "Surely mortal man is a broomstick."

This "bite" presumably cured Lady Berkeley of her devotion to Boyle's works. In the same way, Johnson was fond of teasing Mrs. Thrale's mother, too credulous, he thought, of political and military news in the papers, by secretly having inserted in the newspapers accounts of "battles and plots," as Mrs. Thrale tells us, "which had no existence, only to feed her with new accounts of the division of Poland, perhaps, or the disputes between the states of Russia and Turkey." Johnson's own recollection of these proceedings is both funny and poignant. Sir Brooke Boothby reports:

He related that a lady of his acquaintance implicitly believed everything she read in the papers; and that, by way of curing her credulity, he fabricated a story of a battle between the Russians and the Turks, then at war: and 'that it might,' he said, 'bear internal evidence of its futility, I laid the scene in an island at the conflux of the Boristhenes and the Danube, rivers which run at the distance of a hundred leagues from each other. The lady, however, believed the story, and never forgave the deception; the consequence of which was that I lost an agreeable companion, and she was deprived of an innocent amusement.' And he added, as an extraordinary circumstance, that the Russian ambassador sent in haste to the printer to know . . . whence he had received the intelligence.

Against this we can set what he once said in conversation on the theme that "The happiness of society depends on virtue": "Without truth there must be a dissolution of society. As it is, there is so little truth that we are almost afraid to trust our ears; but how should we be if falsehood were multiplied ten times? Society is held together by communication and information . . . ." How do we reconcile his treatment of Mrs. Thrale's mother with these improving sentiments? The answer is that we don't.

His skill at telling lies gracefully is of the kind that can reach its apogee only in a literary world where known styles replace unique personal mannerisms as the focus of literary interest. If the speaker in any work, thus, is not necessarily the author, why not go all the way? We see then that the practice of literary fraud is the ultimate logical end of the conscious practice of the genres. Literary frauds and even forgeries are rhetoric writ large.

The various roles enjoined by the various genres accustom the writer to exercising himself in numerous different objective voices: the Johnson who writes letters to children or political handbills for Henry Thrale is not the Johnson who reviews Soame Jenyns's *A Free Inquiry into the Nature and Origin of Evil.* Robert Voitle has drawn attention to Johnson's "constantly shifting personae." "He was," Voitle observes,

always aware of the occasion, of his purposes, and of the nature of his audience. . . . It would be folly indeed to lump together indiscriminately the preacher *in absentia* at Ashbourne [writing the sermons delivered by his clerical friend John Taylor], the raconteur of the Club, the anguished sinner of the *Prayers and Meditations,* the biographer, the lexicographer, the sober moralist of the *Ramblers,* and the sometimes sportive bear of [Mrs. Thrale's household at] Streatham.[7]

It is because Johnson is skilled in shifting from voice to voice that comments about his "style" can be so misleading. The nineteenth-century recoil from his writings largely took the form of attacks, like Macaulay's, on what was thought of as his "style." It was assumed that he wrote always in his own sincere person and that therefore he had one style; and that this style was unremittingly polysyllabic, fraudulently—that is, merely mechanically —antithetical, and hence uniformly pompous. William Hazlitt's objection[8] to a fancied uniformity is typical: "The fault of Dr. Johnson's style is that it reduces all things to the same artificial and unmeaning level." But such a view will not survive close application to the writings in all their variety.

The charge of ostentatious polysyllabism is easiest answered. Often the polysyllables complained of are not Johnson's at all: they belong to his ridiculous characters, and on such occasions Johnson flourishes big words with a cunning satiric consciousness of their absurdity and its effect on the reader. The brag of the silly virtuoso in *Rambler* 82 is a good example: "As Alfred re-

ceived the tribute of the Welsh in wolves' heads, I allowed my
tenants to pay their rents in butterflies, till I had exhausted the
papilonaceous tribe." Often, as in *Rambler* 202, it is irony that
is dictating the choice of a Latinate over an Anglo-Saxon word.
Someone inattentive to the ironic potential of incongruous diction
would write: "Nor was Diogenes much mortified by living in a tub,
where he was honored with the visit of Alexander the Great."
Johnson writes: "Nor was Diogenes much mortified by residence
in a tub, where he was honored with the visit of Alexander the
Great."

When in a piece of writing Johnson does establish an elevated
stylistic norm, giving us much antithesis and balance and offering
an abnormal number of Latinate polysyllables, he frequently does
so to provide himself with a grid against which the blunt and the
monosyllabic will show with special energy. In this he behaves
like a poet who establishes a regular texture of meter and rhyme
and line-length so that significant variations from these things can
take place and the spectrum of expression be widened. Thus, in his
review of Jenyns, after preparing the effect with a plethora of
terms like *contemplating, analogous, advantage, argument, operations, philosopher*, and *vicissitudes*, he is able to jolt the reader by
dropping to a final clause built only of the bluntest monosyllables:

Many a merry bout have these frolic beings [the superior spirits posited
by Jenyns 'who may deceive, torment, or destroy us for the ends only
of their own pleasure or utility'] at the vicissitudes of an ague, and
good sport it is to see a man tumble with an epilepsy, and revive and
tumble again, *and all this he knows not why* [my emphasis].

In the same way we can notice how, in the *Preface to Shakespeare*,
he can move from one stylistic level to another and drop suddenly
into blunt simplicity. Here the bluntness operates to enforce a
transition between expectation, on the one hand, and actuality, on
the other:

But the admirers of this great poet have most reason to complain
when he approaches nearest to his highest excellence, and seems fully

resolved to sink them in dejection, and mollify them with tender emotions, by the fall of greatness, the danger of innocence, or the crosses of love. *What he does best, he soon ceases to do.* He is not soft and pathetic without some idle conceit, or contemptible equivocation. He no sooner begins to move, than he counteracts himself; and terror and pity, as they are rising in the mind, are checked and blasted by sudden frigidity [my emphasis].

Indeed, Johnson is a master of the unpretentious monosyllabic utterance whose force is especially heartbreaking because of the more rococo medium in which it is set. The letters are full of such effects. Writing to his friend John Taylor the day after Tetty's death, he says:

Let me have your company and your instruction. Do not live away from me. My distress is great.

Commiserating with Mrs. Thrale upon the sudden death of her nine-year-old son Harry, her favorite and the repository of all her hopes, he writes: "Poor dear sweet little boy." Elegiac occasions urge him to such usages in the poems as well. Consider the descent to the immitigable facts of life in *The Vanity of Human Wishes*:

> Now kindred merit fills the sable bier,
> Now lacerated friendship claims a tear.
> Year chases year, decay pursues decay,
> *Still drops some joy* from with'ring life away.

And in his written Prayers also we perceive that he is by no means the captive of any one style. Simplicity is his as well as complexity:

I profess my faith in Jesus. I declare my resolution to obey him. I implore in the highest act of worship grace to keep these resolutions.

Or again:

I have outlived many friends. I have felt many sorrows. I have made few improvements . . . . I am dejected, but not hopeless. O God, for Jesus Christ's sake, have mercy upon me.

It is clear that he learned a style as well as a substance from *The Book of Common Prayer*, where we find such irreducible simplicities as

We have done those things which we ought not to have done; and there is no health in us,

and

O Lord, from whom all good things do come. . . .

Once, reading *A Liberal Translation of the New Testament* (1768), by Dr. Edward Harwood, he came to John 11:35, the verse rendered in the King James version "Jesus wept." Harwood translates, "Jesus, the Savior of the world, burst into a flood of tears." Johnson, we are told, "hurled the book aside with the exclamation, 'Puppy!'"

In conversation as well as in writing and reading, one of his delights is the significant avoidance of the sesquipedelian. At the age of seventy-five he is reminded by Boswell of "Thomas Lord Lyttelton's vision, the prediction of the time of his death, and its exact fulfillment." Conscious of his own nearness to death, he says: "I am so glad to have every evidence of the spiritual world that I am willing to believe it." Dr. William Adams reassures him: "You have evidence enough; good evidence, which needs not such support." And Johnson, in a style reminding us of his response to the death of Desdemona ("It is not to be endured"), answers simply, eloquently: "I like to have more." And no one was better than Johnson at calling a spade a spade. To him the Reverend Kenneth Macaulay, met during the Scottish tour, was "the most ignorant booby and the grossest bastard." Thanks to the recovery of the Boswell papers, we now know what Johnson actually said when he finally gave up visiting David Garrick's premises backstage. In the *Life* Boswell presents a version done into Johnsonese:

I'll come no more behind your scenes, David; for the silk stockings and white bosoms of your actresses excite my amorous propensities.

This would gratify Macaulay's expectations. But what Johnson actually said is more likely to satisfy us:

No, David, I will never come back. For the white bubbies and the silk stockings of your actresses excite my genitals.

Thus Johnson's exquisite sense of occasion. His styles are those appropriate to a number of occasions, or genres. Even various kinds of conversations are genres, and in them as well as in written occasions he senses the necessity of literary conventions. Indeed, in conversation "stated and prescriptive" actions and reactions constitute the essential dynamics. He often chided Mrs. Thrale for her practice of gross flattery, and it is true that much of his criticism of her usages was moral in intent: envy is so powerful a human passion that to praise anyone highly in company is immediately to rouse against him as many secret enemies as there are persons present. But in addition, much of his criticism of Mrs. Thrale's flattery is more purely literary: flattery that deviates from the conventional is like bad writing—it produces the opposite rhetorical effect from the one designed by its practitioner. As he tells Mrs. Thrale:

Unusual compliments, to which there is no stated and prescriptive answer, embarrass the feeble, who know not what to say, and disgust the wise, who, knowing them to be false, suspect them to be hypocritical.

Johnson's terms are rich with his instinct for genre and literary conventions: the bad kind of compliments are the *unusual* ones; properly "coded" conversational intercourse consists largely of *stated and prescriptive* answers; the feeble, addressed in an unprecedented way, *know not what to say*.

Surely one of Johnson's pleasures in being the last of the Renaissance polymaths was the sheer multiplicity of roles available to him. We have seen him playing lawyer and legal scholar. We have seen him playing a Ciceronian member of the House of Lords. We have seen him facetiously playing foreign correspondent. His mastery of the "stated and prescriptive" form of every kind of written material—especially, perhaps, the humblest—enabled him even to play physician. As Boswell reports: "He went into an apothecary's shop and ordered some medicine for himself, and wrote the prescription in technical characters. The boy took him for a physician." He was equally learned in the conventions of the written medical "case history": there were more than twenty medical treatises in his library, and we remember that at one stage of his career he had written—secretly, of course—a part of Dr. Robert James's *Medicinal Dictionary*. His letters of June, 1767, to Dr. Thomas Lawrence describing the condition of his Lichfield friend Kitty Chambers are couched in the precise and entirely objective language of the medical case history, just as if Kitty Chambers were a mere scientific object and patient and not, as Johnson says, "an old friend whom I am extremely desirous to keep alive whether her disease does or does not admit of cure." And he is troubled that both she and her local medical men are less skilled than he is in the conventions of the genre "case history." As he says, "Neither she nor her attendants are very good relators of a case." We know that when he was twenty he wrote a Latin case history of his own melancholia for a Lichfield physician, and when we find him at fifty-nine pondering the desirability of writing "the history of my melancholy," we gather that the term *history* implies a formal, conventional case history rather than anything like an autobiography.

Just as he can assume the role of physician, he can as readily assume the role of political candidate. Since Henry Thrale, the real parliamentary candidate, was not skilled in the "stated and prescriptive" style which one uses to give the illusion that one actually is a political candidate, he called upon Johnson—knowing him to be an adept at roles and devices—to speak for him. The stated style of the campaign utterance involves a very subtle mixture of both "manly" self-respect and, at the same time, due "democratic" abasement before one's constituency. In this kind of writing, one obligation is to use the term *representative*—as one must—without allowing that term to convey the impression that the candidate means it literally, that he has in any way ceded his total freedom of action. Johnson achieves exactly the right illusion in this statement which he wrote for Thrale's use in the campaign of 1780:

TO THE WORTHY ELECTORS
OF THE BOROUGH OF SOUTHWARK

Gentlemen,

A new Parliament being now called, I again solicit the honor of being elected for one of your representatives; and solicit it with the greater confidence, as I am not conscious of having neglected my duty, or of having acted otherwise than as becomes the independent representative of independent constituents; superior to fear, hope, and expectation, who has no private purposes to promote, and whose prosperity is involved in the prosperity of his country. . . .

If in the role of a parliamentary candidate Johnson invites something of a manly self-sufficiency into the prose as appropriate to its function, such a tone must be largely excluded from another brief prose genre in whose conventions he is likewise skilled, the dedication to a royal, noble, or important personage. Here the matter is homage; and "the known style," as he once declared, "is flattery." A dedication is no more to be "believed" than an epitaph. The presiding convention of each is that it implicitly depict someone as exempt from normal human weaknesses. Johnson of course, of all people, knows better. The ultimate effect of both dedication and epitaph is the creation of a character—addressee or subject respectively—akin either to the faultlessly heroic figures of heroic drama or epic or opera, or to the unremittingly virtuous ones of sentimental drama or romance. It is wonderfully typical of Johnson that he never did dedicate one of his own works to nobility—that lurking, subterranean adhesion to the ideal of sincerity again!—but that he obliged countless frailer friends by writing theirs for them, and writing them with both accuracy and *brio*.

One especially happy dedication is the one he wrote for his Italian friend Joseph Baretti to promote Baretti's *Dictionary of the English and Italian Languages* (1760). This is especially successful because it is witty, and it is witty because it disavows any syco-

phantic design by openly confessing that such is a known convention of the genre. But in this process of disavowal, the dedication
manages to flatter the addressee anyhow. In addressing the dedicatee, the Italian ambassador to the Court of St. James's, the fictive
"Joseph Baretti" begins thus:

MY LORD,

That acuteness of penetration into characters and designs, and that
nice discernment of human passions and practices, which have raised
you to your present height of station and dignity of employment, have
long shown you that Dedicatory Addresses are written for the sake of
the author more frequently than of the patron; and though they profess
only reverence and zeal, are commonly dictated by interest or vanity.

Having momentarily admitted the dedicatee into the secret, and
having thus taken a lien on his good will, the speaker goes on to
expose the essential artifice of what he's doing, and to expose it
specifically as a way of proclaiming his candor. The declaration of
absolute candor makes even more telling the flattery that follows:

I shall therefore not endeavor to conceal my motives, but confess
that the Italian Dictionary is dedicated to Your Excellency that I might
gratify my vanity by making it known that in a country where I am a
stranger, I have been able, wthout any external recommendation, to
obtain the notice and countenance of a nobleman so eminent for knowledge and ability. . . .

But that sort of thing is easy, indeed child's play, for Johnson.
A harder task of role-playing fell to him in 1777, when his secret
solicitations on behalf of Dr. William Dodd involved him in a
variety of genres and obliged him to enact a number of rhetorical
roles at once. Dodd was an Anglican priest renowned both for his
preaching and for living well beyond his means. He had once
been tutor to Lord Chesterfield's booby son. Deeply in debt at one
point, it struck him as plausible to forge the son's name to a bond.
He was exposed, tried, convicted, and sentenced to be hanged. "In
his distress," Boswell writes, "he bethought himself of Johnson's
persuasive power of writing, if haply it might avail to obtain for

him the Royal mercy." Johnson did do all he could as a writer to help Dodd. And what he did he did less for the cause of Dodd, whom he actually thought a scoundrel, than for the cause of the Church, which he perceived to be already severely enfeebled and not likely to be strengthened by the spectacle of a divine hustled toward the gallows in his canonicals and baited by the delighted mob all the way through the London streets.

In the course of his anonymous writing for Dodd, which occupied about two months—months when he was also planning and sketching out *The Lives of the Poets*—he wrote at least a dozen fictive documents in Dodd's voice, including an address to the court before sentence was passed, a confessional autobiography, a Newgate sermon directed to Dodd's fellow convicts, letters to the Lord Chancellor, the Lord Chief Justice, and the King, and petitions to the King and Queen. Most of these documents manage to develop one theme: the desirability of commuting the capital sentence to deportation and lifetime exile in order to give Dodd ample time to perform a full expiation through prayer and penitence.

As "Mrs. Dodd," Johnson addressed the Queen, petitioning for mercy with the special arguments most natural for a female speaker and most likely to be efficacious with a female addressee. In emphasizing her husband's good works, for example, Mrs. Dodd contrives to strike the chord of "family" rather than focus on individual beneficiaries of Dodd's charitable ministry. She says,

Many are the families whom his care has delivered from want; many are the hearts which he has freed from pain, and the faces which he has cleared from sorrow.

(The subliminal appeal through the word *freed* is a nice touch.) And Johnson goes on digging at the vein most likely to yield the richest ore:

[Mrs. Dodd] most humbly throws herself at the feet of the Queen, earnestly entreating that the petition of a distressed wife asking mercy for a husband may be considered as naturally soliciting the compassion of Her Majesty; and that, when her wisdom has compared the offender's good actions with his crime, she will be pleased to represent his case to our most gracious sovereign in such terms as may dispose him to mitigate the rigor of the law.

So prays Your Majesty's most dutiful subject

> and supplicant,
> Mary Dodd.

Notice how it works: not "charitable actions" or "exemplary actions," as Johnson might put it in another context, but "good actions"—it is the exact idiom of sincere and troubled simplicity.

The appeals to the King, on the other hand, go about their work in a different way. Their style is less opulent, more manly and blunt. The argument changes from a focus on past acts of charity to an appeal for time for an adequate penance. The appeals to the King emphasize less that justice should be suspended—presumably an argument which might operate on the Queen—than that it should remain rigorous but should be redefined in a way the wisdom and piety attaching to sovereignty would want to redefine it. When "Dodd" is addressing the King, he openly admits that his past has been distinguished less for charity than for enormity:

I confess the crime, and own the enormity of its consequences and the danger of its example. Nor have I the confidence to petition for impunity; but humbly hope that public security may be established without the spectacle of a clergyman dragged through the streets to a death of infamy, amidst the derision of the profligate and profane; and that justice may be satisfied with irrevocable exile, perpetual disgrace, and hopeless penury.

And now Johnson-Dodd arrives at the heart of the argument, signaled by a shift to short, abrupt, quasi-candid clauses:

My life, Sir, has not been useless to mankind. I have benefitted many. But my offenses against God are numberless, and I have had little time for repentance. Preserve me, Sir, by your prerogative of mercy, from the necessity of appearing unprepared at that tribunal, before which Kings and subjects must stand at last together.

After this implicit invitation for the King to meditate on his own failings and thus on his own need for the prayers of others, Dodd concludes by asserting that if his life is spared, he will spend the remainder of it in prayer for an addressee now mindful of his need for such prayers:

Permit me to hide my guilt in some obscure corner of a foreign country, where, if I can ever attain confidence to hope that my prayers will be heard, they shall be poured out with all the fervor of gratitude for the life and happiness of Your Majesty.

Johnson knew that this sort of thing would do only if the illusion of sincerity were not compromised. Therefore, in sending this document to Dodd for him to copy out in his own hand, he enclosed a note containing this crucial injunction:

Sir,
    I most seriously enjoin you not to let it be at all known that I have written this letter. . . . Tell nobody.

But despite the skill of the hand that wrought them, all these rhetorical performances failed. The sentence was not commuted. The day before the hanging, Johnson senses that he has one last rhetorical obligation to fulfill: the comforting of a man now in irrevocable despair. Consulting the public armory of conventional arguments fit for this occasion, he finds there materials for the following points: (1) that all men are existentially condemned to death, and that therefore Dodd's fate rather binds him to common humanity than excludes him from it; (2) that in a context of eternity, earthly public opinion and earthly ignominy—that is, the forthcoming jeers of the populace—are of no consequence; (3) that compared with bribery or murder, Dodd's crime of forgery dwindles to something like a misdemeanor; and (4) that the God of mercy will very probably judge him less severely than an earthly tribunal worried about the stability of credit in a money society. Finally, perceiving that what a man about to be hanged needs to support himself is a conviction of his own untarnished value as a human soul, Johnson implies that Dodd's efficacy as a soul and as a priest has not been impaired—his prayers are still efficacious.

As if to enforce the point beyond doubt, Johnson closes by earnestly and convincingly begging a prayer for himself. The letter is one of the subtlest pieces of rhetoric Johnson was ever to contrive:

Dear Sir,

That which is appointed to all men is now coming upon you. Outward circumstances, the eyes and the thoughts of men, are below the notice of an immortal being about to stand the trial for eternity before the Supreme Judge of heaven and earth. Be comforted: your crime, morally or religiously considered, has no very deep dye of turpitude. It corrupted no man's principles; it attacked no man's life. It involved only a temporary and reparable injury. Of this, and of all other sins, you are earnestly to repent; and may God, who knoweth our frailty and desireth not our death, accept your repentance, for the sake of His Son JESUS CHRIST our Lord.

In requital of those well-intended offices which you are pleased so emphatically to acknowledge, let me beg that you make in your devotions one petition for my eternal welfare.

                    I am, dear sir, your affectionate servant,
                                        Sam. Johnson.

"Your affectionate servant"! Actually Johnson had been in Dodd's company only once, at a gathering years before the crime; he saw him not at all while writing on his behalf; and, as M. J. C. Hodgart says, he "had a low opinion of [Dodd's] writings and morals."[9] But one is not upon oath in composing a letter of comfort:

> O, reason not the need! Our basest beggars
> Are in the poorest things superfluous.

One useful thing emerging from this spectacle of Johnson's assuming so many foreign identities and creating so many real speakers and real addressees who are not the actual ones is a more subtle definition of *fiction* than we are perhaps accustomed to entertain. If we look in Johnson for "fiction" in the common sense—if we go with this hope to *Rasselas*, say, or to *Irene*—we are bound to be disappointed. But if we look for the powers and effects of fiction in the operations of Johnson's alleged "discursive" or "expository" work, we will find them in abundance. It is here that characters are created, suspense generated, plots resolved. And it is all done because of the very conventionality of the genres within which he is working. They are little theaters of fabrication, fabrication in the highest sense.

In *The Achievement of Samuel Johnson*, W. J. Bate notices the way Johnson seems to anticipate something like a Freudian concept of "repression" in personality and general motive.[10] And in an essay on "Freud's Aesthetics," E. H. Gombrich, writing about Freud, comes very close to talking about Johnson. Gombrich is at pains to explode the naïve assumptions of "expressionistic"— actually "self-expressionistic"—criticism:

Expressionism and its derivatives in criticism appear to take the word *ex-pression* almost literally. They believe that an unconscious thought troubles the artist's inside and is therefore expelled outward by means of art to trouble the minds of the public as well. Form, on this reading, is little more than a wrapping for the unconscious contents which the consumer in his turn unwraps and discards. Freud's view [and, I would add, Johnson's practice] clearly allows us to look at the matter from the other angle. It is often the wrapping that determines the content. Only those unconscious ideas that can be adjusted to the reality of formal structures become communicable, and their value to others rests at least as much in the formal structure as in the idea. The code generates the message.[11]

(One must apologize for the vulgar associations of Gombrich's final sentence, associations for which he is not to blame.) His point is quite correct. James Boswell was a superb writer *in potentia*. The reason he has achieved a position as a writer of the second rank only is, as F. A. Pottle has pointed out, that "the accepted public genres of Boswell's day offered him none that quite suited him."[12] Hence his commitment to his *private* journal. Johnson's case is different. His literary character was made by the prevailing genres and by the accident that an age recognizing an abundance of genres brought forth a man who could work in an immense variety of almost ventriloquial stances and voices.

It is clear that the public value attaching to various genres at any given point in history will largely determine not only who becomes a writer but what that writer will say. As we have seen, Johnson's talent was for embracing the literary and even the sub-literary genres readily available in a world conceived as a social, judicial, empirical place. His repeated literary action is that of redeeming the commonplace by showing us how we have mis-defined it, how in our snobbery or thoughtlessness we have ignored the possibilities of beauty in what we take to be ordinary things. He shows us how the humblest form can be made the vehicle of the subtlest art.

Johnson's sense of the force of genre does not always appear in likely places. Consider his reaction to the news that his young friend Bennet Langton had just made his Last Will. Langton had clearly enjoyed playing the self-important role of testator assisted in the genre of the Will by Robert Chambers. When Johnson heard about it, Boswell says, "he . . . laughed immoderately," and said,

'I dare say he thinks he has done a mighty thing. He won't stay till he gets home to his seat in the country, to produce this wonderful deed: he'll call up the landlord of the first inn on the road; and, after a suit-able preface upon mortality and the uncertainty of life, will tell him that he should not delay making his will; and here, Sir, will he say, is my will, which I have just made, with the assistance of one of the ablest lawyers in the kingdom; and he will read it to him ([Johnson] laugh-ing all the time). He believes he has made this will; but he did not make it: you, Chambers, made it for him. I trust you have had more conscience than to make him say, "being of sound understanding." Ha, ha, ha! I hope he has left me a legacy. I'd have his will turned into verse, like a ballad.'

Boswell proceeds, puzzled by "the mighty sage's" immoderate mirth:

In this playful manner did he run on, exulting in his own pleasantry, which certainly was not such as might be expected from the author of *The Rambler*, but which is here preserved that my readers may be acquainted even with the slightest occasional characteristics of so eminent a man.

Boswell doesn't get it, but perhaps now we can. Johnson is of course morally amused at the pretentiousness of it all, at so little a creature as Langton affecting such consequence. But a further trigger of Johnson's cosmic hilarity is the ironical tyranny of literary genres—even Wills—over the naïve minds that have to work within them, the ultimately comical illusion of personal self-sufficiency which writing, whether "creative" in the Romantic sense or not, is capable of giving to the one who writes. Boswell concludes his report of the episode:

Johnson could not stop his merriment, but continued it all the way till we got without the Temple Gate. He then burst into such a fit of laughter that he appeared to be almost in a convulsion; and, in order to support himself, laid hold of one of the posts at the side of the foot pavement, and sent forth peals so loud, that in the silence of the night his voice seemed to resound from Temple Bar to Fleet Ditch.

It is like Chaucer's Troilus laughing, finally, at a naughty world.

CHAPTER 4

The Sacrament of Authorship

By this time we may wonder whether the spectacle of Johnson's literary behavior has not brought us to the brink of open skepticism not only about his own trustworthiness but, worse, about the accepted relations between "life" and "literature." In a sense, it has. But Johnson is infinitely complex. It is true that nothing he feels, thinks, or says about writing can be understood outside the context of the powerful system of genres in which his writing takes place: in that context, the emphasis on rhetoric urges the writer toward something very like a career of literary duplicity. But it is equally true that nothing he feels, thinks, or says about writing can be understood outside the context of his personal religious life, especially his sense of the Christian obligation to write "sincerely" and to criticize responsibly. It is this sense that engenders his odd, contradictory adherence to an ideal of absolute literary honesty.

In his own lifetime his piety was legendary. It was so conspicuous that when Edward Lye listed the subscribers to his *Dictionarium Saxonico- et Gothico-Latinum* (1772) he quite naturally wrote Johnson down as "Rev. Samuel Johnson, LL.D." His piety was especially notable because of the general context of skepticism in which it shone out. He was fully aware that in an age marked, as he put it, by an "inundation of impiety," he was one of the very few vigorous defenders of Christian usages and the Christian conception of virtue. Sir John Hawkins perceived how much of Johnson's writing was undertaken to supply a counterforce to Deism and Freethinking. Of the *Rambler*, he says:

Johnson has remarked that malevolence to the clergy is seldom at a great distance from irreverence for religion. He saw the features of that malevolence in the writings of [Freethinkers like] Thomas Morgan and Matthew Tindal, and the point at which Freethinking was likely to terminate; and taking up the defense of religon where Mr. Addison had left it, he made it a part of his design as well to adduce new arguments for its support. . . .

And his friend Dr. William Maxwell remembered: "He lamented that all serious and religious conversation was banished from the company of men. . . ."

Everyone was impressed by his piety, but everyone was not impressed in the same way. Adam Smith reports:

I have seen that creature [he means Johnson] bolt up in the midst of a mixed company, and, without any previous notice, fall upon his knees behind a chair, repeat the Lord's Prayer, and then resume his seat at table. He has played this freak over and over, perhaps five or six times in the course of an evening. It is not hypocrisy, but madness.

And even the worshipful Boswell, recording in his Journal Johnson's habit of uttering pious ejaculations under his breath, deviates into that passive voice which he often employs when he must depict some slightly discreditable Johnsonian attribute (as he does, for example, when he says, "his appetite . . . was so fierce and indulged with such intenseness that while in the act of eating, the veins of his forehead swelled, and generally a strong perspiration was visible"). Of the mighty sage's manifestations of piety he says, "Mr. Johnson is often uttering pious ejaculations when he appears to be talking to himself; for sometimes his voice grows stronger, and parts of the Lord's Prayer are heard."

Readers of Johnson's *Diaries, Prayers, and Annals* will have noticed the frequency with which he marks his own auctorial occasions with prayers or with written Christian meditations. Thus, beginning a strenuous two-year writing project in 1750, he utters and records this

PRAYER ON THE RAMBLER

Almighty God, the giver of all good things, without whose help all labor is ineffectual, and without whose grace all wisdom is folly, grant, I beseech Thee, that in this my undertaking Thy Holy Spirit may not be withheld from me, but that I may promote Thy Glory, and the salvation both of myself and others—Grant this, O Lord, for the sake of Jesus Christ, Amen. Lord Bless me. So be it.

And he never forgot his intention, in the *Rambler*, to promote "the salvation both of myself and others." Thirty-four years later, having heard of a Russian translation of the *Rambler*, he included this prayer in a letter to Mrs. Thrale:

Grant, O Lord, that all who shall read my pages may become more obedient to Thy laws, and when the wretched writer shall appear before Thee, extend Thy mercy to him, for the sake of Jesus Christ. Amen.

He sounds a similar note, we remember, when he brings to a close the *Lives of the Poets* and his own literary career:

I am now to review the last year, and find little but dismal vacuity, neither business nor pleasure; much intended, and little done. My health is much broken; my nights afford me little rest. I have tried opium, but its help is counterbalanced with great disturbance; it prevents the spasms, but it hinders sleep. O God, have mercy on me.

After this registration of his need, both physical and intellectual, for assistance and support, he goes on to write:

Last week I published the *Lives of the Poets*, written, I hope, in such a manner as may tend to the promotion of piety.

His famous idiosyncrasies in the *Lives*—the odd hostility to Swift, for example, the dismissal of *Lycidas*, even the suspicion of blank verse—take on more than idiosyncratic meaning when we locate them, as we must, within their larger context of theological and redemptive purpose, the purpose of "promoting" something more important than artistic truth and taste. That purpose is always there whether Johnson is at work on a poem, a letter, an essay, a preface, or a critical dissertation.

For he senses that we are much more than writers. As he himself put it in the *Life of Milton,* "We are perpetually moralists, but we are geometricians only by chance." We can alter the language of this formulation without radically altering the meaning, and put it this way: "We are perpetually religious creatures, but we are writers only by chance." In his commitment to the public and social obligations of the writer, his feeling for the writer's duty to redeem society by having a rhetorical impact upon it, Johnson seems to detach himself from his own time to adhere either to the Renaissance Christian tradition of Walton or Herbert, or—curiously—to the Victorian activist tradition of Wells or Butler or Shaw. As Eric Bentley has observed, "It was not Karl Marx but Samuel Johnson who said: 'It is always a writer's duty to make the world better.'"[1]

From the beginning, he knew that he was extraordinarily gifted with literary talent. We may assume that this awareness brought him only a sort of delight, or at least satisfaction, until his fateful religious conversion, if that's what it is to be called, at Oxford in his twentieth year. From that moment, his awareness of his literary superiority became his curse as he meditated always more despairingly on the divine axiom that of him to whom much is given, much will be required. Boswell is acute on this matter. He says:

The solemn text, 'of him to whom much is given, much will be required,' seems to have been ever present to his mind, in a rigorous sense, and to have made him dissatisfied with his labors and acts of goodness, however comparatively great; so that the unavoidable consciousness of his superiority was, in that respect, a cause of disquiet.

Perhaps Johnson was unlucky in having been so deeply moved by William Law's *Serious Call*: for that book is notable for its stress not just on goodness or a tendency to goodness but on perfection. From his Oxford days to the very end of his life he played out a perpetual *agon* of self-torment, nagged by a debt that perhaps could not be paid even by a *Dictionary*, a *Rasselas*, a *Vanity of Human Wishes*, or a *Lives of the Poets*. It was his cool awareness of his own distinction, an awareness uniquely without a trace of vanity or pride, that generated in him the conviction that he had had laid upon him an obligation that, write as he might, he never could fulfill. Hence his obsession with his own idleness, his neurotic hatred of entering the lists by writing at all.

His favorite emblem of his own literary circumstances is the Parable of the Talents (Matthew 25:14–30): the "wicked and slothful servant" who has not returned an investment on the talent entrusted to him is ordered "cast . . . into outer darkness." And the nature of the "outer darkness" is particularized in Christ's narrative: "there shall be weeping and gnashing of teeth." It is true that Johnson's fear of death is in part a fear of sheer intellectual extinction and physical metamorphosis. As Arthur Murphy remembers,

The contemplation of his own approaching end was constantly before his eyes; and the prospect of death, he declared, was terrible. For many years, when he was not disposed to enter into the conversation going forward, whoever sat next his chair might hear him repeating, from Shakespeare [*Measure for Measure*, III, i, 119-123],

> Ay, but to die and go we know not where;
> To lie in cold obstruction and to rot;
> This sensible warm motion to become

> A kneaded clod, and the delighted spirit
> To bathe in fiery floods. . . .

The idea of physical dissolution does give Johnson the creeps more than it does most people: he is astonishingly delicate and sensitive. But his fear of death is more importantly a fear of judgment; and the judgment he fears is less for his presumed sexual irregularities when Richard Savage was his guide, philosopher-manqué, and friend, than for his failure to exploit his literary talent unremittingly "for the salvation both of himself and others." His talk about his fear of death often seems to hint at the "conditions" implied by the Parable of the Talents. Thus the following colloquy in his seventy-fifth year:

Dr. Johnson surprised [the Oxford scholar John Henderson] not a little by acknowledging with a look of horror that he was much oppressed by the fear of death. The amiable Dr. Adams suggested that GOD was infinitely good. JOHNSON. 'That he is infinitely good, as far as the perfection of his nature will allow, I certainly believe; but it is necessary for good upon the whole that individuals shall be punished. As to an *individual*, therefore, he is not infinitely good; and as I cannot be *sure* that I have fulfilled the conditions on which salvation is granted, I am afraid I may be one of those who shall be damned.' (Looking dismally). DR. ADAMS. 'What do you mean by damned?' JOHNSON. 'Sent to Hell, Sir, and punished everlastingly!'

The same imagery of crime and punishment attends his talk about writing even when he is being whimsical. Writing to Thomas Warton in 1755 and begging a letter from him, he says: "Not to write when a man can write so well is an offense sufficiently heinous."

At moments of literary despair the image of the Talents is always at hand, always available for his use in goading himself on. In 1753, most of the first volume of the *Dictionary* finished but the second volume looming depressingly before him, he writes in his *Prayers and Meditations*:

I began the second volume of my Dictionary, room being left in the first for Preface, Grammar, and History, none of them yet begun.

O God, who hast hitherto supported me, enable me so to proceed in this labor and in the whole task of my present state that when I shall render up at the last day an account of the talent committed to me, I may receive pardon for the sake of Jesus Christ. Amen.

Notable here is the parallelism by which he relates—and almost equates—"this labor" of the *Dictionary* with "the whole task of my present state," that is, his entire life, conceived as an arena of obligation. The part is like the whole: the dynamics of obligation in the one literary task are like the dynamics of obligation defining the whole life of writing. The making of literature, even unto the meeting of deadlines, becomes an image of the conditions and demands of the life of Christian obligation. We are reminded by the prayer above of the one sent to Mrs. Thrale, where assonance helps him to suggest a distinct relation between "*my* pages" and "*Thy* laws."

The implications of the Parable of the Talents for the life of writing seem to strike him with special force at Easter, his conventional moment for reviewing literary and moral accomplishments—it is impossible to distinguish the two—and determining on improvement for the future. On these annual occasions of literary and moral bookkeeping one of his favorite works of devotion is Nelson's *Festivals and Fasts*.

Nelson is Robert Nelson (1656–1715). It is said of him in his epitaph, as it could be said of Johnson, that "though a layman, he shone among the clergy." In his own time he was known as a pious but amiable defender of Anglican devotional usages against Popery, on the one hand, and against Puritanism, on the other. A product of St. Paul's School, he resisted an invitation to join the court of Charles II and instead expended himself in good works, especially those of the new Society for the Promotion of Christian Knowledge, founded in 1698 and still Nelson's publisher. His systematic, proto-Methodistic temper attracted him to a conception of Christianity in which stated festivals of the calendar assume special importance. This conception of a systematic Christian year

—available already in The Book of Common Prayer but fleshed out and dramatized by Nelson—is one of the things that drew Johnson to the *Festivals and Fasts*. Johnson's regard for Nelson's virtues was such that he was pleased to regard him as the original of Richardson's saintly Sir Charles Grandison. But some complication is present even in Johnson's conception of "the learned and pious Nelson," and it is a complication that will remind us of the relation in Johnson between the impulse to rhetoric and the impulse to sincerity. As he says of Nelson in *Adventurer* 131,

He was remarkably elegant in his manners, and splendid in his dress. He knew that the eminence of his character drew many eyes upon him; and he was careful not to drive the young or the gay away from religion by representing it as an enemy to any distinction or enjoyment in which human nature may innocently delight.

The full title of Nelson's book is *A Companion for the Festivals and Fasts of the Church of England, with Collects and Prayers for Each Solemnity*. It was published in 1703. It is hard now to appreciate the fantastic popularity of this book during the eighteenth century. As a *vade mecum* which everyone owned and used, it enjoyed the kind of popularity which we choose to accord only to, say, the *Guide Michelin*. According to Boswell, Nelson's book was distinguished by having "the greatest sale of any book ever printed in England, except the Bible." Johnson so venerated it that on one occasion he expressed astonishment when a bookseller supplied him with a copy bound in mere sheepskin—limp black leather, presumably, was what he had in mind.

It is Nelson's *Festivals and Fasts* that Johnson is reading on Good Friday, 1765, in his fifty-sixth year. On that evening he makes this entry in his Diary: "In reading Nelson, thought on death *cum lachrimis*." The passage that has the power to draw tears from Johnson on this occasion is doubtless Nelson's excursus on the Christian's approach to death (Part II, Chapter v), the passage constituting the reading for Easter Eve. It goes this way, in Nelson's catechistical form:

Q. What farther care should we exercise about preparation for death?

A. We should use great circumspection about the spending our time, which is the precious Talent entrusted to us by God to fit and prepare our souls for a happy eternity; and ought not to be consumed in impertinent visits, nor to be squandered in vain diversions, nor to be loitered away in unaccountable sloth, as if mirth and doing nothing were the business of life. . . . If we have . . . the advantages of power and understanding, let us look upon ourselves as under greater obligations to spend our time well; because in such circumstances there is greater capacity and leisure to attend to the good of others, as well as the salvation of our own souls. . . . Let our zeal be never so great, when we come to die we shall wish we had done more.

It will not be hard to imagine the force with which such a passage will penetrate Johnson's heart, even though by this time he has so devotedly invested his talent that he has produced *The Vanity of Human Wishes*, 208 papers of the *Rambler*, 29 papers of the *Adventurer*, a complete *English Dictionary* in two volumes folio— the forty members of the French Academy took forty years to make theirs—105 papers of the *Idler*, and *Rasselas*.

But the trouble at this moment, the cause of his tears, is the fact that his edition of Shakespeare isn't out yet, and he is nervously conscious that he has delayed with it for close to ten years and disappointed the subscribers. Indeed, he has long ago spent all the subscription money. Thus, translating Nelson's equation of Time and Talent into his own more complex equation of literary opportunity and literary talent, Johnson not only experiences but makes a careful literary record of the tears of self-accusation and remorse. At this moment the life of writing becomes a vast metaphysical contract under whose terms he stands arraigned as the debtor severely in arrears. It is to repay these arrears that he struggles from the beginning to the end. It is his consciousness of having perhaps discharged them finally with the *Lives of the Poets* that helps him to reject the last opiates proferred by his physicians and to present his soul for judgment clear and unclouded. The sacrament of authorship has been enacted: Samuel Johnson has saved his own soul. And by writing with a specific moral design on readers, he has perhaps saved the souls of others too. As he once wrote a young clergyman of his acquaintance, "All means must be tried by which souls may be saved."

There is another passage in Nelson which also clearly shaped Johnson's feelings about literary obligation. This is Nelson's treatment of the terms of Christian judgment:

Q. For what shall we be judged?

A. For all things 'we have done in the body, whether they be good or bad.' All our thoughts, words, and actions shall then undergo the severest scrutiny; for they being all in some measure subject to God's laws, they shall then be examined as to the breach or observance of them. We must then give an account how we have performed our duty to God, our neighbor, and ourselves; how we have improved the talents we have been entrusted with. . . .

. . .

Q. But will the degree of [men's] good and bad actions be considered, as well as the nature and quality of them?

A. The Scripture is plain and express in this matter: 'To whomsoever much is given, of him shall be much required'; 'he which soweth sparingly shall reap also sparingly; and he which soweth bountifully shall reap also bountifully.' And in the Parable of the Talents our Savior plainly teacheth us that men are rewarded according to the improvements they make. . . .

The force with which the sowing-and-reaping metaphor struck Johnson we can infer from *Rambler* 154, an essay on the ethics of study. Although the essay is sedulously impersonal in tone, we sense that he is fully mindful of his own circumstances when he asserts, "He that neglects the culture of ground naturally fertile is more shamefully culpable than he whose field would scarcely recompense his husbandry."

The precarious state of Johnson's health from his infancy to his death, his miraculous survival of a score of chronic diseases and grave malformations, gave him a sense of special obligation very like that of a battle-scarred veteran whose life has been repeatedly very narrowly spared. We would have to go to an actual soldier to find something like Johnson's intense conviction of special obligation. To someone like Hugh Dormer, the English soldier-author of the Second World War, who writes just before his death,

If I survive, I shall again have passed under the shadow of the sword, and I do not believe that any man's life would be so spared unless God intended it for some special purpose.[2]

Johnson's version of this conviction is this passage in his "first solemn prayer," written on his twenty-ninth birthday, in 1738:

In the days of childhood and youth, in the midst of weakness, blindness, and danger, Thou hast protected me; amidst afflictions of mind, body, and estate Thou hast supported me; and amidst vanity and wickedness Thou hast spared me. Grant, O merciful Father, that I may have a lively sense of Thy mercies. . . . And O Lord, enable me by Thy grace . . . to make use of Thy gifts to the honor of Thy name.

Johnson has good reason for imploring power to "make use of Thy gifts to the honor of Thy name": he has just begun his campaign to burst into literature. *London* had been out for four months, and he was about to commence Swiftian imitator with *A Complete Vindication of the Licensers of the Stage* and *Marmor Norfolciense.* He was also beginning to contribute to the *Gentleman's Magazine,* notably, in 1739, the "Life of Boerhaave."

Boerhaave had just died, and Cave sensed that readers would happily consume an account of his life. In assigning the task to Johnson he knew or cared not at all that Johnson would find in Boerhaave's life a paradigm of his own future, that in this minor journalistic work he would come close to erecting a model for himself as a moral writer.

Herman Boerhaave (1668–1738) was a Dutchman distinguished in his own time for his achievements in medicine, botany, and chemistry. His public identity was that of a professor of medicine; his private reputation was that of a pious empiricist, and it is in his private character that Johnson finds a reflection of his own ambitions toward useful virtue. As W. K. Wimsatt has noticed,

Boerhaave, deeply religious and orthodox, antagonistic to the philosophies of Hobbes and Spinoza, may well have been something like a hero for the young Johnson, such an exponent of rhetoric as well as of physical and metaphysical sciences as Johnson set himself to become.[3]

Like Johnson's, Boerhaave's origins were in poverty and physical suffering: we are told of "a painful and malignant ulcer" on his thigh which tormented him for five years; we hear of his Johnsonian struggles to educate himself by winning university prizes.

At Leyden, Boerhaave's thesis in philosophy "discussed the important and arduous subject of the distinct natures of the soul and body," Johnson writes, and the thesis was argued "with such accuracy, perspicuity, and subtlety that he entirely confuted all the sophistry of Epicurus, Hobbes, and Spinoza, and equally raised the characters of his piety and erudition." As Johnson goes on, we catch him in the interesting act of committing biography and autobiography simultaneously: "Divinity," he says of Boerhaave, "was still his great employment, and the chief aim of all his studies." And surely in the following, where Johnson glances at Boerhaave's amalgamation of theological and physical studies, we perceive something of Johnson's own dignified self-awareness. We sense both his full knowledge of the value of his yet uninvested Talents and his sense of his capacity for realizing their investment:

It is, I believe, a very just observation, that men's ambition is generally proportioned to their capacity. Providence seldom sends any into the world with an inclination to attempt great things, who have not abilities to perform them.

Boerhaave is praised also for a Johnsonian disinclination to specialize unduly: "Yet did he not suffer one branch of science to withdraw his attention from others: anatomy did not withhold him from chemistry, nor chemistry, enchanting as it is, from the study of botany, in which he was no less skilled than in other parts of physic." And still,

In conjunction with all these enquiries he . . . pursued his theological studies, and still, as we are informed by himself, proposed, when he had made himself master of the whole art of physic, and obtained the honor of a degree in that science, to petition regularly for a license to preach, and to engage in the cure of souls. . . .

But Boerhaave's hopes of a calling in divinity were blasted by a very Johnsonian sort of conversational incident. He was calumniated with an imputation of Spinozism, or, as Johnson puts it, "of atheism itself." Johnson presents this part of his narrative as an *exemplum* on the general depravity of human nature as manifested in the normal human passions of vanity and envy and the normal human propensity to "malicious designs." He lays the ground for the actual narrative of the crucial incident with this moral generalization:

We shall give the relation, not only to satisfy the curiosity of mankind, · but to show that no merit, however exalted, is exempt from being not only attacked, but wounded, by the most contemptible whispers. Those who cannot strike with force can, however, poison their weapon, and weak as they are, give mortal wounds, and bring a hero to the grave; so true is that observation that many are able to do hurt, but few to do good.

After this somber but energetic overture, he proceeds to the incident itself:

As Boerhaave was sitting in a common boat, there arose a conversation among the passengers upon the impious and pernicious doctrine of Spinoza, which, as they all agreed, tends to the utter overthrow of all religion. Boerhaave sat and attended silently to this discourse for some time, till one of the company, willing to distinguish himself by his zeal, instead of confuting the positions of Spinoza by argument, began to give a loose to contumelious language and virulent invectives, which Boerhaave was so little pleased with that at last he could not forbear asking him whether he had ever read the author he declaimed against.

The orator, not being able to make much answer, was checked in the midst of his invectives, but not without feeling a secret resentment against the person who had at once interrupted his harangue and exposed his ignorance.

This was observed by a stranger who was in the boat with them; he inquired of his neighbor the name of the young man whose question had put an end to the discourse, and having learned it, set it down in his pocket-book, as it appears, with a malicious design, for in a few days it was the common conversation at Leyden that Boerhaave had revolted to Spinoza.

Envy sufficed to maintain and spread this calumny, and Boerhaave, "finding this formidable opposition raised against . . . his design of assuming the character of a divine, thought it neither necessary nor prudent to struggle with the torrent of popular prejudice, as he was equally qualified for a profession [that is, medicine], not indeed of equal dignity or importance, but which must undoubtedly claim the second place among those which are of the greatest benefit to mankind." Notice Johnson's implicit ranking of the professions: divinity is at the top, followed by medicine, and, we can infer from what we already know, law: the man who finds himself a professional writer instead of any of these will already have a considerable load of guilt and sense of failure to expiate.

The career of divine placed now out of his grasp, Boerhaave pursued his medical and scientific studies instead, and he pursued them in a notably Johnsonian way: "Superior to any discouragement, he continued his search after knowledge, and determined that prosperity, if ever he was to enjoy it, should be the consequence not of mean art or disingenuous solicitations, but of real merit and solid learning." What Johnson means by solid learning we can deduce from his praise of Boerhaave's empiricism in the science of medicine, the equivalent of Johnson's affectivism in literary criticism. Johnson writes,

In 1715 he made an oration [at the University of Leyden] upon the subject of 'attaining to certainty in natural philosophy'; in which he declares, in the strongest terms, in favor of experimental knowledge, and reflects with just severity upon those arrogant philosophers who are too easily disgusted with the slow methods of obtaining true notions by frequent experiments, and who, possessed with too high an opinion of their abilities, rather choose to consult their own imaginations than inquire into nature, and are better pleased with the charming amusement of forming hypotheses than the toilsome drudgery of making observations.

Here, in the character of Boerhaave jousting with "those arrogant philosophers" impatient to form hypotheses, we have a prefiguring of Johnson twenty-six years later, in the *Preface to Shakespeare* going instinctively to the empirical behavior of actual people witnessing actual plays to deflate the hypothesis of the dramatic unities dear to neoclassical criticism. As a result of his solid inquiries, Boerhaave, as Johnson is pleased to notice, acquired "a reputation not casually raised by fashion or caprice, but founded upon solid merit...."

The nature and purpose of elegance in prose style is what Johnson chooses to consider next. Elegance is, he finds, a function of benevolence, that benevolence which loves the audience enough to aim at transmitting matter in a delightful way. Obscurity and clumsiness in prose are here associated with fraud and vanity. Johnson's occasion for these findings is the oration Boerhaave delivered in 1718, when he attained the Professorship of Chemistry at Leyden. In this oration, Boerhaave

treated [chemistry] with an elegance of style not often to be found in chemical writers, who seem generally to have affected not only a barbarous but unintelligible phrase, and to have, like the Pythagoreans of old, wrapped up their secrets in symbols and enigmatical expressions, either because they believed that mankind would reverence most what they least understood, or because they wrote not from benevolence but vanity. . . .

Thus morally considered, the signals of elegance in eighteenth-century prose—parallelism, syntactical doubling, periodic sentence structure—betoken not affectation but virtue, the virtue of the writer who seeks to recommend his moral substance by clothing it in an appropriate garment of delightful clarity and order. To the affective functions of prose elegance Johnson returns in a later passage, where he says,

Nor was [Boerhaave] unacquainted with the art of recommending truth by elegance, and embellishing the philosopher with polite literature; he knew that but a small part of mankind will sacrifice their pleasure to their improvement, and those authors who would find many readers must endeavor to please while they instruct.

Boerhaave knew the importance of his own writings to mankind, and lest he might, by a roughness and barbarity of style too frequent among men of great learning, disappoint his own intentions, and make his labors less useful, he did not neglect the politer arts of eloquence and poetry.

Next Johnson glances at one of the overwhelming questions in dispute among contemporary moralists, the relative excellence of Classical as opposed to Christian ethics. During an illness which, like Johnson's lifetime afflictions, deprived him of sleep, Boerhaave "found no method of diverting his thoughts so effectual as meditation upon his studies, and . . . he often relieved and mitigated the sense of his torments by the recollection of what he had read, and by reviewing those stores of knowledge which he had reposited in his memory." But lest this kind of intellectual control sound merely Stoical, Johnson hastens to impute it rather to Christian ethics:

This is perhaps an instance of fortitude and steady composure of mind which would have been forever the boast of the Stoic schools, and increased the reputation of Seneca or Cato. The patience of Boerhaave, as it was more rational, was more lasting than theirs; it was that *patientia Christiana* which Lipsius, the great master of the Stoical philosophy, begged of God in his last hours; it was founded on religion, not vanity; not on vain reasonings, but on confidence in God.

And when Johnson, anticipating the central or "character" sections of the *Lives of the Poets*, offers a brief physical characterization of Boerhaave, we have more self-portraiture: the scholar is presented now as a physical hero as well as an intellectual and

moral one. There are few words in this physical vignette of Boerhaave that a biographer of Johnson would feel any need to change:
"He was of a robust and athletic constitution of body, so hardened
by early severities and wholesome fatigue that he was insensible of
any sharpness of air or inclemency of weather." We remember
Johnson's response to a remark of Boswell's during a severe storm
in the Hebridean seas. Their boat is tossing about melodramatically,
but when Boswell shouts, "We are contending with seas," Johnson
answers, "Not much."

Johnson continues his physical description of the character which
by now we can only call Boerhaave-Johnson:

He was tall, and remarkable for extraordinary strength. There was in
his air and motion something rough and artless, but so majestic and
great at the same time that no man ever looked upon him without veneration, and a kind of tacit submission to the superiority of his genius.

We may go so far as to suspect that Johnson arrived at his unique
later physical style and mannerisms in part by imitating Boerhaave,
or by translating Boerhaave's qualities of mind and heart into
visible physical terms. For in physical as well as written styles, a
man has to imitate someone: a man acting absolutely "naturally"
would gesture, for example, in a way that would transmit nothing
to his audience. John Hollander has perceived the presence of
convention in even "the natural act," sexual intercourse itself. As he
says in "Movie-Going,"

> Try to see a set
> Of old blue movies every so often, that the sight
> Of animal doings out of the clothes of thirty-five
> May remind you that even the natural act is phrased
> In the terms and shapes of particular times and places.[4]

The image of Boerhaave's mind and person was deeply impressed
on Johnson's consciousness, and the fabric of much of his later life
can be seen as a continual act of homage to his memory. "Almost
every man, if closely examined," he writes in *Rambler* 164,

will be found to have enlisted himself under some leader whom he expects to conduct him to renown; to have some hero or other, living or dead, in his view, whose character he endeavors to assume, and whose performance he labors to equal.

When the original is well chosen, and judiciously copied, the imitator often arrives at excellence. . . .

He concludes his hagiography of Boerhaave in a way that can leave little doubt of the impact Boerhaave's image is making on his biographer. He bursts out into a series of optative ejaculations so enthusiastic that we feel suddenly transported to the rhetorical world of Thomas Carlyle himself:

May [Boerhaave's] example extend its influence to his admirers and followers! May those who study his writings imitate his life! and those who endeavor after his knowledge aspire likewise to his piety!

Rhetoric of this overheated, exclamatory sort is extremely rare in Johnson. His customary way of handling a passionate wish is not to let it out openly but to circumscribe it, as if ironically, with close syntactical pressures and complex but precise subjunctive constructions. A good example of his usual way with passionate wishes is his treatment, in *A Journey to the Western Islands*, of the news that there was a plan afoot among certain entrepreneurs to melt down and sell the lead from the roof of Lichfield Cathedral. He writes: "There is now, as I have heard, a body of men . . . longing to melt the lead of an English cathedral. What they shall melt, it were just that they should swallow." The warmth of this baroque wish, contained even as it is within a rigorously Latinate syntax, finally embarrassed him, and he was persuaded to cancel the page on which it appeared and to substitute an inoffensive general lament for the "unregarded delapidation" of "monuments of sacred magnificence." The writer of sixty-six has learned to handle passion in a way that the writer of thirty, fired by the model of learned and sincere piety he is engaged in constructing, has not. His warm exhortation to the reader at the end of the *Life of Boerhaave* to go and for God's sake do likewise is one of the most revealing moments in Johnson's lifetime commitment to the conception of the sacrament of authorship.

The conviction of divine literary obligation assumes a theater of time inexorably and significantly contracting. Johnson's earliest extant New Year's Day prayer, written in 1745 when he was thirty-six, is heavy with the Christian sense that time is to be conceived of as an arena of redemptive action: "Let me remember, O my God, that as days and years pass over me, I approach nearer to the grave where there is no repentance. . . ." And we recall the inscription on the dial-plate of his pocket watch, "a short Greek inscription," as Boswell notes, "taken from the New Testament, . . . being the first words of our Savior's solemn admonition to the improvement of that time which is allowed us to prepare for eternity: 'the night cometh, when no man can work.'" Another prayer, composed in 1752, registers his consciousness both of the risks of waste and of the means of redemption, namely, literary production:

Grant, O Lord, that I may not lavish away the life which Thou hast given me on useless trifles, nor waste it in vain searches after things which Thou hast hidden from me.

Enable me, by Thy Holy Spirit, so to shun sloth and negligence, that every day may discharge part of the task which Thou hast allotted me. . . .

What he is doing is impregnating with Christian meaning the classical proverb *Nulla dies sine linea.* Applied to Apelles by Pliny, in its original context the words suggest an injunction merely artistic and even commercial. Johnson seizes on its substance and subsumes it into his system of productive Christian anxiety. The theme of discharging tasks divinely set returns in another prayer, this one written fourteen years later:

Grant that I may no longer linger in perplexity, nor waste in idleness that life which Thou hast given and preserved. Grant that I may serve

Thee with firm faith and diligent endeavor, and that I may discharge the duties of my calling with tranquillity and constancy.

And twelve years later, while at work on the *Lives of the Poets*— he has finished Cowley and is deep in Waller, Denham, and Butler—he prays to be kept mindful of his Christian literary mission: "Make me to love all men, and enable me to use Thy gifts, whatever Thou shalt bestow, to the benefit of my fellow creatures."

In the face of all this evidence of Johnson's theological seriousness about his own life of writing, what are we to make of his insistence in conversation that his motive in writing is the mere making of money? Everyone remembers such sallies as "No man but a blockhead ever wrote, except for money." Here it's well to recall Boswell's final, summary paragraph in the *Life of Johnson,* a paragraph delivering the thesis of the whole book: "Man is . . . made up of contradictory qualities." Johnson is the example used to argue the thesis:

In him were united [is this the right word?] a most logical head with a most fertile imagination, which gave him an extraordinary advantage in arguing: for he could reason close or wide, as he saw best for the moment. Exulting in his intellectual strength and dexterity, he could, when he pleased, be the greatest sophist that ever contended in the lists of declamation; and, from a spirit of contradiction and a delight in showing his powers, he would often maintain the wrong side with equal warmth and ingenuity; so that, when there was an audience, his real opinions could seldom be gathered from his talk; though when he was in company with a single friend, he would discuss a subject with genuine fairness: but he was too conscientious to make error permanent and pernicious, by deliberately writing it; and, in all his numerous works, he earnestly inculcated what appeared to him to be the truth . . .

And Boswell concludes with the assertion which requires no qualification:

his piety being constant, and the ruling principle of all his conduct.

Thus when in talk Johnson blusters about money-making as the essential literary motive, he is doing many things at once, but the one thing he is not doing is registering his own convictions on the matter. "Nobody at times talks more laxly than I do." In talking about money as the motive for writing, he intends to startle the genteel and the sentimental, to undermine easy cant on the subject of literary motive by making the whole question, as it is discussed in public, appear naïve and stupid. For another thing, he is engaged in reminding the fortunate in his audience of his own dismal origins in obscurity and poverty. But he is also wryly drawing his own attention to the gulf between private motive—always covert, secret, complex; and public—always oversimplified, over-schematized, and unworthy of human beings as souls to be saved. His feeling for the gulf between public and private, the apparent and the actual, emerges from what he tells Mrs. Thrale three years before his death:

I have through my whole progress of authorship honestly endeavored to teach the right, though I have not been sufficiently diligent to practice it, and have offered mankind my opinion as a rule, but never proposed my behavior as an example.

Actually, if Johnson really believed, as he was fond of arguing in public, that he wrote only to make money, he was, compared with, say, Pope, oddly incompetent at his calling. Many times he let his works go at a low figure when he could have driven a much more profitable bargain. Initially he asked only £200 for the whole *Lives of the Poets*, a work which Edmond Malone, who knew all about such things, assures us could have brought £1,000 or even £1,500. And for a man whose literary motive was commercial, he had a strange habit of wasting his substance by giving away his works to all comers. In fact, his generosity in giving away copies of the *Lives* acutely distressed his publisher, who feared that these excessive donations would injure the sale. The case was really very different from what Johnson wanted to make it seem. As

Boswell perceived, "[Johnson] had less attention to profit from his labors than any man to whom literature has been a profession."

Johnson, then, conceives of writing as something very like a Christian sacrament, defined in the Anglican catechism as "an outward and visible sign of an inward and spiritual grace given unto us." It is this conception that lies behind his adherence at odd critical moments to an ideal of literary sincerity, even though he is simultaneously committed to the idea of an objective world of fixed genres in which certain things are to be said in certain ways regardless of the temporary disposition of the writer. At moments when he is especially conscious of divine obligation, he conceives of all writing as an oblique mode of prayer. And as he once said: "[Jeremy] Taylor gives a very good advice: 'Never lie in your prayers!' "

A most solemn statement he once made in a letter to Boswell suggests the association in his troubled mind between the ideal of absolute literary sincerity and the theological obligations laid upon the writer by the richness of his talents, the shortness of his time, and the inevitability of his Judgment. Counseling Boswell not to indulge too readily the belief that London offers in St. Paul's richer possibilities of sincere worship than the churches of Scotland, he concludes: "I am now writing, and you, when you read this, are reading under the Eye of Omnipresence." Under the unblinking scrutiny of the Eye of Omnipresence, nothing short of total sincerity will do.

CHAPTER 5

Writing as Imitation

"The critics instruct us," says Georg Christoph Lichtenberg, "to stay close to nature, and authors read this advice; but they always think it safer to stay close to authors who have stayed close to nature."[1] Which is a way of implying that anyone who writes anything well imitates something. Every piece of writing which strikes readers as successful is the realization of a paradigm. When we say that a piece of writing is bad, one of the things we mean is that it has imitated unsuccessfully the archetype we perceive it is trying to resemble. Another way of putting it is to say that every new work—it will be well to abandon the propaganda word *original*—is a virtual translation into local terms of a pre-existing model. In this sense the old, orthodox critical word *imitation* retains its usefulness if we take it to suggest not a naïve *imitatio naturae*—

such an uncoded imitation is, on E. H. Gombrich's demonstration, impossible—but an *imitatio literarum*, an imitation of that which is written.

The best way to test the validity of these assertions is through empirical self-scrutiny and confession. Many of those reading this book will themselves have written scholarly and critical works and will know that it is a convention of such works that they come equipped with a preface. A preface to a modern critical work is by convention a happy form, for it is the last part of the book to be written. The writer of a preface has just finished months or years of labor: he has finally been sprung from his treadmill, and he is proud of his book. Relief and pride, even if disguised with a due humility, are the happy emotions we find in prefaces. A gloomy preface to a learned book is a contradiction in terms. One recent highly successful preface, in Maynard Mack's *The Garden and the City* (1969), positively radiates felicity. It dwells enthusiastically on the "kindness" of a host "who held us for three days enchanted"; it alludes to "an exceptionally gracious audience"; it lavishes terms like *love, joyousness, and blessing*; and it ends with a warm personal compliment to the author's three grown children and their spouses. Every good preface is like every other good preface in conveying the author's happiness. And every good preface is like every other good preface in containing the same materials and in presenting these materials in the same order. The conventional order is bi-partite: (1) a statement of the intent and limits of the inquiry; and (2) acknowledgments to persons living or dead, together with acknowledgments of reprint permissions. It is an inviolable convention of the preface as a literary form that the second element, the acknowledgments, not appear first. If it does appear first, we justly tax the writer with amateurism or incompetence. He has done something, we realize, that is "not done."

Now everyone who has ever written a preface to his own book knows—if he peers into his heart of hearts—that at some point he has carefully and very privately consulted other people's prefaces to see how it is done. It is impossible to write a satisfactory preface simply by wanting to, or by being inspired to, or by instinctively sensing how to. One must copy. I would say that our own experiences of going about such literary actions, our own awareness of how we, as writers, imitate perforce, constitute more trustworthy guides to a general theory of literary making than any amount of metaphysical or psychological speculation, no matter how rich and suggestive. We are all writers, and there seems no reason to suppose that we operate very differently from other people, once we set aside the colorful dramaturgy of illusion and pretension which a lively life of literature enjoins on her devotees.

That the life of writing is attended always with this interesting external dramaturgy Johnson readily recognizes. It is what he is recognizing when he approves of the elegance of Robert Nelson's manners and the splendor of his dress. I am again proposing Johnson as exemplary of the writer in general. He differs from other writers largely in his greater willingness to penetrate beneath the announced dynamics of literary action, his greater willingness—a function of his empiricism—to scrutinize what he and others are actually doing.

Like a preface, a personal letter is a conventional literary performance. The reason children's letters are easy to find droll is that their writers have not yet learned how conventional a letter is supposed to be and don't know that the reader will be either amused or disturbed by departures from convention. One convention of the letter is that the early part of it make some allusion to the occasion that has prompted it, usually the receipt of a letter from the addressee. We are jolted, therefore, when we encounter a letter like this, written from summer camp by a twelve-year-old girl. What jolts us is that it begins, to our surprise, *in medias res*:

Dear Family,

Please send me a Care package. If you don't know what it is, it is a big chock full box of candy and cookies. If you send it up make sure you get no black licorice and get red licorice instead. I like camp a lot.

It's fun. Well, I can't think of anything else to say, but I will think of something.

In its own way the last sentence here seems to illustrate Gombrich's finding that "The code generates the message"; if the code—read "conventions"—is not apparent to writer and reader alike, nothing can get said. It is no wonder that this child "can't think of anything else to say": what she means is that, being innocent of the conventional practice of the letter as a literary form, she can't think of anything else to say that conventionally belongs in a letter. It is doubtful that her friends at camp found her speechless: it is the literary form alone that is imposing speechlessness upon her. Because, as Frye perceives, the style of the personal letter is likely to imitate the style of "associative monologue," convention is even more important in it than in other forms. As he observes,

Convention has had to devise a great number of ways for getting a letter stopped. We must close now and do something else; we are in good health and hope you are the same; and we finally reach yours sincerely like a liner being towed into port.[2]

Although the object of this child's letter is something other than to make us smile, we do smile, and thus we can say, if we are rigorous critics, that it constitutes a rhetorical abortion. As a conveyer of information it did succeed—I did remit the red licorice—but as writing, that is, as conventional rhetoric, it was less successful.

To turn from a child's letters to Johnson's is of course not to play entirely fair. But to consider Johnson's letters in a context like this is to see immediately that his are rhetorically so impressive because he has firmly in mind the paradigm of each of the "kinds" of letters he writes. He instinctively denies that conception of the letter which would hold that it constitutes an opportunity for natural self-expression. Indeed, as we have seen, he goes so far as to perceive that "no transaction offers stronger temptations to fallacy and sophistication than epistolary intercourse." After his death an acquaintance recalled that "He spoke contemptuously of . . . professing to *pour out one's soul* upon paper."

For the Johnsonian theory of the letter we turn to *Rambler* 152. The emphasis throughout is on art and artifice, and Johnson insists that as the substance of the letter is less weighty, the element of art must be more conspicuous. Although in his theory of the letter he is not entirely serious—he seldom is *entirely* serious when registering literary opinions—we can perceive in it the significant analogy he is implying between the personal letter and other fixed literary forms, forms whose fixity arises from the universality and uniformity of the rhetorical occasions in which they take place. He writes:

Letters that have no other end than the entertainment of the correspondents are more properly regulated by critical precepts [than letters with a more serious rhetorical purpose], because the matter and style are equally arbitrary, and rules are more necessary as there is a larger power of choice.

We should pause to notice how remarkably Johnson's rhetorical theory of art anticipates Gombrich's in *Art and Illusion*. Johnson says: "Rules are more necessary as there is a larger power of choice." Gombrich says: "Where [in a work] everything is possible and nothing unexpected, communication must break down."[3] And we should not allow Johnson's term *rules* to mislead us into patronizing him as a mere prescriptive theorist: by *rules* he means publicly accepted conventions; he does not mean the prescriptions of critics which have no demonstrated empirical basis in uniform human reactions to works of artifice. He goes on in *Rambler* 152:

In letters of this kind [he is thinking of the trivial letter as a distinct literary genre], some conceive art graceful, and others think negligence amiable; some model them by the sonnet, and will allow them no means of delighting but the soft lapse of calm mellifluence; others adjust them by the epigram, and expect pointed sentences and forcible periods.

Although the party of the sonnet-analogy and the party of the epigram-analogy are both being lightly satirized, Johnson is rather smiling at the pedantic precision and exclusivism of the two prescriptions than ridiculing the analogies themselves. It strikes him as quite natural to find analogies for the trivial letter in well-known formal genres, in one of which, the sonnet, the verse form is rigorously fixed, and in the other of which, the epigram, substance and tone are as rigorously predetermined. Focusing always on the reader and on his all-important reactions, he concludes *Rambler* 152 this way:

> When the subject has no intrinsic dignity, it must owe its attractions to artificial embellishments, and may catch at all the advantages which the art of writing can supply.

> . . .

> The purpose for which letters are written when no intelligence is communicated, or business transacted, is to preserve in the minds of the absent either love or esteem: to excite love we must impart pleasure, and to raise esteem we must discover abilities. Pleasure will generally be given, as abilities are displayed, by scenes of imagery, points of conceit, unexpected sallies, and artful compliments. Trifles always require exuberance of ornament: the building which has no strength can be valued only for the grace of its decorations. The pebble must be polished with care which hopes to be valued as a diamond.

Of all the "kinds" of letters Johnson practices, from letters of condolence and of moral counsel to artfully trivial letters to children, of no kind is he more a master than of the severe letter, or the letter of abuse. Indeed, his two best-known letters, to James ("Ossian") Macpherson and to Lord Chesterfield, are both of this kind. Both are full of art, but the art in each is very different, to accord with their very different occasions and recipients.

Johnson's quarrel with Macpherson achieved full publicity when, in *A Journey to the Western Island of Scotland* (1775), he commented thus on Macpherson's refusal to produce the Ossianic "manuscripts":

The editor, or author, could never show the original; nor can it be shown by any other; to revenge reasonable incredulity by refusing evidence is a degree of insolence with which the world is not yet acquainted; and stubborn audacity is the last refuge of guilt.

Reading this, Macpherson came alight and, as Arthur Murphy reports, "sent a threatening letter to the author; . . . Johnson answered him in the rough phrase of stern defiance." But we perceive that even "the rough phrase of stern defiance" must find a pre-existing form, indeed, even one single archetype, to couch itself in. Johnson finds that form and that archetype by remembering Richard Savage's distinguished performance in the abusive letter almost fifty years earlier. Johnson's model is this splendid effort sent by Savage to Lord Tyrconnel, who, in Savage's view, had gravely wronged him:

Right Honorable Brute and Booby,

I find you want (as Mr.—— is pleased to hint) to swear away my life, that is, the life of your creditor, because he asks you for a debt.—The public shall soon be acquainted with this, to judge whether you are not fitter to be an Irish evidence than to be an Irish peer.—I defy and despise you.

I am,
Your determined adversary,
R. S.

Johnson's version of Savage's letter goes as follows, and we notice "stern defiance" condescending—wholly for the sake of rhetorical clarity—to observe the convention that the early part of the letter allude to the prompting occasion:

Mr. James Macpherson—I received your foolish and impudent note. Whatever insult is offered me I will do my best to repel, and what I cannot do for myself the law will do for me. I will not desist from detecting what I think a cheat, from any fear of the menaces of a ruffian.

You want me to retract. What shall I retract? I thought your book an imposture from the beginning; I think it upon yet surer reasons an imposture still. For this opinion I give the public my reasons, which I here dare you to refute.

But however I may despise you, I reverence truth, and if you can prove the genuineness of the work, I will confess it. Your rage I defy, your abilities since your Homer are not so formidable, and what I have heard of your morals disposes me to pay regard not to what you shall say, but to what you can prove.

And then the last twist of the knife:

You may print this if you will.

Sam: Johnson.

When we recall the Parliamentary Debates or the law lectures written for Chambers, we realize that Johnson's notions about literary impostures are very complicated. Ours should be too.

It seems indicative of the whole context of literature as admitted rhetoric in which this letter was written and received that the recipient did not—as we should expect—destroy it in a fury but instead treasured it up for a lifetime: indeed, the text printed by R. W. Chapman in his edition of Johnson's letters derives from the original manuscript carefully saved by Macpherson. His interesting behavior is like Chesterfield's: upon receiving Johnson's other famous abusive letter, he kept it on his library table to show people. Robert Dodsley says: "He read it to me; said, 'This man has great powers,' pointed out the severest passages, and observed how well they were expressed." And the Rev. John Hussey, who had not seen the letter, recalls: "Doctor Johnson assured me that so far from being couched in disrespectful terms, his Lordship had returned his thanks for it and added that it was the letter of a scholar and a gentleman."[4]

While the severe letter to Macpherson adopts a roughness of style appropriate to the imputed bucolic boorishness of the Scottish addressee, the severe letter to Chesterfield proceeds with an equally appropriate suavity:

My Lord,

I have been lately informed by the proprietor of *The World* that two papers in which my *Dictionary* is recommended to the public were written by your Lordship. To be so distinguished is an honor which, being very little accustomed to favors from the Great, I know not well how to receive, or in what terms to acknowledge.

It is precisely a powerful focus on rhetoric, occasion, and convention that is generating this opening paragraph and providing the spring of its irony: having in his own experience no model for the present occasion, the speaker confesses that he knows not *in what terms* convention requires him to respond. He goes on:

When upon some slight encouragement I first visited your Lordship, I was overpowered like the rest of mankind by the enchantment of your address, and could not forbear to wish that I might boast myself *Le Vainqueur du Vainqueur de la Terre*, that I might obtain that regard for which I saw the world contending; but I found my attendance so little encouraged that neither pride nor modesty would suffer me to continue it. When I had once addressed your Lordship in public [in *The Plan of a Dictionary of the English Language* (1747)], I had exhausted all the art of pleasing which a retired and uncourtly scholar can possess. I had done all that I could, and no man is well pleased to have his all neglected, be it ever so little.

Seven years, my Lord, have now passed since I waited in your outward rooms or was repulsed from your door, during which time I have been pushing on my work through difficulties of which it is useless to complain, and have brought it at last to the verge of publication without one act of assistance, one word of encouragement, or one smile of favor. Such treatment I did not expect, for I never had a patron before.

The shepherd in Virgil grew at last acquainted with Love, and found him a native of the rocks. Is not a patron, my Lord, one who looks with unconcern on a man struggling for life in the water, and when he has reached ground, encumbers him with help? The notice which you have been pleased to take of my labors, had it been early had been kind: but it has been delayed till I am indifferent and cannot enjoy it, till I am solitary and cannot impart it, till I am known and do not want it.

I hope it is no very cynical asperity not to confess obligation where no benefit has been received, or to be unwilling that the public should consider me as owing that to a patron which Providence has enabled me to do for myself.

Having carried on my work thus far with so little obligation to any favorer of learning, I shall not be disappointed though I should conclude it, if less be possible, with less; for I have been long wakened from that dream of hope in which I once boasted myself with so much exultation, my Lord, your Lordship's most humble, most obedient servant,

Sam: Johnson.

The implicit metaphoric or even mythic dynamics here would repay months of study. The structure of the action realizes Johnson's usual theme: the ironic and pathetic—that is, the human—distance between the world of enchantment or dream, the world of wishing, hoping, and boasting, and the world of actuality, of waking, loneliness, uncertainty, hopelessness, and confessing. What these dynamics say is that no man, not even one who writes so well, is immune from the temptations emanating from the domain of sleep and dream. It is Johnson's version of the myth of the Lotus-Eaters.

If the model of the letter to Macpherson is Savage's letter to Tyrconnel, the paradigms of the letter to Chesterfield are two: the general Ciceronian oration with the irony subtilized (one of Johnson's contemporaries referred to the letter as "that epistolary Philippic")[5] and the Horatian satire conceived as occurring in the mode of the Horatian epistle. For all his ill luck with his patron, Johnson was fortunate that the neglect had lasted the actual time of seven years. As Niall Rudd has suggested, the sentence beginning "Seven years, my Lord, have now passed since I waited in your outward rooms . . . " glances at Horace's Sixth Satire of the Second Book (*"Septimus octavo proprior iam fugerit annus"*) and thus brings Chesterfield as a patron into a distinctively disadvantageous comparison with Horace's Maecenas.[6] In the fictive character of the addressee which the letter establishes, we can find traces also of Pope's Atticus and even of Pope's Sporus. But the letter has not merely taken from the past—it has given to the future. It would be hard to calculate the dependence of modern London High Journalism on the little matrix of irony provided by Johnson's phrase "no very cynical asperity." John Carey is one of many who find it unforgettable: writing of a television interview with Noel Coward, he says,

Ronald Bryden, presumably trying to rouse us to a spirit of gay challenge, tossed out comparisons with Congreve and Molière. . . . These might have seemed a trifle optimistic. Loose, too: related to no very strenuous thinking on Mr. Bryden's part.[7]

But instead of tracing all Johnson's borrowings and bequests, it is more important here to emphasize his conviction that in the genre of the abusive letter the writer is no more "upon oath" than he is, as Johnson insisted, when writing an epitaph. The object of the letter of this "kind" is to insult the recipient appropriately and plausibly. As genre, it is the dedication turned inside out. A remark made by Johnson to Bennet Langton testifies abundantly to his sense of the precedence of genre even in the abusive letter. Langton reports:

Dr. Johnson, when he gave me this copy of his letter [to Chesterfield], desired that I would annex to it his information to me, that whereas it is said in the letter that 'no assistance has been received,' he did once receive from Lord Chesterfield the sum of ten pounds; but as that was so inconsiderable a sum he thought the mention of it could not properly find place in a letter of the kind that this was.

Actually, ten pounds was quite a lot of money: it approaches the fifteen guineas Johnson earned by major works like the *Life of Savage* or *The Vanity of Human Wishes*. Pope got only fifteen pounds for the five-canto version of *The Rape of the Lock*, and only seven for the two-canto version. But the paradigm Johnson is engaged in realizing in the letter to Chesterfield can admit mention of *no* act of assistance. Two words in Langton's comment particularly invite scrutiny: *properly* and *kind*. *Properly* asserts the precedence of the genre over mere occasional fact or mere idiosyncratic personal circumstance—too local to be important, as it were. And *kind* means something much more specific than we might imagine. In the *Dictionary* Johnson defines *Kind* as "generical class"; and whenever he speaks of a literary work of a certain "kind," he does

not mean anything so loose as a work of a certain sort. In critical
contexts he uses *kind* very exactly to mean a received public genre
with well-known conventional differentia.

We must turn now to some of Johnson's poems and inquire, as
we have of these letters, what they are and what they are made
of. What pre-existing models are they translating into their own
terms? With *The Vanity of Human Wishes* the answer is given in
the subtitle: "The Tenth Satire of Juvenal Imitated." Equally
obvious is the model in Proverbs 6:6 for "The Ant," which begins,

> Turn on the prudent ant thy heedful eyes;
> Observe her labors, sluggard, and be wise.

Somewhat less obvious is the provenance of the materials out of
which some other poems are made. I use *materials* consciously to
suggest the inert pre-existence of the quasi-architectural stuff of
poems, stuff which must have achieved the status of public property
before it can be disposed successfully as an element of compositions.

Again, as with his performance in dedications and political
advertisements, Johnson's great art is the art of redeeming the
received and even the commonplace. It is entirely typical of his
literary procedure for him to take up a commonplace literary
(or frequently sub-literary) kind, put into it exactly the sort of
materials that belong there by sheer rhetorical right, and so redeem
the ordinary by an extraordinary rhetorical acuteness.

By Johnson's time hardly any genre had more of the commonplace about it than the theatrical prologue. Like the dedication and
the petition, the theatrical prologue is dramatic writing in the sense
that the author speaks not in his own person but in the role of the
speaker assigned to deliver his words. In Johnson's *Drury Lane
Prologue* of 1747 the speaker is not Johnson but David Garrick,
and further, David Garrick not in his off-stage role of an amiable
if vain companion but in his official role as actor-manager of a playhouse. Consequently, the vignette history of the English drama
which Johnson writes for Garrick to speak is appropriately couched
in a raised, flamboyant style of the sort a showman would conven-

tionally affect. The images Johnson uses are a bit too bold, the antitheses a little too melodramatic, the issues over-schematized and oversimplified both to lend verisimilitude to the speaker and to flatter the audience into imagining that it constitutes an appropriate tribunal of literary criticism. We can understand Johnson's task if we imagine ourselves assigned the job of writing a brief comparison between the poetry of William Carlos Williams and Wallace Stevens that will sound entirely natural when spoken by David Susskind.

Johnson hated to write so much that he generally wrote as fast as possible to get it over with. In composing poems his usual method was to do the whole thing in his head before recording any of it on paper. In this way he could himself wield the stick from which the carrot before him depended. Of *The Vanity of Human Wishes* he says: "I wrote . . . the first seventy lines . . . in the course of one morning. . . . The whole number was composed before I threw a single couplet on paper." Notice the language here: *composed*, not created; *threw*, as if the couplets are inert, almost material objects. Johnson's comment on *Throw* in the *Dictionary* seems to imply a very accurate image of his own compositional practices: "[The word *Throw*] always comprises the idea of haste, force, or negligence." Of the *Drury Lane Prologue* he says: "The same method [as in writing *The Vanity of Human Wishes*] I pursued in regard to the Prologue on opening Drury Lane Theater. I did not afterwards change more than a word of it, and that was done at the remonstrance of Garrick. I did not think his criticism just, but it was necessary he should be satisfied with what he was to utter." (Actually, it turned out that Garrick didn't utter the lines at all: he was sick on the crucial evening. The play, by the way, was *The Merchant of Venice*.)

We can appreciate Johnson's ventriloquial powers if we compare the way Johnson-Garrick goes about praising Shakespeare with the way Johnson-as-"critic" praises him in the *Preface* to his formal edition of Shakespeare. Johnson-Garrick's emphasis is all on the wonderful, on Shakespeare's powers of fancy, his capacity for exhausting known worlds and then imagining new ones, and for disdaining the boundaries of real existence:

> When Learning's triumph o'er her barb'rous foes
> First reared the stage, immortal Shakespeare rose;
> Each change of many-colored life he drew,
> Exhausted worlds, and then imagined new:
> Existence saw him spurn her bounded reign,
> And panting Time toiled after him in vain.

But in the *Preface*, Johnson in his role as a judicious critic praises Shakespeare for quite contrary qualities, namely, his fidelity to the natural—that is, the expected and familiar—in human character. Indeed, what Johnson-Garrick locates as a Shakespearian virtue Johnson-as-critic singles out as a defect: "He had no regard to distinction of time and place," we are told in the *Preface*; and this readiness to spurn the bounded kingdom of real existence leads Shakespeare into anachronism and confusion. Mrs. Thrale is one who would have been capable of perceiving the distinction between Johnson-Garrick and Johnson-as-critic. She notes "his extreme distance from those notions which the world has agreed . . . to call Romantic," and she continues: "It is indeed observable in his *Preface to Shakespeare* that while other critics [!] expatiate on the creative powers and vivid imagination of that matchless poet, Dr. Johnson commends him for giving so just a representation of human manners. . . . "

With the second verse-paragraph of the *Drury Lane Prologue* we begin to see what publicly-available materials Johnson is inviting into the poem:

> Then Jonson came, instructed from the school,
> To please in method, and invent by rule;
> His studious patience and laborious art
> By regular approach essayed the heart;
> Cold approbation gave the ling'ring bays,
> For those who durst not censure scarce could praise.

The Shakespeare-Jonson antithesis had been a standard piece of literary goods ever since Dryden's *Essay of Dramatic Poesy* of 1668, where Jonson is taxed with elegant frigidity: "You seldom find him . . . endeavoring to move the passions," says Dryden. The antitype is Shakespeare, whose passion, as Johnson-Garrick is pleased to conceive of it, storms and immediately conquers the breast of the apprehender.

For the paradigm of the next two paragraphs, which trace the history of Restoration comedy through its career of bawdiness and that of post-Restoration tragedy through its career of declamation and dullness, we need search no further than Pope's imitation of the First Epistle of the Second Book of Horace, the *Epistle to Augustus*, and the versified literary history embedded there. And the sinister transformations that follow, where theater is metamorphosed into raree-show, will remind us of the similar transformations already enacted in the *Dunciad*.

Up to this point in the poem, we have heard, as it were, two voices speaking as one, Johnson's and Garrick's performing a sort of recitative duet. But as the last two verse-paragraphs begin at line 47, each speaker seems to remain silent for a moment to allow the other an unmodified development of his own position in his own verbal way. Thus the speaker in the penultimate paragraph is Garrick taking over:

> Hard is his lot [the actor's], that here [on the
>   front of the stage] by Fortune placed,
> Must watch the wild vicissitudes of taste.

(*Wild vicissitudes*, although emerging from Garrick's lips, is a fine example of Johnson's poetic practice of juxtaposing the Anglo-Saxon with the Latinate, the Northern monosyllabic with the Southern polysyllabic.) But in the last paragraph it is Garrick's turn to stand silent while Johnson takes over, which is to say that theatrical values yield, finally, to moral ones. The final injunction to the audience assumes an intimate connection between the artistic virtues of plays and the moral virtues of those who witness them.

The redemption of the drama is to be accomplished only by a more important redemption of the audience:

> Then prompt no more the follies you decry.

This sober, moralistic call to the audience to change its well-known ways is unexampled in Dryden's prologues, which are unremittingly frivolous: he can't even address the King and Queen without striking out conceits and descending to gags. The model for Johnson's solemn address to the audience is instead Pope's Prologue to Addison's *Cato* (1713). Pope's speaker shares the assumptions of Johnson's that the office of writing is to do something to the audience, and at the outset of the *Prologue to Cato* we are lodged firmly in the same world in which Johnson-Garrick easily imagines Shakespeare's passion storming the breast:

> To wake the soul by tender strokes of art,
> To raise the genius, and to mend the heart;
> To make mankind in conscious virtue bold,
> Live o'er each scene, and be what they behold:
> For this the Tragic Muse first trod the stage.

Irresistible as Shakespeare's passion, the power of the tragic drama is to be withstood by neither the tyrannical nor the vicious:

> Tyrants no more their savage nature kept,
> And foes to virtue wondered how they wept.

After twenty-four lines devoted to the argument that the theme of *Cato*—patriot virtue—is nobler as material for tragedy than the common themes of heroic grandeur or love, Pope "turns" in the last ten lines, just as Johnson does in his last eight, exhorting the audience to moral improvement specifically as a means of theatrical redemption:

> Britons, attend: be worth like this approved,
> And show you have the virtue to be moved.
> With honest scorn the first famed Cato viewed
> Rome learning arts from Greece, whom she subdued;

Our scene precariously subsists too long
On French translation and Italian song.
Dare to have sense yourselves; assert the stage,
Be justly warmed with your own native rage.
Such plays alone should please a British ear
As Cato's self had not disdained to hear.

Johnson knew this poem by heart: he knew even its textual variants. As he writes in the *Life of Addison,*

When Pope brought [Addison] the Prologue . . . there were these words, 'Britons, *arise*, . . . ' meaning nothing more than, Britons, erect and exalt yourselves to the approbation of public virtue. Addison was frighted lest he should be thought a promoter of insurrection, and the line was liquidated to 'Britons, attend.'

It is significant that Johnson seems to know most about precisely that part of Pope's *Prologue* which has had the strongest impact on his own, that is, the final "turn" to direct moral-artistic exhortation. Arthur Murphy was striking very near the truth when he said of Johnson's *Drury Lane Prologue* that it "may at least be placed on a level with Pope's to the tragedy of *Cato.*"

Even Johnson's apparently most direct, natural, and "sincere" poem, the domestic elegy *On the Death of Dr. Robert Levet*, cannot take place without the mechanism of imitation. Its essential paradigm is the Anglican hymn in long measure. Its images of "Hope's delusive mine" and "Misery's darkest caverns" seem to remember both Toplady's cleft Rock of Ages and the "unfathomable mines" of Cowper's *Light Shining Out of Darkness*. Johnson's curious final image,

Death broke at once the vital chain
And freed his soul the nearest way,

seems to recall Toplady's equally curious

When my eye-strings break in death,

as well as Isaac Watts's

> Dear Sovereign, break these vital strings
> That bind me to my clay.

In the matter of address, Toplady's and Watts's hymns are really prayers. But Johnson's poem, although overtly an elegy, is visited by the mode of prayer. Consider the seventh stanza:

> His virtues walked their narrow round,
> Nor made a pause, nor left a void;
> And sure th' Eternal Master found
> The single talent well employed.

What this glance at the Parable of the Talents implies is Johnson's awareness of the multiplicity of his own talents, which contrast so strikingly with Levet's single one. What is implied in this stanza is the prayer, "May the Eternal Master find my talents equally well employed." The poem, as Edward A. Bloom has perceived, is "more about Johnson than Levet."[8]

To attend to Johnson's work thus closely is to perceive everywhere its pervasive reliance on the pre-existent. And the important point is this: the compositional process of imitation I have been examining is in no way unique to Johnson, or to "the eighteenth century," or even to a vanished world in which writers are presumed to be learned and bookish. William Blake, for all his dramaturgy of inspiration and uniqueness of vision, requires Thomas Chatterton very much the way Johnson requires Dryden, Pope, Toplady, and Watts, as we realize when we perceive something familiar in this impressive image from the most inventive of Blake's early works, *The Marriage of Heaven and Hell*:

> How do you know but every bird that cuts the airy way
> Is an immense world of delight, closed to your senses five?

What generates the shock of recognition here is our memory of Charles Bawdin's speech in Chatterton's *Bristowe Tragedie*:

> 'Howe dydd I knowe thatt ev'ry darte
> Thatt cutte the airie waie

Myghte nott fynde passage toe my harte
And close myne eyes for aie?'

And Blake goes even further. He imitates not only Chatterton, who is easily conceived as an appropriate soulmate. Unlikely as it might seem, he imitates Matthew Prior—wit, diplomatist, and Augustan, representative of exactly that Lockean skepticism and that social sophistication and cynicism which Blake's literary identity obliges him to appear to repudiate. In 1718 Prior committed this witty, patronizing epigram in the mode of the smoking-room story:

A TRUE MAID

'No, no! for my virginity,
When I lose that,' says Rose, 'I'll die.'
'Behind the elms last night,' cried Dick,
'Rose, were you not extremely sick?'

Seventy-six years later Blake recovers this by resuming the voice of Dick and addressing Rose—transmuted now into "the Rose"—for very different ends:

THE SICK ROSE

O Rose, thou art sick!
The invisible worm
That flies in the night
In the howling storm,

Has found out thy bed
Of crimson joy,
And his dark secret love
Does thy life destroy.

Blake drains the wit out of Rose's sickness and re-directs it toward the portentous and the wonderful. And the love-in-darkness of Prior's epigram, where it is an expression of mere social and sexual play, Blake manages to attach to the principle of dissolution. He has taken Prior's song of experience and made it one of his own. But we must emphasize that he has had to begin with a literary artifact to transmute.

Sometimes imitations are so subtle that our perception of them is fainter. But they are always there nevertheless. Consider, for example, the syntax and pattern of vowel sounds in the line from Yeats's *Sailing to Byzantium* where the speaker apostrophizes the sages to come

> And be the singing-masters of my soul.

The imitation here is of the last line of Keats's sonnet *To Sleep*:

> And seal the hushèd casket of my soul.

The vowel sound of Keats's *seal* gives birth to Yeats's *be*; and Keats's *casket*, by its invitation to a near-rhyme, creates Yeats's *masters*.

If we proceed in this direction, a suspicion capable of troubling our sleep will now and then steal upon us: that given sufficient time, sufficient perceptiveness, sufficient analytic patience, and sufficient literary memory, we could ultimately track every written thing to all its imitations and end with no distinguishable separate works at all but only with one great *Ur*-source. "In the Beginning was the Word." Which is to say, in less baroque language, that the main condition of being a writer is being a reader. William Bowles remembered of Johnson that "He had . . . projected . . . a work to show how small a quantity of real fiction there is in the world; and that the same images, with very little variation, have served all the authors who have ever written."

One would imagine that the act of prayer would be among the least literary and artificial of things. If a man can't be "natural" when privately addressing his Maker, when *can* he be? But Johnson's practice in his prayers indicates that even if one is going to pray, one must perforce imitate something. What Johnson imitates, even in his most open, anguished, "lyric" moments, is The Book of Common Prayer.

In praying, as in any other mode of utterance, one has to adopt a style. Christian prayers are conventionally uttered in an archaic style less because of the dignity of the occasion than because of the flagrant archaism of the literary models available. Because his chosen model for prayers is The Book of Common Prayer, the style Johnson must adopt is, as Stella Brook has designated it, "a sixteenth-century liturgical vernacular with a seventeenth-century overlay."[9] What makes the prayers so startling in something like *Are You Running With Me, Jesus?*, by the Rev. Malcolm Boyd, is not so much their substantive endorsement of fornication as their embrace of an unprecedented stylistic model for prayers, the non-chalant Hip or "mixed-up" vernacular.

The version of the Prayer Book used by Johnson was the revision of 1662, the first to include the Psalms and to employ for the Gospels and Epistles the text of the Authorized Version rather than the Great Bible. In Johnson's day The Book of Common Prayer, for all the conspicuous archaism of its usages, could be regarded as almost a work of contemporary literature. Its chronological relation to Johnson was roughly that of Shaw's *Widowers' Houses* to us. The Prayer Book imitated by Johnson appeared in the same year as Part I of Butler's *Hudibras* and only six years before Dryden's *Essay of Dramatic Poesy*. For the style of the Prayer Book Johnson felt the sort of enthusiasm he reserved for rare (and disturbing) masterpieces like *Paradise Lost*. One reason he hated to go to church was the painful literary contrast he witnessed there between the all-but-illiterate idiom of the sermon and the sublime rhetoric of the liturgy:

I am convinced [he once said] that I ought to be present at divine service more frequently than I am; but the provocations given by ignorant and affected preachers too often disturb the mental calm which otherwise would succeed to prayer. I am apt to whisper to myself on such occasions—How can this illiterate fellow dream of fixing attention after we have been listening to the sublimest truths, conveyed in the most chaste and exalted language, throughout a liturgy which must be regarded as the genuine offspring of piety impregnated by wisdom?

His way with the prayer as genre is like his way with the other kinds: it is the method of redeeming the received, of fusing the individual and local with the public and external, of advertising by practice the all-important equipose between individual-consciousness and species-consciousness. A function of his method is to locate reality by mediating precisely between the unknowable inside and the cliché outside, bringing into harmony the new and the known. A typical performance is the first prayer of any length he recorded, set down in 1738, on his twenty-ninth birthday. We have seen before how it registers his conviction of being under a special obligation because of his extraordinary survival. The prayer transmits an effect of naked sincerity, but paradoxically it does so only because we recognize in it Johnson's mastery of the elements of the genre "Anglican prayer." The effect of sincerity is a function of the imitation of prayers already firmly in the public domain.

Johnson begins this prayer by adapting the salutation of the Prayer Book's "Prayer for All Conditions of Men": "O God, the Creator and Preserver of all Mankind." He then skips to the ascription part of the next prayer in the book, "A General Thanksgiving," and imitates it very closely:

Father of all Mercies, I thine unworthy servant do give thee most humble thanks [the model reads "most humble and hearty thanks"] for all thy goodness and lovingkindness to me. I bless thee for my creation, preservation, and redemption, for the knowledge of Thy Son Jesus Christ, for the means of Grace, and the hope of Glory.

Launched now with the indispensable aid of imitation and adaptation, he is free to turn the paradigm to his own individual purposes. The necessity he feels for *beginning* conventionally here is like the similar necessity he recognizes when he begins the letter to Macpherson, "I received. . . ." As he continues composing, bringing himself to his obsessive theme of investing his talents and thus redeeming the time, he animates what he says by echoing the same syntactical parallelism—taking the form primarily of triplets —he has begun by imitating:

In the days of childhood and youth, in the midst of weakness, blindness, and danger, Thou hast protected me; amidst afflictions of mind, body, and estate, Thou hast supported me; and amidst vanity and wickedness Thou hast spared me. . . . Create in me a contrite heart, that I may worthily lament my sins, acknowledge my wickedness, and obtain remission and forgiveness through the satisfaction of Jesus Christ. And O Lord, enable me by Thy Grace to use all diligence in redeeming the time which I have spent in sloth, vanity, and wickedness; to make use of Thy gifts to the honor of Thy name; to lead a new life in Thy faith, fear, and love. . . .

But even in writing so apparently intimate as this we must be careful to assign to the writer what belongs to the writer and to literature what belongs to literature. As R. W. Chapman has observed,

Not even the *Prayers and Meditations* comprehend their author. Johnson, an accomplished writer of dedications, said that 'the known style of dedication is flattery.' He would have said that the proper topic of a Christian's and a sinner's meditations is self-examination and self-abasement. The *Prayers and Meditations* are true; but they are not autobiography.[10]

In this process of imitating prayers Johnson is quite capable of redeeming his original, even when his original is the Authorized Version. In his borrowings as well as his criticism what M. J. C. Hodgart says about his essential method holds true: "He keeps his eye firmly on the text, and works through it like an editor or a publisher's reader: from his long experience as a practical journalist, he knows that almost everything, except short passages of poetry, can be improved in argument or polish. . . ."[11] During April, 1752, he is mourning for Tetty, who died on March 17. Perceiving that his despair must be brought to at least a formal end, he writes this prayer on May 6:

O Lord, our heavenly Father, without whom all purposes are frustrate, all efforts are vain, grant me the assistance of Thy Holy Spirit, that I may not sorrow as one without hope, but may now return to the duties of my present state with humble confidence in Thy protection, and so govern my thoughts and actions that neither business may withdraw my mind from Thee, nor idleness lay me open to vain imaginations; that neither praise may fill me with pride, nor censure with discontent; but that in the changes of this life I may fix my heart upon the reward which Thou hast promised to them that serve Thee; and that whatever things are true, whatever things are honest, whatever things are just, whatever are pure, whatever are lovely, whatever are of good report, wherein there is virtue, wherein there is praise, I may think upon and do, and obtain mercy and everlasting happiness. Grant this, O Lord, for the sake of Jesus Christ. Amen.

What he is doing near the end here is improving in rhythm and economy the sentence in Philippians 4:8:

Finally, brethren, whatsoever things are true, whatsoever things are honest, whatsoever things are just, whatsoever things are pure, whatsoever things are lovely, whatsoever things are of good report; if there be any virtue, and if there be any praise, think on these things.

Philippians 4 is set as the Second Lesson for Evening Service for April 27: perhaps he had it especially in mind as a model because he had heard it from the pulpit that day. But even though he can use Biblical texts—and improve them—he never loses a sense of their awful solemnity and a conviction that they are too sacred to be trifled with or even invoked on unholy occasions. W. J. Bate and Albrecht B. Strauss have found 669 quotations or literary allusions in the *Rambler*: only seven are from the Bible.[12]

Thus Johnson—and everyone else, in my view—writes by imitating. And he thinks by imitating too. "The point," says E. D. Hirsch,

is not [merely] that the author cannot communicate a totally unfamiliar type of meaning, but the less obvious one that he cannot even *formulate* [my emphasis] such a type. Pre-existing type conceptions are apparently as necessary to the imagination as they are to the exigencies of communication.[13]

Which is a way of expressing in the modern context of "codes," "roles," and "games" what Sir Joshua Reynolds was aware of in 1776. He emphasizes in his *Sixth Discourse*: "It is vain for painters or poets to endeavor to invent without materials on which the mind may work and from which invention must originate. Nothing can come of nothing." The process of literary invention is thus a function of the process of recollection. Mickey Rooney, distinguished as a professional if not as an intellectual, has had enough experience of the actual world to sense that this is so. He accounts this way for the formula of the Andy Hardy films: "I realized that this family imagery came about through the picture of *Ah Wilderness*, Eugene O'Neill's great play. I did [that] picture with Lionel Barrymore, who was in a sense the first Judge Hardy."[14] Thomas Hobbes gets at the principle this way: "Imagination and memory are but one thing, which for divers considerations hath divers names." That Johnson, candid as usual about literary process, is sensitive to the difficulty of distinguishing these two things is clear in his *Preface to Shakespeare*, where he observes about what he may owe unconsciously to earlier commentators,

Whatever I have taken from them it was my intention to refer to its original author, and it is certain that what I have not given to another I believed when I wrote it to be my own. . . . If I am ever found to encroach upon the remarks of any other commentator, I am willing that the honor, be it more or less, should be transferred to the first claimant, for his right, and his alone, stands above dispute; the second can prove his pretensions only to himself, nor can himself always distinguish invention, with sufficient certainty, from recollection.

He would have relished a passage in Harold Nicolson's recent *Diaries and Letters*: Nicolson sends Vita Sackville-West the remark of the poet Edward Shanks that one sign of increasing age is his not knowing "Whether a line is one of his own lines or something which he has read years ago." She replies:

As to remembering whether a line is by me or by someone else, you know very well that I never could. The first shock of this realization came when I very laboriously hammered out a line, choosing every word most carefully, and arrived at:

Men are but children of a larger growth.

[Dryden, *All for Love*, IV, i, 43]

Since then I have been cautious.[15]

The theory of literary process which Johnson and his world take for granted does seem odd to a modern world dominated by images of individualism and "free-enterprise" and sustained by laws about copyright and plagiarism. Northrop Frye is acute on this matter:

All art is equally conventionalized, but we do not ordinarily notice this fact unless we are unaccustomed to the convention. In our day the conventional element in literature is elaborately disguised by a law of copyright pretending that every work of art is an invention distinctive enough to be patented.

(It would be interesting, by the way, to scrutinize the assumptions about "originality" which generated the nineteenth-century laws of patent and to locate their origins in Romantic theory of creation.) Frye goes on:

Hence the conventionalizing forces of modern literature . . . often go unrecognized. Demonstrating the debt of A to B is merely scholarship if A is dead, but a proof of moral delinquency if A is alive. This state of things makes it difficult to appraise a literature which includes Chaucer, much of whose poetry is translated or paraphrased from others; Shakespeare, whose plays sometimes follow their sources almost verbatim; and Milton, who asked for nothing better than to steal as much as possible out of the Bible. It is not only the inexperienced reader who looks for a *residual* originality in such works. Most of us tend to think of a poet's real achievement as distinct from, or contrasted with, the achievement present in what he stole, and we are thus apt to concentrate on peripheral rather than on central critical facts.

The real state of literary affairs, Frye concludes, "was much clearer before the assimilation of literature to private enterprise concealed so many of the facts of criticism."[16] Or the facts of writing, as I have called them.

In emphasizing the imitative mechanism in writing I have of course started some embarrassing critical questions, among them: Where do literary genres come from? Are they generated *ex nihilo?* How do new ones come into being? In Johnson's time these questions were more easily answered. Assuming a static image of human character, most eighteenth-century critics found little difficulty in associating the main genres and even the main modes in writing with universal, unchanging elements in the more or less uniform human personality. Thus an older theorist of genres could reason somewhat as follows: each element of the unalterable and perpetually re-created human mind has a literary genre which accords with its expectations; since human nature is historically uniform and since, therefore, the same very few essential human actions are played over and over *ad infinitum*, the genres devised (or better, "discovered") by the Ancients may serve for eternity. Thus the part of the mind which gratifies itself with gentle, "safe" melancholy leans toward and sanctions elegy. The part that relishes enthusiasm or devotion sanctions the ode. The part delighting in ideas of justice is gratified by tragedy, comedy, or satire. The part that delights in fantasies of dissipation and irresponsibility has song or pastoral for its gratification. The part hankering after an ideal of heroism sanctions the epic. And so on. Relying always on the Lockean image of the mind as a repository of all-but uniform experience, the critics of Johnson's day, if they could ignore new things like the novel—and most of them did—embraced an account of the origin of genres which made them co-terminous with the origin of the human mind itself.

In thinking about the matter we will find ourselves in a more difficult position, although, like earlier theorists, we will necessarily start from our habitual way of reasoning about—or imaging— genetics and trying to account for origins. When we engage in this activity our own bent is probably toward the Hegelian and the sexual. We thus may find ourselves speculating as follows.

All distinct literary genres are the result of a "dialectical" synthesis between two earlier genres. The Gothic novel, for ex- ample, is the result of a synthesis between the picaresque romance and the spooky eighteenth-century discursive poem like Young's *Night Thoughts*, a genre which, in its turn, synthesizes elements of revenge play (*Hamlet*) and Christian epic (*Paradise Lost*), in the process domesticating, lowering, and sentimentalizing the mélange. The epistolary novel, as practiced by Richardson or Smollett, can be seen to be a synthesis of Renaissance prose romance, on the one hand, and the early eighteenth-century manual of letter-writing, on the other. And we can perform the same operation in trying to account for the shape of modern genres like, say, the Absurd Play, which would appear to derive from a fusion of nineteenth-century domestic melodrama with nineteenth-century nonsense fiction of the sort derived by Peacock from Sterne, and bequeathed by Peacock to Lewis Carroll.

The indispensable principle underlying this theory of genres is that nothing can come of nothing; for to be accepted as a genre by readers, that is, to be recognized as a coded context or grid in which "literature" can occur, a literary form must carry with it something of the familiar, something that reminds the reader, however dimly, of an earlier form with which he is familiar and which he habitually regards *as a form,* as a well-known arena in which apparent literary purpose and value can show themselves. As Hirsch puts it:

In every new genre [a] process of assimilation is at work. No one would ever invent or understand a new type of meaning unless he were capable of perceiving analogies and making novel subsumptions under previously known types.

And he continues:

Every new verbal type is . . . a metaphor that required an imaginative leap. The growth of new genres is founded on this quantum principle that governs all learning and thinking: by an imaginative leap the unknown is assimilated to the known, and something . . . new is realized.[17]

Instructive here is the theatrical producer E. Martin Browne's experience with T. S. Eliot when the two of them had undertaken to compose and present a church pageant, the work which ultimately became *The Rock.* The problem facing these two devisers was that they had no form available in which to cast their material, "pageant" meaning to a lettered audience less a literary form than a vague mode of circus or non-verbal processional. As Browne recalls:

We used to meet for lunch, about once a month . . . , to search for a form in which to cast the show. . . . We talked round and round the problem each month, seeing no light until at last, the day before the deadline for a scenario, some broke upon me. We could model it upon the type of revue, bound together by a thin thread of plot, currently presented by C. B. Cochran. It would allow both for spectacular scenes acted to music and for a chorus, who instead of displaying their physical charms would use their speaking voices in delivering verse.[18]

Thus the girlie-show was selected as the form with which the audience was already familiar—that is, prepared to regard as "a form"—and Eliot and Browne could now proceed to transmute it to their own uses.

It is important to see, as this example shows, that audiences are really more consequential in determining genres than writers are. As Frye says, "The basis of generic criticism . . . is rhetorical, in the sense that the genre is determined by the conditions established between the poet and his public."[19] We can appreciate how little a writer by himself can contrive a new genre by recalling things like the curtal sonnets of Gerard Manley Hopkins, which, for all their technical interest, reveal themselves to be one-shot performances *because* their readers sense in them no profound new reason for such an abbreviation of sonnet form and consequently decline to call for more. While the activity of literature is clearly a great many other things as well, one crucial thing it is is a market, and we will not get far in understanding writing if, dazzled by the presumed metaphysics of its creation, we lose sight of the supply-and-demand mechanics of its transmission.

In the way I have been suggesting, then, literary elements and forms imitate organic history, reaching back irrecoverably into the abysm of time but, within our limited view, procreating and occasionally mutating like the creatures depicted for us by biology. It is ironic that the theory of the production of new genres I have been suggesting accords exactly with the scandalous vision of the Goddess of Dullness in the *Dunciad*; peering down into the murky chasm of Grub Street, she perceives

> How Tragedy and Comedy embrace,
> How Farce and Epic get a jumbled race.

From Johnson to Blake, Yeats, Sackville-West, and Eliot would seem a long distance, but it may seem long because a generation later than Johnson's has chosen to surround the act of writing with a novel, essentially propagandistic "creative" terminology which implies that the actual nature of the literary process changed during the nineteenth century. If we will inspect what writers do rather than what they say they are doing, we may want to conclude otherwise.

CHAPTER 6

"The Anxious Employment of a Periodical Writer"

So much for theory. It is now time to turn to Johnson's main writing enterprises—the *Rambler*, the *Dictionary, Rasselas*, and *The Lives of the Poets*—and to consider what they are and what their meaning is within the context of his paradoxical critical and moral equipment. First, the *Rambler*.

"I purpose to endeavor the entertainment of my countrymen by a short essay on Tuesday and Saturday": thus, with an appearance of security and even jauntiness, Johnson announced his plans for the *Rambler* in the first number, on Tuesday, March 20, 1750. Two years and 208 essays later, he looked back over his accomplishment and began the last of the *Ramblers* in the tone of a man sadly illuminated by experience. We hear now of "labors" and anxiety instead of "entertainment" and an easy brevity: "Time, which puts an end to all human pleasures and sorrows, has likewise concluded the labors of the Rambler. Having supported for two years the anxious employment of a periodical writer, and multiplied my essays to upwards of two hundred, I have now determined to desist."

Finding a title had been the first problem, and Reynolds recalls Johnson's report of the way he solved it: "What *must* be done, Sir, *will* be done. When I was to begin publishing that paper, I was at a loss how to name it. I sat down at night upon my bedside and resolved that I would not go to sleep till I had fixed its title. The *Rambler* seemed the best that occurred, and I took it." This must be one of the very few times that one of his "resolutions" came to anything. On this occasion he was perhaps assisted by recalling the title of Savage's poem *The Wanderer*, a work he admired and often alluded to. And he was certainly assisted by recalling the title chosen in similar circumstances by two of his predecessors: the *Spectator*.

Once the title was settled, the next problem—an unremitting one—was to get down to work, which meant encountering for two years an irrevocable deadline twice a week. For a man so given to procrastination as Johnson, this experience must have been ghastly. Indeed, the twice-weekly crises would remind him in many ways of his twice-weekly examinations (every Thursday and Saturday) by his master Humphrey Hawkins at the Lichfield Grammar School. Or if writing the *Rambler* was not like going to school again, it was at least like presiding over one, and a depressing one at that: Boswell quotes from one of Johnson's notebooks, "I do not remember that since I left Oxford I ever rose early by mere choice, but once or twice at Edial, and two or three times for the *Rambler*." Writing regularly invited him to conceive of regularity as a theme for the *Rambler*. As he encountered his first and second deadlines every week, he was reminded of that week's Christian meaning, and often he devoted Saturday's essay to a Christian exhortation appropriate to the following day. And regular performance month in and month out excited a similar consciousness of the meaning of the Christian year. Robert Voitle has noticed "how much the tone of the *Ramblers* changes around Christmas and Easter.... [On these occasions] the *Ramblers* became grave largely because he feels that during these seasons his readers should also meditate on how pitifully weak man is and how little he can accomplish on his own."[1]

Taken as a whole the papers of the *Rambler* are much too rich and complicated to be described easily. They range from the gay to the austere, from the whimsical to the solemn. It can be said, however, that one important object of the *Rambler* is to describe and recommend the psychological technique by which contentment is to be achieved, by which a degree of happiness is to be derived from an acceptance of unalterable circumstance. As Johnson puts it in No. 178, "The reigning error of mankind is that we [not *they*, notice] are not content with the conditions on which the goods of life are granted." Where Christian mechanisms are appropriate for securing content, Johnson invokes them; but almost as often the techniques he suggests derive from pagan commonplaces or from his understanding of his own experience, very closely scrutinized for real motive, or the experience of others he has observed closely. In the many papers devoted to psychological and moral problems, he tries to look at life purely, disregarding the adventitious ornaments and temporary details which give a delusive appearance of specialness or uniqueness to one place or one time. By focusing on the essential springs of human action, by analyzing human desires and their customarily ironic or otherwise unsatisfactory results, he takes us deep into the heart of human psychological experience. His topics are the universal human feelings, the same now as they ever have been and ever will be, of joy, guilt, shame, curiosity, boredom, excitement, frustration, satiety. What the *Rambler* provides is a virtual anatomy of the human emotional life. And there is an unforgettable tenderness in many of Johnson's inquiries; here is no rigorous anatomist like Swift. One of his recurrent topics is the torment of self-consciousness; another is the social desire to be liked; another is, as he designates it in No. 132, "the anxiety of irresolution"; and a favorite is the embarrassments occasioned by social awkwardness. The poles of Johnson's focus are individuals and society; and his topics come alive when he mediates between these poles, studying that point where the individual makes contact, sometimes satisfying, more often humiliating, with society.

As W. J. Bate has perceived, well over a fourth of the *Ramblers* deal in some way with the motive of envy as a primary disturber of the human peace and as the main social cause of discontent and self-imposed misery.[2] In these papers he may have been mindful of Savage's treatment of this theme in *The Wanderer* (lines 353–410). Although the treatment of envy is generally somber and sermonesque, occasionally Johnson brings a severe levity to bear, and we get witty syntactical exhibitions comparable to Popian couplets: "Let it . . . be constantly remembered that whoever envies another confesses his superiority, and let those be reformed by their pride who have lost their virtue" (No. 183). An indication of the curious neglect of Johnson by what might be called the intellectual community is the fact that Professor Helmut Schoeck has recently managed to write 408 pages on *Envy: A Theory of Social Behavior* (London, 1969) without once alluding to Johnson or the *Rambler*.

But he is not always busy analyzing viciousness. Sometimes he turns to anatomize mere folly. As Bate says,

Johnson seems to become most light-hearted and amusing . . . when he is discussing either marriage, the pursuit of wealth, or the hopes we place in retirement to country retreats. The expectations we feel, in all three cases, also serve for Johnson as recurring symbols of the way in which the imagination, in common and daily life, is always simplifying the endless desires of the heart into specific wants, and then finding them insufficient.[3]

In other words, what he is doing in these gently satiric papers on the pathetic folly of most human wishes is discovering in domestic or low life the same self-destructive motives which, in *The Vanity of Human Wishes*, he has imputed to heroes and scholars and administrators and which, in *Rasselas*, he will disclose as animating the builders of the Pyramids. His ultimate topic, as he puts it in *Rasselas*, is "That hunger of imagination which preys incessantly upon life."

Something of the quality of the whole collection of essays is projected in *Rambler* 208, the paper where Johnson announces his determination to desist. In appearing to reveal the reason why he is quitting he behaves typically: that is, he behaves ironically and frustrates expectation by declining to offer a reason. "The reasons of this resolution," he says, "it is of little importance to declare, since justification is unnecessary when no objection is made." Launched now on the rhetoric of apparent self-pity, he conceals the reason for terminating within a sentence asserting that no reason is going to be vouchsafed: "I am far from supposing that the cessation of my performances will raise any inquiry, for I have never been much · a favorite of the public, nor can I boast that, in the progress of my undertaking, I have been animated by the rewards of the liberal, the caresses of the Great, or the praises of the eminent." In announcing that in the role of the Rambler he has "never been much a favorite of the public," Johnson may be comparing his popularity with Addison's, for it is only in comparison with the *Spectator* that the *Rambler* will appear to have been neglected by readers. Although the print-order in London was 500 copies, provincial newspapers all over England picked up and reprinted the essays; and it has been estimated that "within a few days of the first printing, many, if not all, of the *Rambler* papers were being read by thousands of people who did not live in London."[4] Some *Ramblers* even crossed the channel. In 1754 Johnson's friend Arthur Murphy, desperate for copy, came across an appealing Near Eastern morality tale in a French journal. He hastily appropriated and published it, translated, in *Gray's Inn Journal*. It proved to be *Rambler* 190. Johnson was amused.

If, as Johnson says, he cannot "boast" one wild kind of success, he is proud to claim a better sort of triumph, the result of his declining to confuse the momentary and trivial with the permanent and essential:

If I have not been distinguished by the distributors of literary honors, I have seldom descended to the arts by which favor is obtained. I have seen the meteors of fashion rise and fall without any attempt to add a moment to their duration. I have never complied with temporary curiosity, nor enabled my readers to discuss the topic of the day. I have rarely exemplified my assertions by living characters; in my papers no man could look for censures of his enemies or praises of himself; and they only were expected to peruse them whose passions left them leisure for abstracted truth, and whom virtue could please by its naked dignity.

It is this complicated sound of mingled failure and success, this subtle interweaving of humility and pride and self-pity, that gives *Rambler* 208 its distinction as an eminently characteristic piece of complex Johnsonian orchestration.

He was especially sensitive to the endings of things ("Time . . . puts an end to all human pleasures and sorrows"), not least literary projects and pieces of writing. The complex tone with which he invests the valedictory *Rambler* anticipates the great conclusion of the Preface to the *Dictionary* three years later. There shame and pride, self-pity and self-congratulation displace each other by turns to bring him to his final confession of foolish procrastination and subsequent misery. But in the Preface he has devised a complex prose world: the proclaimed misery and despair are belied stylistically in his final clause, which achieves a proud, self-sufficient harmony, balance, and rhythm (the final nine words constitute a line of iambic pentameter) suggesting a state of mind and soul quite different from the announced hopelessness: "I have protracted my work till most of those whom I wished to please [he is thinking especially of the dead Tetty] have sunk into the grave, and success and miscarriage are empty sounds: I therefore dismiss [the *Dictionary*] with frigid tranquillity, having little to fear or hope from censure or from praise." As usual, what Johnson's writing "means" is to be searched for where opposites and contradictions encounter each other. As usual, Johnson appears less an annunciator of "views" and conclusions than a complicator of the apparent. If the positions asserted in the prose are noble, the means by which they become asserted are sly.

After the paragraph in *Rambler* 208 describing his ideal readers—and flattering them in the act of describing them—he descends to necessary housekeeping details, acknowledging the assistance of others for contributions to seven of the essays. But even here, pride and humility merge inextricably: "My obligations having not been frequent, my acknowledgments may be soon dispatched. I can restore to all my correspondents their productions with little diminution of the bulk of my volumes, though not without the loss of some pieces to which particular honors have been paid." What remains is entirely his own, he goes on to say, and he will neither apologize for it nor seek a patron to protect it: "Having hitherto attempted only the propagation of truth, I will not at last violate it by the confession of terrors which I do not feel; having labored to maintain the dignity of virtue, I will not now degrade it by the meanness of dedication." The parallelism of syntax here implies strongly that the violation of truth and the writing of dedications are close to synonymous: no matter that Johnson was in actual fact the greatest eighteenth-century writer of dedications.

Conscious as always of his own inappropriateness as a moral example and consequently aware of the necessity of a salutary duplicity, he next sets forth his theory of the moral mask under which he has been conducting the *Rambler*. He has expatiated before on this theme, in *Rambler* 14, where he equates the homely human weakness of "oriental monarchs" with the natural frailty of the moral writer considered as a man:

It has long been the custom of oriental monarchs to hide themselves in gardens and palaces, to avoid the conversation of mankind, and to be known to their subjects only by their edicts. The same policy [defined by Johnson in the *Dictionary* in this sense as "stratagem"] is no less necessary to him that writes [didactically], than to him that governs; for men would not more patiently submit to be taught than commanded by one known to have the same follies and weaknesses with themselves.

And with himself clearly in mind, he goes on in *Rambler* 14: "It may be prudent for a writer who apprehends that he shall not enforce his own maxims by his domestic character to conceal his name that he may not injure them." So concealment is required, not merely as a cloak to cover the actual weaknesses of the author but also as a device of freedom. As he says in *Rambler* 208, quoting Castiglione—an author he never mentions without high praise— "'A mask . . . confers a right of acting and speaking with less restraint, even when the writer happens to be known.'"

In the *Rambler* Johnson assumes many masks. The main one is that of the "Rambler" himself, the moral instructor who speaks with secure authority, entertaining no doubts about his right to instruct others. He is an elderly man who, unlike the actual forty-one-year-old Johnson, has long ago learned to command his passions by studying "the severest and most abstracted philosophy" (No. 18). But the roles played in the essays are not always so austere: Johnson clearly enjoys wearing the masks of the various letter-writers who send in their contributions: these fictive correspondents are male and female, young and empty as well as experienced and wise—maltreated servants, eccentric collectors, impatient heirs, awkward scholars embarrassed in fine society. By this gallery of masks Johnson constructs an image of a whole society deeply dipped in folly but capable of a step toward redemption through literary means, that is, though its capacity for regretting and confessing its follies in letters to the *Rambler*.

As Johnson continues in No. 208, we are reminded that the whole series of essays is inextricably bound up with his work on the *Dictionary*, from which it served as a twice-weekly respite, if that is the right word to describe a self-imposed disciplinary task. "Only a language experiment" is what Whitman was to call *Leaves of Grass*, and there is a sense in which this formulation describes the *Rambler* as well, despite its overt didacticism and piety. Johnson indicates that while producing the *Rambler* he has been conscious of something much more technical than moral virtue. "I have labored," he says, "to refine our language to grammatical purity, and to clear it from colloquial barbarisms, licentious idioms, and irregular combinations." And then a sentence which syntactically and rhythmically enacts beautifully what it is saying: "Something, perhaps, I have added to the elegance of its construction, and something to the harmony of its cadence." Immersed at the moment in the lexicographer's concern with accurate definition, he goes on to record his reliance on scientific ("philosophic") terminology to clarify the principles of human motivation and its results: "When common words were less pleasing to the ear, or less distinct in their signification, I have familiarized the terms of philosophy by applying them to popular ideas, but have rarely admitted any word not authorized by former writers...." The pressure of the continuing work on the *Dictionary* appears in many other places in the *Rambler*: in No. 125, for example, a disquisition on the text "Definitions are hazardous"; or in No. 143, where we are told that "Descriptions . . . are definitions of a more lax and fanciful kind." But the most revealing signs of the impact on the *Rambler* of the too-slowly-advancing *Dictionary* are the frequent wry allusions to large, difficult tasks airily undertaken. These allusions are abstract, just as if Johnson were not, in fact, recognizing and deploring in each his own personal victimization by hope. He writes in No. 122: "Nothing is more subject to mistake and disappointment than anticipated judgment concerning the easiness or difficulty of any undertaking, whether we form our opinion from the performance of others, or from abstracted contemplation of the thing to be attempted." *Rambler* 127 considers the unsuspected impediments that can be counted on by the experienced to threaten and delay "great undertakings." And in No. 137, he seems engaged largely in an attempt to cheer himself up: formidable tasks, overwhelming in their magnitude, *can* be accomplished if they are undertaken in small parts. "Divide and conquer," he assures himself, "is a principle equally just in science [that is, learning] as in policy." In No. 145 he behaves as if he has just depressed himself by contriving the famous witty *Dictionary* definition of a lexicographer as "a harmless drudge"; for in this essay he breathes a sigh of sympathy for the pathetic, anonymous hacks of literature, for "the abridger, compiler, and translator," and exhorts all such to a mutual affection based on a grave mutual need: "The common interest of learning requires that her sons should cease from intestine hostilities, and, instead of sacrificing each other to malice and contempt, endeavor to avert persecution from the meanest of their fraternity."

The *Rambler* throughout seems impressed by a somberness deriving perhaps less from Johnson's general "personality" than from the implications of the specific professional trap in which he found himself during the early 1750's. Obsessed by his own contractual obligations, he instinctively made obligation—both divine and social—one of the central topics of the *Rambler*. It would not be going far wrong to say that the *Rambler* constitutes a translation into objective moral and psychological terms of much of the personal anguish Johnson felt in forcing himself to fulfill the *Dictionary* contract. In No. 207 he quotes "the malicious remark of the Greek epigrammatist [Palladas of Alexandria] on marriage": "Its two days of happiness are the first and the last." Similarly with a large literary project, as Johnson was intensely aware: the only two moments when the heart leaps up are at the signing of the contract and the delivery of the manuscript—in between stretches a desert of boredom diversified only by occasional outcrops of self-contempt.

He concludes the retrospective *Rambler* 208 by classifying in ascending order of importance and dignity the four sorts of essays he has been writing for two years. Lowest in the hierarchy are the few papers aiming largely at "harmless merriment" with no very elevated moral intent, papers like Nos. 132, 194, and 195, which retail the narrative of a feckless tutor frustrated by the folly of his noble pupil. Next in Johnson's hierarchy, but still in a very unexalted position, are "the disquisitions of criticism, which . . . is

only to be ranked among the subordinate and instrumental arts."
He is thinking of essays like No. 4, on romance and novel as
literary kinds; Nos. 36 and 37, on pastoral; or No. 60, on biography. Ranking above these because more broadly applicable in
moral terms are papers dealing with what he calls "pictures of
life": he is thinking of essays like No. 59, which depicts Suspirius,
the lugubrious prophet of evil and disaster, or No. 200, which
satirizes Prospero, the *nouveau riche* who receives his old friend
only so that he can lord it over him. Johnson ranks these essays
higher than the critical ones simply because life is more important
than literature. And in these "pictures of life" resemblance (that is,
"Nature") is essential. Talking about the danger of deviating too
far toward burlesque in monitory character-sketches, he warns that
"as they deviate farther from reality, they become less useful,
because their lessons will fail of application. The mind of the
reader [notice his rhetorical focus] is carried away from the contemplation of his own manners; he finds in himself no likeness to
the phantom before him; and though he laughs or rages, is not
reformed."

It is efficiency of moral rhetoric, then, that determines Johnson's
own hierarchy of *Rambler* papers, and in the highest position he
ranks "the essays professedly serious," which he earnestly hopes
"will be found exactly conformable to the precepts of Christianity,
without any accommodation to the licentiousness and levity of the
present age." An example of this sort of paper would be No. 32,
on Christian patience, or No. 185, on forgiveness. These differ from
sermons only in the way they begin: they start not from some
Biblical text but from some general proposition of psychology or
ethics. Thus the opening of No. 185: "No vicious dispositions of the
mind more obstinately resist both the counsels of philosophy and
the injunctions of religion than those which are complicated with
an opinion of dignity." Or No. 21: "Every man is prompted by
the love of himself to imagine that he possesses some qualities
superior either in kind or in degree to those which he sees allotted
to the rest of the world; and, whatever apparent disadvantages he

may suffer in the comparison with others, he has some invisible distinctions, some latent reserve of excellence, which he throws into the balance, and by which he generally fancies that it is turned in his favor." Or No. 14—and here we come very near to autobiography: "Among the many inconsistencies which folly produces or infirmity suffers in the human mind, there has often been observed a manifest and striking contrariety between the life of an author and his writings...."

Having arrived by ascending steps to specify the only one of the four sorts of *Ramblers* of which he is genuinely proud—and implying by the way his faith in the superior moral efficacy of overt discursive instruction to even powerful fictional representation—he concludes the final *Rambler* with his moralist's mask intact to the end: "I shall never envy the honors which wit and learning obtain in any other cause if I can be numbered among the writers who have given ardor to virtue, and confidence to truth." And just as he began work on the *Rambler* by inscribing a prayer, so he ends it, translating a passage from Dionysius' *Periegesis*:

> Celestial powers, that piety regard:
> From you my labors wait their last reward.

Why is writing the periodical essay such *anxious* employment, even if one is not, at the same time, slogging slowly ahead on an enormous dictionary? Johnson offers one answer to the question in the middle of this final *Rambler*. Despite his later insistence in conversation that "A man may write at any time if he will set himself doggedly to it," he reveals here that he knows that compositional occasions are never faced and resolved so simply. Even the well-conducted will does not—as perhaps "schematically" it should—urge the writer smoothly to the writing table and prompt him to the immediate and fruitful exercise of memory, intelligence, and expression. As Johnson admits:

He that condemns himself to compose on a stated day will often bring to his task an attention dissipated, a memory embarrassed, an imagination overwhelmed, a mind distracted with anxieties, a body languishing with disease: He will labor on a barren topic till it is too late to change it; or, in the ardor of invention, diffuse his thoughts into wild exuberance which the pressing hour of publication cannot suffer judgment to examine or reduce.

When he asserted the contrary in 1773, saying that a man may write at any time if he will merely set himself doggedly to it, he was in Edinburgh, suspicious of his company and ready to contradict all their utterances. "Somebody," says Boswell, "talked of happy moments for composition; and how a man can write at one time and not another." "Nay," said Johnson—and he continued that day saying Nay, deprecating the locals' romantic view of Scottish independence, condemning the dirtiness of Scottish churches, belittling Scottish learning as well as the literary achievement of Swift, denying the authenticity of Ossian's poetry, ridiculing Lord Monboddo's hope that the orangutan might be taught to speak English, and even denying the force of theatrical illusion. Such is the importance of context and genre in deducing what we may still be tempted to call Johnson's "real" views.

If in *Rambler* 208 the vision of composing "on a stated day" resembles a nightmare of anxiety, quite a different image of enforced composition surfaces in *Rambler* 184, written less than three months before. Here it all sounds dreadfully easy, even mechanical:

The writer of essays escapes many embarrassments to which a large book would have exposed him: he seldom harasses his reason with long trains of consequences, dims his eyes with the perusal of antiquated volumes, or burdens his memory with great accumulations of preparatory knowledge. A careless glance upon a favorite author, or transient survey of the varieties of life, is sufficient to supply the first hint or seminal idea, which, enlarged by the gradual accretion of matter stored in the mind, is by the warmth of fancy easily expanded into flowers, and sometimes ripened into fruit.

It sounds even farcical: we are reminded of Holofernes, in *Love's Labor's Lost*, accounting for his talent in extemporaneous composition:

This is a gift that I have, simple, simple; a foolish extravagant spirit, full of forms, figures, shapes, objects, ideas, apprehensions, motions, revolutions. These are begot in the ventricle of memory, nourished in the womb of *pia mater*, and delivered upon the mellowing of occasion. But the gift is good in those in which it is acute, and I am thankful for it.

To both the speaker in *Rambler* 184 and Holofernes, it is an image of a seed sprouting indomitably under even a rather careless—or at least automatic—nurture that depicts the compositional process. Is this Johnson's real view? What, then, do we make of what he says in *Rambler* 208?

The answer is that it all depends upon context and rhetorical purpose. The object in *Rambler* 208 is to take a sentimental farewell and to generate sympathy for the Rambler, who has been toiling for two years solely in our interests. The object in *Rambler* 184 is to discourse on the domination of chance (rather than "schemes") in human affairs; and the image of the natural growth of an essay like a plant is there in the service of this larger idea, the idea which brings the Rambler finally to the pious but not entirely logical conclusion that "nothing in reality is governed by chance, but . . . the universe is under the perpetual superintendance of Him who created it; . . . our being is in the hands of Omnipotent Goodness, by Whom what appears casual to us is directed for ends ultimately kind and merciful. . . ."

One of Boswell's great handicaps in understanding Johnson as a writer is his naïveté about literary contexts such as these and about the ascendancy of rhetoric in Johnson's literary behavior. The popular simplification of Johnson as an odd wise man who is most interesting because he "says" witty and outrageously dogmatic things upon all occasions derives largely from Boswell's deficiency in literary sophistication, his lack of interest in what belongs to a given genre or literary moment. If Boswell is a great biographer, he is an appalling critic. And what makes him a great biographer, his devotion to "truth," to the unambiguously demonstrable and documentable, is one of the things that disables him as a critic. He thinks that a statement means simply what it says. And so do many later interpreters of Johnson's writings and conversation. The weakness of an otherwise excellent book like Joseph Wood Krutch's *Samuel Johnson* is its lumping together as if of equal weight and force and "reality" various Johnsonian utterances, whether barked out in the heat of conversational passion, where Johnson often said things merely to annoy people he didn't at the moment approve of, or embodied with various kinds of care in quite other contexts—prayers, dedications, moral essays, letters of various "kinds," poems of various genres, or fictions and allegories operating within very strict conventions. A statement about poetry embedded in the *Life of Cowley* is a statement of a very different weight and density from a statement about poetry put into the mouth of Imlac in *Rasselas*. And even in recognizing this we must go still further: the function and meaning of both statements will depend on their operation within the specific dynamics of the passages in which they are lodged. All this seems obvious enough once we articulate it: the problem is to keep it obvious when we find ourselves caught up in the act of reading Johnson or listening to him via Boswell's reproduction of his remarks.

Self-condemned to write upon a stated day whether ready or not, Johnson found himself in a recurring compositional predicament which turned out to determine the *ad hoc* structure of most of the *Rambler* essays as well as a great part of their substance. As we will see, many of them complicate their presumed topics surprisingly by setting out in one direction and then turning, oddly, in another. The anxiety-ridden compositional circumstances in which the *Ramblers* got written were inappropriate for the registration of any dogmatic certainties, or even for the achievement of a very seamless consistency. And in subject as in method they bear the mark of the way they were composed. The bulk of them are either openly or covertly about the insufficiency of pre-concerted "schemes" or plans to deal with the actual occasions of life. The "outline" is the compositional analogue of schemes and plans: it proposes an easy articulation, but the number of times a writer has been betrayed by one is a measure of his experience and maturity. Schemes, plans, and outlines all prove ironically deficient, defeated always by the surprising and unpleasant actualities of the *ad hoc*.

One pre-concerted scheme with which Johnson was living while producing the *Rambler* was the result of commercial necessity. The papers were advertised in advance by the publication in newspapers of their epigraphic mottoes, the equivalent of indicating their subjects in advance. Johnson had to supply these mottoes considerably beforehand. As publication day approached, he was thus obliged to flesh out something like a predetermined scheme.[5] No wonder the bulk of the *Ramblers* glance either at anxiety or at the irony and pathos of the flagging will ridden by a consciousness of predetermined schemes.

There are numerous witnesses of the way Johnson wrote the *Ramblers*. All agree that twice a week he left the hated job until the very last moment (often until late on the night before publication), and then, and only then, forced himself to write compulsively, rapidly, and conclusively. What he says later of Dryden describes himself perfectly:

Of labor, notwithstanding the multiplicity of his productions, there is sufficient reason to suspect that he was not a lover. To write [like Pope, for example] *con amore,* with fondness for the employment, with perpetual touches and retouches, with unwillingness to take leave of his own idea, and an unwearied pursuit of unattainable perfection, was, I think, no part of his character.

Johnson's way of writing was so little *con amore* that he seldom even looked over what he had just written before handing the sheets to the waiting printer's boy; and sometimes he found himself so close to his deadline that the boy was running the first sheet to the compositor while Johnson was agonizing over the remainder, holding in memory as well as he could what he had already irrevocably committed to the press. Boswell says: "He told us 'almost all his *Ramblers* were written just as they were wanted for the press; and that he sent a certain portion of the copy of an essay, and wrote the remainder while the former part of it was printing. When it was wanted, and he had fairly sat down to it, he was sure it would be done.'" According to another observer, the Rev. Mr. Parker, "Mrs. Gastrell was on a visit at Mr. Hervey's, in London, at the time that Johnson was writing the *Rambler*; the printer's boy would often come after him to their house, and wait while he wrote off a paper for the press in a room full of company." And Mrs. Thrale testifies that "the fine *Rambler* on the subject of procrastination [No. 134] was hastily composed . . . in Sir Joshua Reynolds's parlor, while the boy waited to carry it to press."

Indeed, in this *Rambler* 134, Johnson becomes his own witness to the ironic dynamics of his accustomed compositional process, and does so by exposing as usual the ironic distance between "schemes"—here, "this dream of study"—and actualities—"a summons from the press"; the distance is like that in the letter to Chesterfield between "that dream of hope" and "no act of assistance":

I sat yesterday morning employed in deliberating on which among the various subjects that occurred to my imagination I should bestow the paper of today. After a short effort of meditation by which nothing was determined, I grew every moment more irresolute, my ideas wandered from the first intention, and I rather wished to think, than thought, upon any settled subject; till at last I was awakened from this dream of study by a summons from the press; the time was come for which I had been thus negligently proposing to provide, and however dubious or sluggish, I was now necessitated to write.

It is like going on stage without having learned one's lines. What arises is guilt: "I could not forbear to reproach myself for having so long neglected what was unavoidably to be done, and of which every moment's idleness increased the difficulty." But he now has found his topic, generalized from his own pathetic, farcical experience of delay followed by frantic composition: "Thus life is languished away in the gloom of anxiety, and consumed in collecting resolutions which the next morning dissipates; in forming purposes which we scarcely hope to keep, and reconciling ourselves to our own cowardice by excuses which, while we admit them, we know to be absurd."

This sort of pathological irresolution he now proceeds to objectify in a number of "characters": one man hesitates to choose until a rival takes all; another delays to choose until "some accident intercepts his journey"; another sees too far ahead—his lively imagination "extends to remote consequences," with the result that "he is entangled in his own scheme, and bewildered in the perplexity of various intentions"; another employs the neurotic technique of perfectionism to sanction doing nothing. Johnson ends *Rambler* 134 in quite a different mode from the one in which he began it: if he starts with ironic confessions of irresolution, by the time he has devised and contemplated all these human examples he enables himself to end it on a fairly resolute note: "The certainty that life cannot be long, and the probability that it will be much shorter than nature allows, ought to awaken every man to the active prosecution of whatever he is desirous to perform." But even here the imagery of dreams and waking, the recourse to *ought to,* and even the embarrassed prolixity with which the sentence ends remind us of what he is really writing about: unsatisfactory, backsliding human beings, the author included. Instead of certainty or any sort of dogmatism, what we find in *Rambler* 134 is pathos, doubt, and the essential incertitude inseparable, we should notice, from the process of extemporaneous composition. Where the simple Boswell, lusting for unambiguous guidance, saw the Johnson of the *Rambler* only as "a majestic teacher of moral and religious wisdom," more sophisticated readers will perceive that the *Rambler* papers are dynamic enterprises in which real doubts and uncertainties are constantly at war with the mere appearance of order and faith.

What we find in *Rambler* 134 we find throughout the series—Johnson, caught short at deadline time, is working things out *ad hoc* from page to page. His situation is quite different from the traditional image accepted, for example, by F. E. Halliday, who writes, "The matter was all in his head, neatly arranged, and it was merely a question of transcription."[6] This view ignores the very many *Ramblers* in which Johnson finds that he must virtually retract in the final paragraphs what he has set forth with every appearance of confidence early on. Even if the first sheet has not already gone to the compositor, Johnson is too impatient of labor to go back and begin again when a contradiction presents itself. Frequently he will not even expunge the evidence of a contradiction by revising. Instead, he plunges on, writing rapidly and hating to write: "What *must* be done, . . . *will* be done." Where he cannot resolve inconsistencies, he ignores them; where he cannot ignore them, he embraces them. All this is to say that the psychological dynamics of his compositional predicament give him his essential critical method, in the *Rambler* as well as in *The Lives of the Poets*.

Johnson's conduct of *Rambler* 23 exemplifies what I am saying. Here his topic is the appropriate amount of advice a writer should solicit from critics and friends. As we should expect, Johnson's position on this matter is one of obstinate self-sufficiency. As he says,

Whoever is so doubtful of his own abilities as to encourage the remarks of others will find himself every day embarrassed with new difficulties, and will harass his mind in vain with the hopeless labor of uniting heterogeneous ideas [contributed by a multitude of critics], digesting independent hints, and collecting into one point the several rays of borrowed light, emitted often with contrary directions.

Better for the writer to keep his own counsel and to do in his own way what must be done, knowing that, like any work of man, what he writes will always be capable of improvement, but at the same time knowing that what he writes must finally be concluded and uttered, imperfect though it will certainly be.

Johnson goes on developing this idea, and as he arrives at his seventh paragraph he remembers an observation by the Younger Pliny that he thinks might be useful to his purpose, the observation that the speaker should "not so much . . . select the strongest arguments which his cause admits, as . . . employ all which his imagination can afford: for, in pleading, those reasons are of most value which will most affect the judges; and the judges . . . will be always most touched with that which they had before conceived." By the time Johnson perceives where this point is taking him— to the position that the utterer should closely adapt what he says to the expectations of the audience, of which critics constitute an important segment—it is too late to expunge it. What he does is simply let it stand and audaciously change direction instead. He begins the next paragraph: "But, though the rule of Pliny be judiciously laid down, it is not applicable to the writer's cause. . . ." This is typical: Johnson embarks on one direction of argument, but sees that it is inapplicable; instead of returning and striking it out, he lets it stand and extricates himself later on as well as he can.

A similar act is visible in *Rambler* 139, where he criticizes *Samson Agonistes*. But here the technique we can call "the involuntary 'turn'" occurs within a single sentence. He has begun the essay by citing Aristotle's perception that the events of the most affecting tragedies are causally connected. He goes on to say that Aristotle's observation applies rather to plot than to stylistic "decorations" like meter, diction, and metaphors; as he says, "This precept is to be understood in its rigor only with respect to great and essential events, and cannot be extended in the same force to minuter circumstances and arbitrary decorations"—he gets this far when he begins to subject what he has just said to the strictest logic, asking himself, "But wouldn't even the 'decorations' be better the more organically they're connected with everything else in the

work?" Perceiving now what logic requires of "decorations," he proceeds thus: "—which yet are more happy as they contribute more to the main design." He goes on to present the reasons which have urged this odd reversal: "For it is always a proof of extensive thought and accurate circumspection to promote various purposes by the same act, and the idea of ornament admits use, though it seems to exclude necessity." This "turn" is especially interesting, for it shows Johnson first lazily embracing one of the critical clichés of his age, the assumption that substance and style are readily separable, and then bravely perceiving that the cliché won't really do. But what is pre-eminently Johnsonian about this performance is that he allows the first part of the sentence simply to stand: it is not hard, indeed, to imagine it written at the bottom of a sheet just snatched away by the printer's boy.

To the attentive reader of the *Rambler*, these *buts* and *yets* become something like its very substance. Consider No. 151. Here his topic is the several ages of man and the general uniformity of desires in infancy, youth, age, and senility. By the time he arrives at his final paragraph, he perceives what he may have been implying: that man in his uniformity is essentially a mechanical, determined creature with very little real control over his successive follies. Aware only at the end of the essay of the confidence he may innocently have supplied to determinism, he proceeds to take it all back:

I have in this view of life considered men as actuated [he still can't rid himself entirely of the quasi-mechanical and passive imagery in which he's been conducting the essay] only by natural desires, and yielding to their own inclinations, without regard to superior principles, by which the force of external events may be counteracted, and the temporary prevalence of passions restrained. Nature will indeed always operate, human desires will be always ranging; but these motions [that is, impulses], though very powerful, are not resistless; nature may be regulated, and desires governed; and to contend with the predominance of successive passions, to be endangered first by one affection, and then by another, is the condition upon which we are to pass our

time, the time of our preparation for that state which shall put an end to experiment, to disappointment, and to change.

Thus he returns, and with great skill, to the position and tone appropriate to "The Rambler"; but he can do so here only by tacking on a conclusion which follows not at all from the premises.

This is what he does again in No. 184, another essay coming dangerously close to an impious determinism and relativism. He writes: "It is not commonly observed how much even of actions considered as particularly subject to choice is to be attributed to accident, or some cause out of our own power, by whatever name it be distinguished." He proceeds through the whole essay to present one example after another of "the dominion of chance." And again, by the time he is ready to write the last paragraph, he sees where he has been led: instead of canceling what he has written, he executes one of his "turns," and suggests now that what he has been saying is virtual nonsense consisting of "unideal sounds." He now insists that

nothing can afford any rational tranquillity but the conviction that . . . nothing in reality is governed by chance, but that the universe is under the perpetual superintendance of Him who created it; that our being is in the hands of Omnipotent Goodness, by whom what appears casual to us is directed for ends ultimately kind and merciful; and that nothing can finally hurt him who debars not himself from the divine favor.

This is lame, having the effect of substituting one determinism for another; and the lameness seems to betray itself in the wooden rhetoric ("debars not himself"). But no matter: the essay must be finished, and yet it must not finish in anything that might comfort determinism or irresponsibility. Besides, tomorrow is Sunday—this is a Saturday essay—and a pious ending will not come amiss. If a jack is seen, a spit will be presumed—maybe the reader won't notice that the final paragraph is attached rather than integral.

Terrible temptations, Johnson knew, await the author who is near the end of a work. When in the *Preface to Shakespeare* he

observes that Shakespeare must often have tired of the latter parts of the plays and hustled willy-nilly to a conclusion, he knew sympathetically the experience he was describing. As he says in *Rambler* 207:

In some of the noblest compositions of wit, the conclusion falls below the vigor and spirit of the first books; and as a genius is not to be degraded by the imputation of human failings, the cause of this declension is commonly sought in the structure of the work, and plausible reasons are given why in the defective part less ornament was necessary, or less could be admitted.

But Johnson, knowing himself, knows better:

But perhaps the author would have confessed that his fancy was tired and his perseverance broken; that he knew his design to be unfinished, but that, when he saw the end so near, he could no longer refuse to be at rest.

It is not only with the most serious moral topics that Johnson performs the act of public mind-changing that we have been looking at. Sometimes his second thoughts are elicited by lighter matter. *Rambler* 177, for example, is devoted almost wholly to an odd letter from one Vivaculus, odd because the letter begins with unconscious self-satire of its writer's autistic complacency and then shifts to ridicule a gang of virtuosos comprising three idiot book collectors and a coin collector whose felicity is complete because his collection of halfpence is. "Every one of these virtuosos," says the suddenly wise Vivaculus, "looked on all his associates as wretches of depraved taste and narrow notions. Their conversation was, therefore, fretful and waspish, their behavior brutal, their merriment bluntly sarcastic, and their seriousness gloomy and suspicious." Johnson thus devotes more than nine-tenths of his space to mounting a standard eighteenth-century attack on grubbers of the silly or the remote. But with a final paragraph to go—a little over one hundred words—he bethinks himself, considers what he's done, and, to the surprise of the reader, concludes this way:

It is natural to feel grief or indignation when anything necessary or useful is wantonly wasted or negligently destroyed; and therefore my correspondent cannot be blamed for looking with uneasiness on the waste of life. Leisure and curiosity might soon make great advances in useful knowledge were they not diverted by minute emulation and laborious trifles.

And now the "turn":

It may, however, somewhat mollify his anger [which has clearly been Johnson's as well] to reflect that perhaps none of the assembly which he describes was capable of any nobler employment, and that he who does his best, however little, is always to be distinguished from him who does nothing.

And finally the "conclusion," which a careful reader will perceive to be at variance with the tendency of the bulk of the essay:

Whatever busies the mind without corrupting it has at least this use, that it rescues the day from idleness, and he that is never idle will not often be vicious.

Johnson's treatment of Vivaculus's satire has its counterpart in the crucial relation between two *Ramblers*, Nos. 82 and 83. No. 82 consists of a ridiculous letter from Quisquilius (cf. Latin *quisquiliae*, rubbish), "long . . . known," by his own account, "as the most laborious and zealous virtuoso that the present age has had the honor of producing. . . ." He has ill-spent a lifetime and a fortune accumulating stones, mosses, shells, hornet-stings, butter-flies, grubs and insects, "the longest blade of grass upon record," an albino mole, various shabby antique fragments, and innumerable historical relics chosen with an audacious disregard of their mean-ing. But he has overextended himself and is now the victim of his creditors. His whole letter constitutes a comic self-exposure of an energetic man who has brought disaster on himself wholly by his silliness and egotism. And Johnson leaves it at that.

But in Tuesday's paper he is entertaining serious second thoughts about what he has done on Saturday. He begins *Rambler* 83: "The publication of the letter in my last paper has naturally led me to the consideration of thirst after curiosities, which often draws contempt and ridicule upon itself. . . ." He goes on:

There are, indeed, many subjects of study which seem but remotely allied to useful knowledge and of little importance to happiness or virtue.

And then, as if thinking of himself last Saturday:

Nor is it easy to forbear some sallies of merriment or expressions of pity when we see a man wrinkled with attention and emaciated with solicitude in the investigation of questions of which, without visible inconvenience, the world may expire in ignorance.

But now, the crucial *yet*:

Yet it is dangerous to discourage well-intended labors or innocent curiosity; for he who is employed in searches which by any deduction of consequences tend to the benefit of life is surely laudable in comparison of those who spend their time in counteracting happiness and filling the world with wrong and danger, confusion and remorse.

And again, the obsessive theme of idleness:

No man can perform so little as not to have reason to congratulate himself on his merits when he beholds the multitudes that live in total idleness and have never yet endeavored to be useful.

He concludes with an elaborate justification of just such activities as his previous paper has been at pains to deride.

The crucial *yet* performs its humane work not only in the *Rambler*: in the *Idler* as well it operates as a brake upon dogmatism. *Idler* 66 is a good example. It begins by lamenting very plausibly the losses of classical literary texts (like the missing plays of Sophocles and Euripides) occasioned by the destruction of ancient libraries. But halfway through (at the beginning of his second sheet of manuscript?) he takes quite a new direction: "Such are the thoughts that rise in every student when his curiosity is eluded and his searches are frustrated; yet it may perhaps be doubted whether our complaints are not sometimes inconsiderate, and whether we do not imagine more evil than we feel." And he proceeds to offer every reason he can think of why we should be satisfied that we have enough classical literature already.

Another *Idler* pivoting on the interesting *yet* is No. 85. Here the subject, always good for a few hundred words in weekly journalism, is the lamentable "multiplication of books." During the first half of the essay we get the impression that Johnson deplores— as we would expect—the gross flux of shallow compilations, encyclopedias, digests, and other productions of those "who have no other task than to lay two books before them, out of which they compile a third . . . ." As we read, we are led to embrace Johnson's apparent view that this is a racket practiced on the half-educated and lazy by the slick and cynical:

> It is observed [by Tacitus] that 'a corrupt society has many laws'; I know not whether it is not equally true that 'an ignorant age has many books.' When the treasures of ancient knowledge lie unexamined, and original authors are neglected and forgotten, compilers and plagiaries are encouraged, who give us again what we had before and grow great by setting before us what our own sloth had hidden from our view.

So far, so good. But, Johnson realizes, this is too simple: some good is produced even by intentions which the moral dogmatist would have to brand as unambiguously evil. Johnson thus executes his "turn":

> Yet are not even these writers to be indiscriminately censured and rejected. Truth, like beauty, varies its fashions, and is best recommended by various dresses to different minds; and he that recalls the attention of mankind to any part of learning which time has left behind it may be truly said to advance the literature of his own age.

This barrister-like defense presented, Johnson is still not satisfied. He goes on worrying the question, and before he arrives at the end of the essay he gives us one more *yet* and two more *buts*, and terminates in something very close to naked indecision. He concludes, significantly, by telling us not what he has decided about the question he has introduced but what Callimachus might think:

> But such is the present state of our literature that the ancient sage who thought 'a great book a great evil' would now think the multitude of books a multitude of evils. He would consider a bulky writer who engrossed a year, and a swarm of pamphleteers who stole each an hour, as equal wasters of human life, and would make no other difference between them than between a beast of prey and a flight of locusts.

The final attitude and image would recommend themselves to our memories as "typically Johnsonian" if we did not notice how shy, tentative, and essentially uncommitted the rhetoric here really is, supported by "He would consider" rather than "It is true." Its method betrays an uncertainty about how the essay should be ended, an uncertainty registering Johnson's genuine puzzlement over the (conventional) "two sides" of the question.

One of the best known of all Johnson's periodical papers is *Rambler* 200. Most of it is taken up with a brilliant and memorable letter from "Asper" (cf. Latin *asper*, harsh, rough) exposing the insufferably snobbish behavior of his former friend Prospero. All contemporaries agree that in Prospero Johnson had in mind the sensationally successful David Garrick, once his own pupil in the doomed school at Edial and his companion on his ragged passage to London. "We set out in the world together," says Asper, "and for a long time mutually assisted each other in our exigencies, as either happened to have money or influence beyond his immediate necessities." But Asper is awakened from this dream of reciprocated beneficence by paying a call which the newly rich Prospero has insisted upon. Asper finds now that Prospero's wish to be visited arises "not from any desire to communicate his happiness, but to enjoy his superiority":

> When I told my name at the door, the footman went to see if his master was at home, and by the tardiness of his return gave me reason to suspect that time was taken to deliberate. He then informed me that Prospero desired my company, and showed the staircase carefully secured

by mats from the pollution of my feet. The best apartments were ostentatiously set open that I might have a distant view of the magnificence
which I was not permitted to approach; and my old friend, receiving
me with all the insolence of condescension at the top of the stairs,
conducted me to a back room, where he told me he always breakfasted
when he had not great company.

From this inauspicious beginning, the visit goes from bad to
worse as Prospero's house-pride takes over completely. Asper is
cunningly denied contact with fine carpets, upholstery, tea, and
china at the same time that he is made aware of their suitability for
finer guests than he. He finally departs in a fury "without any
intention of seeing [Prospero] again, unless some misfortune should
restore his understanding."

At the end of Asper's letter, we feel that his sense of injury is
entirely justified, which is to say that we naturally identify Asper
with Johnson. But to our surprise, Johnson follows Asper's letter
with two paragraphs in which a very different attitude presides.
This attitude can be described as that of "The Rambler":

Though I am not wholly insensible of the provocations which my
correspondent has received, I cannot altogether commend the keenness
of his resentment, nor encourage him to persist in his resolution of
breaking off all commerce with his old acquaintance.

And the voice of moderation goes on to observe that performances
like Prospero's, while undoubtedly offensive, issue rather from
stupidity and folly than outright malice. Besides, the wise man will
learn to bear, friends being always desirable but always imperfect:

He that too much refines his delicacy will always endanger his quiet.
Of those with whom nature and virtue oblige us to converse, some are
ignorant of the art of pleasing, and offend when they design to
caress; some are negligent, and gratify themselves without regard for
the quiet of another; some, perhaps, are malicious, and feel no greater
satisfaction in prosperity than that of raising envy and trampling
inferiority. But whatever be the motive of insult, it is always best to
overlook it, for folly scarcely can deserve resentment, and malice is
punished by neglect.

We could say of *Rambler* 200 that its dynamics are really those of a dialogue: one of Johnson's modes and styles speaks first, and then another is permitted its say. But however we choose to express it, the whole paper makes clear that, as usual, Johnson is apportioning his loyalty between equally attractive attitudes rather than occupying "positions"—very like "schemes," after all—or enunciating "views." The final "official" reprehension of Asper's annoyance does nothing to diminish the attractiveness of his rhetoric and the charm of his narration: those things stick in the mind in dynamic opposition to the cooler second thoughts of the "conclusion"—a conclusion which, not being a logical one, is a conclusion in which nothing is concluded. Johnson is equally committed to both parts of the essay, whose essence is the drama generated by the two parts as they operate to play out the action of "judiciousness" or "honest second thoughts." And as before, it is the *ad hoc* method, the natural attendant of Johnson's neurotic writing habits, that makes oppositions and contraries of this sort offer themselves so naturally to him. What a given *Rambler* tends to be about is the act of Johnson, *agonistes*, making up his mind as he writes.

Johnson's practice in the *Rambler* seems to reveal his prime quality of mind: an instinctive skepticism, no matter what he finds himself saying, of "systems" and unambiguous positions. To his mind, answers are generally determined by the context of the questions that elicit them. That is, genre, occasion, and human rhetorical purpose are the main determinants of truth. It follows that universally applicable or extreme positions—especially those not colored by a meaningful concrete context—are generally wrong. Boswell says: "I mentioned to him a friend of mine [George Dempster] who was formerly gloomy from low spirits, and much distressed by the fear of death, but was now uniformly placid, and contemplated his dissolution without any perturbation." Johnson's reply suggests his suspicion of "uniform" opinions: "Sir, . . . this is only a disordered imagination taking a different turn."

Even his "opinion" of the ventilation of Scottish houses, set forth in *A Journey to the Western Islands*, complicates itself as he writes it down. The trouble with windows in Scotland is that, because the sashes are not equipped with weights, "He that would have his window open must hold it with his hand...." The result is foul air: "The incommodiousness of the Scotch windows keeps them very closely shut . . . and even in houses well built and elegantly furnished, a stranger may be sometimes forgiven if he allows himself to wish for fresher air." But in the very act of writing this, Johnson is visited by shame and uneasiness: hasn't he been too picayune? What does it matter, after all? What he writes next might be written by a critic of his work disappointed to find a writer capable of better things descanting like a school administrator about windows and ventilation: "These dimunitive observations seem to take away something from the dignity of writing...." For this reason, he confesses, they are "never communicated but with hesitation [although we note that little hesitation has been visible in the criticism of Scottish ventilation] and a little fear of abasement and contempt." A sort of resolution of the uncertainty is finally arrived at in the next sentence, where Johnson concludes the little playlet his prose has been enacting: the playlet sets in opposition four ideas (Scottish windows; triviality of criticising them; sense of shame; justification of trivial criticisms), and as before it is the humane *but* that brings us to what offers itself as a resolution:

But it must be remembered that life consists not of a series of illustrious actions or elegant enjoyments; the greater part of our time passes in compliance with necessities, in the performance of daily duties, in the removal of small inconveniencies, in the procurement of petty pleasures; and we are well or ill at ease as the main stream of life glides on smoothly or is ruffled by small obstacles and frequent interruption.

So much for the logical justification. But there seems to lurk still a sense that he really has compromised dignity by noticing fetid air. How else are we to account for the noble, elevated, "Rambler" passage which follows immediately than to see it as Johnson's attempt to efface the undignified passage he has written (and chosen to let stand) two paragraphs back?

The true state of every nation is the state of common life. The manners of a people are not to be found in the schools of learning, or the palaces of greatness, where the national character is obscured or obliterated by travel or instruction, by philosophy or vanity; nor is public happiness to be estimated by the assemblies of the gay or the banquets of the rich. The great mass of nations is neither rich nor gay: they whose aggregate constitutes the people are found in the streets, and the villages, in the shops and farms; and from them collectively considered must the measure of general prosperity be taken. As they approach to delicacy a nation is refined; as their conveniencies are multiplied, a nation, at least a commercial nation, must be denominated wealthy.

We can almost hear one of the voices within Johnson telling him, "Say something dignified and unqualified, something with the appearance of certitude and noble usefulness, to cancel the effect of that window business." The writer that Johnson is sometimes mistaken for would literally have crossed out the window business; the writer that Johnson is lets it stand and then anxiously justifies it.

The *ad hoc* method of composition suits Johnson for more reasons than his mere hatred of revising and rewriting. He observes in *Adventurer* 107: "We have less reason to be surprised or offended when we find others differ from us in opinion, because we very often differ from ourselves." Differing from himself is one of Johnson's activities that has not always been sufficiently appreciated. Boswell's genius in bottling and peddling the Johnsonian ether sometimes gives the impression that the mighty sage operates from a body of principles firmly held and fearlessly applied. But as the method of the *Rambler* suggests, the fact is quite different. Johnson's "thought" is not a great fixed structure, as we might be led to assume from, say, the tables listing his "likes" and "dislikes" at the end of Krutch's *Samuel Johnson.* It is rather a varying, dynamic mélange of reactions recognizing hardly any fixed principles except an adherence to empiricism and a skepticism about the certainties embraced and promulgated by other people. It is this likewise that makes compilations like J. E. Brown's *The Critical Opinions of Samuel Johnson,* for all their air of reasonableness, so useless, for Johnson's criticism operates only within living contexts of actions, reactions, and generic purposes. If you remove the contexts, you misrepresent the criticism. If we want to find out what Johnson is doing, we must, finally, read him.

And reading him brings to light all kinds of interesting contradictions. Everyone who has read the *Lives of the Poets* knows that Johnson "disliked" pastoral poetry. And yet in *Adventurer* 92, as well as in two *Ramblers* (Nos. 36 and 37), he discusses pastoral poetry with no denigration whatever. Indeed, in *Rambler* 36 he specifically awards pastoral the honor of pleasing many and pleasing long: "It is generally pleasing," he says, "because it entertains the mind with representations of scenes familiar to almost every imagination, and of which all can equally judge whether they are well described." Pastoral, just like the plays of Shakespeare, gives "universal pleasure." How do we account for the fact that the views expressed in the *Rambler* quite contradict the views expressed in the *Lives of the Poets*? Simply by understanding that when one has the task of writing 1500 words on pastoral for a general audience, one does not proceed by suggesting that the topic is too contemptible to be written about.

Readers of the *Lives* and the *Preface to Shakespeare* know likewise that Johnson's ultimate critical criterion for judging writings is the skeptical one of "length of duration and continuance of esteem." But as he suggests in *Adventurer* 138, even this criterion, apparently so logical and bed-rock, won't do: "Whoever has remarked the fate of books must have found it governed by other causes than general consent arising from general conviction. If a new performance happens not to fall into the hands of some, who have courage to tell and authority to propagate their opinion, it often remains long in obscurity, and perhaps perishes unknown and unexamined."

Again, readers of the *Lives* as well as eavesdroppers on Johnson's conversation will know that one of his favorite targets of scorn is the notion that weather or climate affect a writer's literary production. In the *Life of Milton* we are assured that "The author that thinks himself weather-bound . . . is only idle or exhausted." And in the *Life of Gray*, Gray's idea that "he could not write but at certain times" is stigmatized as "a fantastic foppery, to which my kindness for a man of learning and virtue wishes him to have been superior." *Idler* 11 also insists that any connection between seasons and literary fecundity is sheer nonsense. What, then, should be our reaction when, turning to *Rambler* 80, we hear a voice earnestly telling us that "To the men of study and imagination the winter is generally the chief time of labor. Gloom and silence produce composure of mind and concentration of ideas. . . . "? The answer is that Johnson's context determines his position. His purpose in *Rambler* 80—written on December 22, 1750—is to justify a severe winter. He goes about this task—a part of his general work of offering techniques of contentment—by marshaling all the arguments he can find on behalf of the idea that the constant change of seasons is really a benefit to man. He descends even to arguments like this: "Winter brings natural inducements to jollity and conversation." His object is to justify the ways of God to man. To argue that men of letters derive particular benefits from winter is to advance another plausible reason for not repining. The rhetorical purpose determines what Johnson says.

In his preface to Lobo's *Voyage to Abyssinia* we have already encountered his skepticism about the reports of travelers. We know that he is almost pathologically skeptical about extraordinary narratives. But if we look at *Idler* 87, we find him warning against just this sort of skepticism and subjecting it to a probing moral analysis: "It is always easier to deny than to inquire. To refuse credit confers for a moment an appearance of superiority, which every little mind is tempted to assume when it may be gained so cheaply as by withdrawing attention from evidence and declining the fatigue of comparing probabilities." In short, "Many relations of travelers have been slighted as fabulous till more frequent voyages have confirmed their veracity." The difference between these two positions is that the purpose of the preface to Lobo is to recommend the book to purchasers and readers as a novelty, while the purpose of *Idler* 87 is to induce the reader to accept the hardly credible myth of the Amazons so that Johnson can make a point about the essential equality of the sexes.

There could hardly be a better example of the point that in Johnson as in other writers the genre determines the message than the relation between a passage in *The Vanity of Human Wishes*, on the one hand, and *Rambler* 202, on the other, works written no more than three years apart. One of the great moments in the poem is the depiction of the foot traveler whose very poverty secures him from assaults:

> The needy traveler, serene and gay,
> Walks the wild heath, and sings his toil away.
> Does envy seize thee [i.e., dear reader]? crush th' upbraiding joy,
> Increase his riches and his peace destroy;
> Now fears in dire vicissitude invade,
> The rustling brake alarms, and quiv'ring shade,
> Nor light nor darkness brings his pain relief,
> One shows the plunder, and one hides the thief.

What the passage is saying is that poverty itself ironically confers benefits, and that a wise man would be cautious about wishing for riches. Yet in *Rambler* 202 he vigorously denies this "point" and subjects the general "poetic" and pastoral conception of poverty to a skeptical inquiry so searching that it is hard to believe that he is not mindful of his own lines in the poem:

Whoever studies either the poets or philosophers will find such an account of the condition expressed by [the term *poverty*] as his experience or observation will not easily discover to be true. Instead of the meanness, distress, complaint, anxiety, and dependence which have hitherto been combined in his ideas of poverty, he will read of content, innocence, and cheerfulness, of health and safety, tranquillity and freedom. . . .

At this point he can hardly help recollecting his own words, "sings his toil away." And as if actually alluding to his poor and therefore happy traveler, he subjects this cliché to his irony: "It is the great privilege of poverty [we are told] to be . . . secure without a guard." The distinction to be kept in mind when we encounter literary behavior like this is between what is appropriate to a poetic satire "imitating" a Roman original—the happy because needy traveler is already present in Juvenal's Tenth—and what is appropriate to a moral essay taking place within a homely, domestic environment. The voice of the poetic satirist is not and must not be the voice of the prose moralist: if the voices become indistinguishable, each form becomes implausible—neither can effect its special kind of illusion.

The Vanity of Human Wishes is, after all, about the folly of human wishes. And yet in *Rambler* 66, written only a year after the poem, we find Johnson performing as if he were subjecting nothing to ridicule so much as his own poem:

> The folly of human wishes has always been a standing subject of mirth and declamation, and has been ridiculed and lamented from age to age, till perhaps the fruitless repetition of complaints and censures may be justly numbered among the subjects of censure and complaint.

This is precisely the sort of thing we must expect from a man who, extraordinarily gifted for the genre, writes scores of brilliant dedications for others and still, in the *Dictionary*, defines a dedication as "A servile address to a patron" and a dedicator as "One who inscribes his work to a patron with compliment and servility." We must likewise expect infinite complication from a man who, hating writing, revising, and retouching as almost no other author ever has and becoming, hence, one of the hastiest of all of them, declares that "Hasty compositions, however they please at first by flowery luxuriance, and spread in the sunshine of temporary favor, can seldom endure the change of seasons, but perish at the first blast of criticism, or frost of neglect" (*Rambler* 169). We are dealing with the man who delighted to conduct experimental, "scientific" inquiries with chemicals, orange-peels, and the growth-rate of his own fingernails, and who was at the same time reprehending such inquiries—in *Rambler* 24, for example—as tending to displace man's genuine business, the scrutiny of his moral nature and obligations. Johnson is the man who feels a natural suspicion of literary criticism and who ends by writing the *Lives of the Poets*, in large part devoted to exhibiting "the characters of authors." But just such books he is at pains to denigrate in *Rambler* 93:

There are few books on which more time is spent by young students than on treatises which deliver the characters of authors; nor any which oftener deceive the expectation of the reader or fill his mind with more opinions which the progress of his studies and the increase of his knowledge oblige him to resign.

For all his skill at literary impersonations, no one is quicker to expose and reject personal or social duplicity. Everyone recalls the delightful *Adventurer* 84 censuring the outrageous dissimulations practiced on each other by a group of stagecoach passengers. "Every man hates falsehood," Johnson asserts in *Rambler* 20, an essay devoted to exposing whimsically the literary masks incompetently assumed by many writers of letters to the Rambler. And in *Rambler* 79 we find this most distinguished wearer of literary masks concluding that "Whoever commits a fraud is guilty not only of the particular injury to him whom he deceives, but of the diminution of that confidence which constitutes not only the ease but the existence of society." These words are written by the hand that sixteen years later was to write for Robert Chambers the law lectures that were to pass as his.

In his personal as well as literary behavior Johnson is equally capable of astonishing anyone who conceives that a degree of consistency belongs to the rational human character. Actually, for all his pretenses to know where he is, Johnson is adrift. Far from being an eighteenth-century man of reason, he is playing by ear. He wants to make up his mind, but he knows he hasn't. His awareness of his plight is in large part what the *Prayers and*

Meditations are about. The tension in him is between the pull, on the one hand, toward an appearance of certainty and firmness of will, and the drift, on the other, toward absurdity and imprudence. Without entirely knowing it, Boswell registers the poles of this opposition. For example:

He said, 'I am very unwilling to read the manuscripts of authors, and give them my opinion. If the authors who apply to me have money, I bid them boldly print without a name [that is, anonymously]; if they have written in order to get money, I tell them to go to the booksellers, and make the best bargain they can.' BOSWELL. 'But, Sir, if a bookseller should bring you a manuscript to look at?' JOHNSON. 'Why, Sir, I would desire the bookseller to take it away.'

And Johnson's firm, well-considered reasons for this disinclination to read manuscripts are both moral and social. "Nobody has a right," he tells Miss Reynolds, "to put another under such a difficulty that he must either hurt the person by telling the truth, or hurt himself by telling what is not true." And yet—and yet: "There was," says Boswell, "perhaps no man who more frequently yielded to the solicitations even of very obscure authors, to read their manuscripts, or more liberally assisted them with advice and correction." A bit of the index to the Hill-Powell edition of Boswell's *Life* makes a pleasant emblem of Johnson's mental posture:

Roman Catholicism . . . Johnson . . . respects it, ii, 105; attacks it, iii, 407.

"*Video meliora proboque,*" says Ovid, "*deteriora sequor*": I see and approve the better course, but follow the worse. Johnson's version of this confession is his perception that "No man practices as well as he writes." He explains, with recourse once again to the all-important *yet*: "I have, all my life long, been lying [abed] till noon. Yet I tell all young men, and tell them with great sincerity, that nobody who does not rise early will ever do any good." Being even more human than most, a moral writer places himself *ipso facto* in an ironical, if not overtly comical, situation, and it is from

this situation that he must write. In *Idler* 27 Johnson considers the value of the exhortation underlying any moralist's advice, even the advice of the most sacred guides: "Know thyself":

This counsel has been often given with serious dignity, and often received with appearance of conviction; but as very few can search deep into their own minds without meeting what they wish to hide from themselves, scarce any man persists in cultivating such disagreeable acquaintance, but draws the veil again between his eyes and his heart, leaves his passions and appetites as he found them, and advises others to look into themselves.

The "majestic teacher of moral wisdom" would be the first to appreciate the inscription written by Mark Twain when he presented a set of his books to the young Winston Churchill: "To be good is noble; to teach others to be good is nobler, and no trouble."[7]

CHAPTER 7

Writing a Dictionary

While anxiously employed with the *Rambler*, Johnson was also deep in the work of writing a dictionary—*writing* is his word for it, and we shall see why he uses it instead of a word like *compiling*. His first public announcement of what he was doing was a thirty-four-page pamphlet which he issued in August, 1747. This document, *The Plan of a Dictionary of the English Language*, is many things at once: it is an advertisement designed to generate publicity and stimulate ultimate purchasers; it is a warning to other aspirants to withdraw lest the competition overwhelm them; it is a formal performance bond between Johnson and himself; it is a sort of preface, in the specifically Johnsonian sense—a preamble announcing, or at least admitting, the limitations of the work to follow; and perhaps most interesting, it is a virtual dialogue on the nature of language and the nature of human life, the protagonists being Johnson, in one corner, and implicitly, Lord Chesterfield in the other.

Those who credit the floating gossip of history—a body of bold simplifications answering to our worst needs—and who consequently conceive of Johnson as some sort of High Priest or Literary Dictator presiding over an Age of Reason should turn to *The Plan of an English Dictionary*, where they will see how very little prescriptive Johnson's conception of lexicography is. The exponent of prescription and "authority" turns out to be Chesterfield, in relation to whom Johnson appears as a skeptical, empirical, "descriptive" registrar of the language. In analyzing the *Plan*, Scott Elledge has perceived "the conflict between [Chesterfield's] notion that the dictionary should have an effect on the language and Johnson's apparently strong conviction that the laws of the life of a language are stronger than any human lawmaker." "From the beginning," Elledge notes, "Johnson's desire to explore was at odds with Chesterfield's desire to civilize."[1] It is Johnson's very unwillingness to adopt the assertive, dictatorial role that Chesterfield has wanted to cast him in that animates the delightful dynamics of the *Plan*.

Its overt form is that of a long respectful "letter" to Chesterfield —the other one, shorter in several senses, would come eight years later. Both letters begin "My Lord" and conclude with the deferential formula, "My Lord, Your Lordship's most obedient, most humble servant, Sam. Johnson," except that in the final letter to Chesterfield *most humble* precedes *most obedient*, as if to emphasize now Johnson's distance from grandeur and pretension, and his ironic pride in his demonstrated independence—his unwillingness "that the public should consider me as owing that to a patron which Providence has enabled me to do for myself."

Actually, it seems likely that the final, satiric riposte to Chesterfield was prompted almost as much by Chesterfield's attitude toward language as by his presumed neglect of Johnson's project. Despite the pains Johnson has taken to indicate in the *Plan* that his approach to language is going to be largely descriptive, Chesterfield's attitude, as embodied in his essay of recommendation in *The World* (Nov. 28, 1754), remains stubbornly, simplemindedly prescriptive: he speaks of a "lawful standard of our language" and deprecates mere word-books in which "all words, good and bad, are . . . jumbled indiscriminately together." Consider how offensive prattle like this, even if spoken in the idiom of the *World's* persona, "Mr. Fitz-Adam," must have sounded to Johnson:

Toleration, adoption, and naturalization have run their lengths. Good order and authority are now necessary. But where shall we find them, and at the same time the obedience due to them? We must have recourse to the old Roman expedient in times of confusion, and choose a dictator. Upon this principle, I give my vote for Mr. Johnson to fill that great and arduous post. And I hereby declare that I make a total surrender of all my rights and privileges in the English language, as a free-born British subject, to the said Mr. Johnson, during the term of his dictatorship.

Most embarrassing. But even worse is to come—an infusion of that sort of frivolity about religion that always stimulates Johnson to some wild revenge:

Nay, more: I will not only obey him, like an old Roman, as my dictator, but like a modern Roman, I will implicitly believe in him as my Pope, and hold him to be infallible while he is in the chair, but no longer. More than this he cannot well require; for I presume that obedience can never be expected when there is neither terror to enforce nor interest to invite it.

The tone could hardly be more disgusting. No wonder Johnson's ironic letter of 1755 begins by coldly noting the "honor" done him by Chesterfield's comments.

Johnson opens the *Plan* with a complex, witty gathering of images of highness and lowness: their effect is both to hint at the amazing, dramatic difference between his unexpected patron's exalted social station and his own, and, at the same time, to derive irony and even comedy from the common conception of the "low" —that is, unexciting—occupation of lexicographer. These themes of high and low begin reverberating in the first paragraph: the opening, through its images, reminds us that Johnson is not only "low" in the relative social sense and "low" in the (mistaken vulgar) idea of the lexicographer's capacity and value—he is also, ironically, half-blind and thus the least likely aspirant to lexicographical honors:

> When first I undertook to write an English Dictionary, I had no expectation of any higher patronage than that of the proprietors of the copy, nor prospect of any other advantage than the price of my labor. I knew that the work in which I was engaged is generally considered as drudgery for the blind, as the proper toil of artless industry; a task that requires neither the light of learning nor the activity of genius, but may be successfully performed without any higher quality [a glance at Chesterfield's?] than that of bearing burdens with dull patience, and beating the track of the alphabet with sluggish resolution.

Later he will define *beat* in this sense as "To tread a path": we are given an image of a sullen, overloaded porter stomping endlessly down a narrow path unrelieved by anything interesting, let alone anything elegant or learned. That, at least, is the popular view of the dictionary maker. It approximates the ironically erroneous view of Johnson's potential entertained by the bookseller J. Wilcox to whom Johnson presented himself when he first arrived in London. "Mr. Wilcox," says Boswell, "on being informed by him that his intention was to get his livelihood as an author, eyed his robust frame attentively and with a significant look said, 'You had better buy a porter's knot.' "

After starting thus with ironic images, Johnson goes on to accept, for the sake of argument, the lowness of the dictionary-maker's role. And in embracing it, he both finds consolation for himself—he is going to become a master, after all, of the voice of "The Rambler"—and manages to avenge himself by returning a series of insulting moral innuendoes on his implied critics:

> On this province, my Lord, I entered, with the pleasing hope that, as it was low, it likewise would be safe. I was drawn forward with the

prospect of employment which, though not splendid, would be useful; and which, though it could not make my life envied, would keep it innocent; which would awaken no passion, engage me in no contention, nor throw in my way any temptation to disturb the quiet of others by censure, or my own by flattery.

So there! Having sufficiently paid off ignorant contemners of lexicography, he turns to develop with new variations the theme of high and low. He is surprised, he says, to find himself with a distinguished patron. He has never expected any enterprise of his to achieve such publicity. As readers we hardly expect his next turn: "Its first effect has been to make me anxious"—the public will expect that miracles are about to be performed, and "expectation, when her wings are once expanded, easily reaches heights which performance never will attain." High and low again, but this time subsumed into his favorite theme of the inevitable self-defeat of hope and wishes. The object of this *Plan*, then, is "not . . . to raise expectation, but to repress it": disappointment with the ultimate achievement will be less likely if the inevitable limitations are clearly understood at the outset.

After these preliminaries, the *Plan* now begins to assume its shape as an implicit dialogue between Chesterfield and Johnson. One cause of the disagreement between them is Johnson's more professional sense of rhetorical address—someone will have to *use* the dictionary and *read* it. Johnson's method in making this point becomes shrewd, dramatic, and even comic. His method is to express Chesterfield's simple, perfectionist views in the guise of his own naïve hopes, and then to complicate them by a rapid descent to real life, where things are discovered not to be rational and systematic but accidental and capricious. Consider the oppositions in this paragraph:

In the first attempt to methodize my ideas I found a difficulty which extended itself to the whole work. It was not easy to determine by what rule of distinction the words of this Dictionary were to be chosen. The chief intent of it is to preserve the purity and ascertain the meaning of our English idiom.

That last sentence sounds like Johnson practically quoting Chesterfield's remote, detached, hopeful view of the job. The *seems* with which he resumes begins to expose the weaknesses of Chesterfield's conception; and before long he is making his antagonist's position sound very much like one held by Dick Minim, the silly, shallow critic satirized in *Idlers* 60 and 61:

This seems to require nothing more than that our language be considered, so far as it is our own; that the words and phrases used in the general intercourse of life, or found in the works of those whom we commonly style polite writers, be selected, without including the terms of particular professions, since, with the arts to which they relate, they are generally derived from other nations [he seems to be thinking especially—as he usually does when focusing on remote diction—of maritime expressions]. . . .

A general, elegant lexicon like this, purged of the "low" terms of trade and the vulgar world, would accord, he admits, with "the exact and pure idea of a grammatical dictionary." But, he goes on, bringing forth now his own position in full opposition to his implied interlocutor's, "In lexicography, as in other arts, naked science is too delicate for the purposes of life." It is "the purposes of life" that determine what books must be like. The theoretician may easily conceive of a perfect dictionary, but complications enter the moment its executant considers, as he finally must, his actual readers:

The value of a work must be estimated by its use: it is not enough that a dictionary delights the critic, unless, at the same time, it instructs the learner; as it is to little purpose that an engine amuses the philosopher by the subtlety of its mechanism, if it requires so much knowledge in its application as to be of no advantage to the common workman.

This criterion, that of rhetorical efficiency, Johnson will rely on thirty years later when he criticizes Thomas Gray's odes, "engines" which may delight the theorist, but which, by failing to "work," leave common readers, Johnson included, quite cold.

It is this opposition between facile rigorous determination and humane relaxation, between "the critic" and the common reader, between the academician who does not solicit a large body of readers and the professional writer who depends wholly upon them, in all their imperfection—an opposition projected implicitly as between Chesterfield and Johnson, and thus between social classes—that runs throughout the *Plan*. The all-important *but* is as frequent here as in the *Rambler*: "The academicians of France, indeed, rejected terms of science in their first essay, but found afterwards a necessity of relaxing the rigor of their determination." Johnson is, after all, writing a dictionary "designed not merely for critics, but for popular use."

Chesterfield has apparently wanted Johnson to rationalize English spelling, and this has appeared a plausible goal for a lexicographer to set himself. And yet—irrational spellings are *there*, and to try to make readers change them is to make their task of being alive even harder than it is already. The principle about spelling which Johnson proposes to follow is therefore "to make no innovation without a reason sufficient to balance the inconvenience of change; and such reasons I do not expect often to find," for—so irrational is mankind—"All change is of itself an evil, which ought not to be hazarded but for evident advantage." It is Richard Hooker's formulation, and we will hear it again before Johnson is finished with the *Dictionary*.

The ultimate basis of the disagreement between Johnson and his patron is profound. It is a disagreement about the nature of human life. Chesterfield, either by something he has said to Johnson or by something Johnson has perceived in his personal style (something strikingly "systematic," the domination of some "scheme" which seems to govern him *a priori*), has apparently implied that he conceives men to be rational creatures, and that consequently their language should show signs of being a rational system. But to Johnson the very opposite seems self-evident, and, as he insists, "What is so much in the power of men as language will very often be capriciously conducted." Indeed, Johnson's conviction of the perversity and unreason of human motives, his recognition of the almost sacred roles of accident and prejudice in human conduct, approximates the vision that animates Edmund Burke's later constructions. As Johnson says,

To our language may be with great justice applied the observation of Quintilian, that speech was not formed by an analogy sent from heaven. It did not descend to us in a state of uniformity and perfection, but was produced by necessity and enlarged by accident, and is therefore composed of dissimilar parts, thrown together by negligence, by affectation, by learning, or by ignorance.

The result is that the principles of English inflection make little sense (*fox, foxes; ox, oxen; sheep, sheep*) and "cannot be reduced to rule." It would be nice, undeniably, to have more regularity and system in language; indeed, who

can forbear to wish that these fundamental atoms of our speech might obtain the firmness and immutability of the primogenial and constituent particles of matter, that they might retain their substance while they alter their appearance, and be varied and compounded, yet not destroyed?

This sounds plausible and attractive: it omits only one crucial thing—just as men are not like units in geometry, words are not like chemical elements. Which is to say that, if God makes elements, man—feckless, corrupt, dying—makes language:

But [an immutable regularity] is a privilege which words are scarcely to expect: for, like their author, when they are not gaining strength, they are generally losing it. Though art may sometimes prolong their duration, it will rarely give them perpetuity; and their changes will be almost always informing us that language is the work of man, of a being from whom permanence and stability cannot be derived.

As they do so often, Johnson's critical and philological findings can be traced back to solid theological origins. Questions that in other minds would remain simply philological stimulate Johnson to elegiac gestures pointing to the contingency, and hence the pathos, of the human situation.

English idiomatic usage is another example of the irrationality of language, and any honest dictionary, says Johnson, must simply register the fact. The only guide in usage, as in law, is precedent, not, surely, a very rational guide, but all we have: "Our syntax therefore is not to be taught by general rules but by special precedents." And again: "Since the rules of style, like those of law, arise from precedents often repeated, [I will] collect the testimonies on both sides and endeavor to discover and promulgate the decrees of custom, who has so long possessed, whether by right or by usurpation, the sovereignty of words." Precedent is the only reason we *put up* both preserves and pictures and *put up with* insults and even *put* people *on*. The only guide to help us here as elsewhere is the discreet principle of imitation, a principle which in itself bespeaks the same frailty in mankind as our necessary dependence on a body of legal precedents: "We must remark how the writers of former ages [or even our friends] have used the same word."

As with spelling, inflection, and idiom, making definitions will also entangle the writer in complications unimagined by the innocent rationalist. How to define a word like *sweet*, for example? And what sort of audience do the definitions assume: does one define *barometer* as "an instrument to discover the weight of the air," or does one, as Johnson clearly wants to do, "spend a few lines upon its invention, construction, and principles"? Again, the criterion of usefulness can be found in nothing but the motive and response of the common reader, the man who will open the dictionary not to criticize definitions but to learn what he does not know. On this principle, Johnson's actual definition of *barometer* turns out to occupy much more than "a few lines": he prints a five-hundred-word technical essay quoted from (and credited to) James Harris's *Lexicon Technicum* (1704). As he explains in the *Plan*: "Since without some attention to such demands [that is, those of the general reader] the dictionary cannot become generally valuable, I have determined to consult the best writers for explanations real as well as verbal; and perhaps I may at last have reason to say . . . that my book is more learned than its author." As it turns out, these long discourses on scientific concepts and apparatus make the *Dictionary* resemble an encyclopedia.

A brief treatment of the need for distinguishing loose or metaphorical from precise or literal meanings becomes, in Johnson's hands, another shrewd hint that Chesterfield is not going to be the patron of exactly the sort of enterprise he fancies:

The strict and critical meaning [of words] ought to be distinguished from that which is loose and popular; as in the word *perfection*, which, though in its philosophical and exact sense it can be of little use among human beings, is often so much degraded from its original signification that the academicians have inserted in their work, the *perfection* of a language, and with a little more licentiousness, might have prevailed on themselves to have added, *the perfection of a dictionary.*

Johnson has no doubt that in dealing with words he is dealing with a very imperfect and disorderly accumulation of signs. The one thing he seems uncertain, even uneasy, about is setting himself up as an authority on usage; and he indicates that it is only Chesterfield's importunity that has half persuaded him that maybe he ought to prescribe usage. His movement into the passive voice ("I have been . . . determined") seems the gauge of his embarrassment:

With regard to questions of purity or propriety, I was once in doubt whether I should not attribute too much to myself in attempting to decide them, and whether my province was to extend beyond the proposition of the question and the display of the suffrages on each side; but I have been since determined, by your Lordship's opinion, to interpose my own judgment, and shall therefore endeavor to support what appears to me most consonant to grammar and reason.

And what follows is clever. At once he both flatters Chesterfield and gets himself off the hook:

I may hope, my Lord, that since you, whose authority in our language is so generally acknowledged, have commissioned me to declare my own opinion, I shall be considered as exercising a kind of vicarious jurisdiction, and that the power which might have been denied to my own claim will be readily allowed me as the delegate of your Lordship.

In other words, the cost of Chesterfield's patronage is going to be more prescriptiveness than is natural to Johnson. In effect, the reader is here being notified that when Johnson prescribes, it will be virtually Chesterfield speaking: Johnson will be assuming yet another mask.

But despite his sort of willingness to sort of agree with Chesterfield on the prescription-of-usage issue, he keeps subtly chipping away at Chesterfield's hopes that the *Dictionary* will "fix" the language. If Chesterfield believes this, he is only inviting his own disillusionment. Notice now the ironic force of *perhaps* and *may be* and *difficult*—*perhaps* and *may be* constitute moments of mock-determination of a question already fully determined; and for *difficult* read *impossible*:

Though, perhaps, to correct the language of nations by books of grammar, and amend their manners by discourses of morality, may be tasks equally difficult, yet, as it is unavoidable to wish, it is natural likewise to hope. . . .

Natural to hope, notice: not sensible.

He brings the *Plan* to an end with a final reminder of his own frailty and a reassertion by implication of the unpredictable, immensely fallible, and unsystematic character of those whose language he is being invited to register "systematically." There is no doubt, he says, that, treading his path through so vast a wilderness of words,

I shall be often bewildered; and in the mazes of such intricacy be frequently entangled: . . . Yet I do not despair of approbation from those who, knowing the uncertainty of conjecture, the scantiness of knowledge, the fallibility of memory, and the unsteadiness of attention, can compare the causes of error with the means of avoiding it, and the extent of art with the capacity of man; and whatever be the event of my endeavors, I shall not easily regret an attempt which has procured me the honor of appearing thus publicly,

> My Lord,
> Your Lordship's most obedient
> and most humble servant,
> Sam. Johnson

The very un-Johnsonian mere swank of this closing flourish makes all the more striking his strenuous attempt in the body of the *Plan*—where genre demands are pressing less powerfully than at beginning and end—to work out for himself dynamically (and almost dramatically) the conception of language and the image of human nature most appropriate for a work of the kind "dictionary." Johnson's conventional close might appear to cancel or resolve most of his earlier uneasiness about the threat of Chesterfield's misapprehensions. But the appearance is only an appearance.

The *Plan* concluded and issued, Johnson is ready for the next (and dreadful) stage, the actual writing of the *Dictionary*. In his notes to his edition of Shakespeare he reveals his complete command of a passage which an earlier editor, William Warburton, had ill understood—a passage depicting a certain state of mind with which Johnson was more intimately acquainted than Warburton. In *Julius Caesar* Brutus muses thus about the moments between decision—"schemes," in Johnson's term—and action:

> Between the acting of a dreadful thing
> And the first motion [i.e., intention, or "plan"], all the interim is
> Like a phantasma, or a hideous dream:
> The genius and the mortal instruments
> Are then in council; and the state of man,
> Like to a little kingdom, suffers then
> The nature of an insurrection.

What Brutus is saying, Johnson observes in his note on these lines, is that decisions, far from settling the mind, disturb it the more; for once a decision is made, "The desire of action and the care of safety keep the mind in continual fluctuation and disturbance." It is a painful psychological circumstance with which every one of Johnson's writing tasks had acquainted him.

How does a man proceed once he has determined singlehandedly to etymologize, define, and illustrate all the essential words of a language? The first job is to find the words. Johnson combined this task with that of selecting the quotations he needed to illustrate usage and to supply by context implicit definitions more subtle than he could devise himself. To find the words and the quotations he proceeded wholly empirically: he read through English writing from the Age of Elizabeth to the early eighteenth century. Decency and taste required some delicate decisions. He admitted common terms for excremental functions (*snot, snotty; arse; fart; piss; turd* —but not, curiously, *shit*), although he excluded popular words for sexual organs and functions. When, reading a book, he came to a word he wanted to include, he underlined it in pencil, indicated by vertical lines at beginning and end the extent of the quotation illustrating it, marked the initial of the word in the margin, and handed the open book to one of his six copyists, who transcribed the passage onto a slip of paper. As a final check against important omissions, he collated his word list with that in Nathan Bailey's folio dictionary of 1736.

When the quotations were all accumulated and filed, he proceeded to write the entries. He marked the stressed syllable of multisyllabic words; he indicated the word's grammatical class; he gave etymology within brackets; he wrote a series of numbered definitions, beginning with the most literal meaning and ending with the most figurative; and he attached to each definition the appropriate quotations. Here is a sample entry:

SÚBSTANCE. *n.s.* [*substance,* Fr. *substantia,* Latin.]

1. Being; something existing; something of which we can say that it is.

> Since then the soul works by herself alone,
> Springs not from sense, nor humors well agreeing,
> Her nature is peculiar, and her own;
> She is a *substance,* and a perfect being.   *Davies.*

> The strength of gods,
> And this empyreal *substance* cannot fail.   *Milton.*

2. That which supports accidents.

> What creatures there inhabit, of what mold,
> And *substance*.   *Milton.*

Every being is considered as subsisting in and by itself, and then it is called a *substance*; or it subsists in and by another, and then it is called a mode or manner of being.   *Watts.*

3. The essential part.

It will serve our turn to comprehend the *substance*, without confining ourselves to scrupulous exactness in form.   *Digby.*

This edition is the same in *substance* with the Latin.   *Burn.*

They are the best epitomes, and let you see with one cast of the eye the *substance* of a hundred pages.   *Addison.*

4. Something real, not imaginary; something solid, not empty.

> Shadows tonight
> Have struck more terror to the soul of Richard
> Than can the *substance* of ten thousand soldiers
> Armed in proof and led by shallow Richard.
>
>   *Shakespeare.*

> He the future evil shall no less
> In apprehension than in *substance* feel.   *Milton.*

> Heroic virtue did his actions guide,
> And he the *substance*, not th' appearance chose:
> To rescue one such friend he took more pride
> Than to destroy whole thousands of such foes.   *Dryden.*

5. Body; corporeal nature.

Between the parts of opaque and colored bodies are many spaces, either empty or replenished with mediums of other densities, as water between the tinging corpuscles wherewith any liquor is impregnated, air between the aqueous globules that constitute clouds or mists, and for the most part spaces void of both air and water, but yet perhaps not wholly void of all *substance* between the parts of hard bodies.   *Newton.*

The qualities of plants are more various than those of animal *substances*.   *Arbuthnot on Aliments.*

6. Wealth; means of life.

> He hath eaten me out of house and home, and hath put all my *substance* into that fat belly of his, but I will have some of it out again. *Shakespeare's Henry IV.*

> We are destroying many thousand lives, and exhausting our *substance*, but not for our own interest. *Swift.*

An entry like this Johnson wrote on a quarto sheet, and each quotation, as copied by the amanuenses, was pasted in its place. To understand what Johnson was doing we must imagine him performing this act 40,000 times. As Ian Watt says, "Every new word was a new and unavoidable challenge."[2] What was apparently supporting him as he worked was both a conviction of religious obligation and a sense that the work on the *Dictionary*—involving as it did almost equal parts of reading and writing—was an emblem of his whole writing career. We remember the prayer in which he equates "this labor" of the *Dictionary* with "the whole task of my present state."

Everyone agrees that the weakest parts of the *Dictionary* are the etymologies. Although a master of Greek, Latin, and Romance philology, Johnson was weak in Germanic, and we must beware when he deals with a word having a "Dutch" (*Deutsch*) original. The word *spider* derives from Old English *spinnan*, to spin; but after quoting and passing by Skinner's correct conjecture about the etymology of *spider*, Johnson arrives at this: "May not *spider* be *spy dor*, the insect that watches the *dor*?" But at the same time he does not hesitate to confess ignorance when he must. Thus his etymology of *tatterdemalion* ("A ragged fellow"): "[*tatter* and *I know not what*]". As Patrick Cruttwell has observed, "The *O. E. D.* does no better, but covers its ignorance with some impressive polysyllables: '*Tatter,* or more prob. *tattered,* with a factitious element suggesting an ethnic or descriptive derivative.'"[3] But if Johnson's etymologies are sometimes faulty by modern standards, it can be said that no one of his contemporaries could have done any better.

Despite his general unwillingness to prescribe usage, now and then, appalled by some monstrosity, he will criticize a word: "*Finesse*: artifice; stratagem. An unnecessary word which is creeping into the language." "*Vaulty*: arched; concave. A bad word." "*Vastidity*: wildness; immensity. A barbarous word." But even such prescriptive activity as we find in the *Dictionary* is attended by a pleasant uncertainty and inconsistency. The expression *To sconce* he defines as "To mulct; to fine," and adds: "A low word which ought not to be retained." And yet we remember his telling Sir John Hawkins of his reply to a college tutor who fined him for absence from a lecture: "Sir, you have sconced me two-pence for non-attendance at a lecture not worth a penny." Sometimes, in amiable defiance of all logic, he will be so charmed by a remote or nonce word that he cannot bear to reprehend it. As with *Incarnadine*: "To dye red. This word I find only once." He illustrates from *Macbeth* and hurries on.

Perhaps the best-known elements of the *Dictionary* are the few whimsical or admittedly personal definitions with which Johnson occasionally alleviated some of the boredom as he went along. Hardly a one has a tendency to deprave or corrupt, and their mode is often much wittier even than we remember. Johnson has considerable fun deploying ambiguities in pronoun reference: the result is that some definitions come close to parodying the literary form "entry." Thus *Giggle*: "To laugh idly; to titter; to grin with merry levity. It is retained in Scotland." A similar maneuver takes place in the definition of *Gratefulness*: "Gratitude; duty to benefactors. Now obsolete." The definition of *Pension* was thought by both friends and enemies to constitute an embarrassment after 1762, and he received many hints that he might revise it. But urged perhaps by his sophisticated shamelessness in advising one thing and doing another, he let it stand: "An allowance made to anyone without an equivalent. In England it is generally understood to mean pay given to a state hireling for treason to his country." *Poetess* has a nice abruptness about it: "A she poet." And *Stock-jobber* is no more serious than many another Johnsonian whimsy:

"A low wretch who gets money by buying and selling shares in the funds." As rhetoric this operates like Johnson's reported remark about a man who has just left the room: "He did not care to speak ill of any man behind his back, but he believed the gentleman was an *attorney.*"

The same conscious irony about performing "low" literary work that plays about the beginning of the *Plan of a Dictionary* visits the definition of *Grubstreet*: "Originally the name of a street in Moorfields in London, much inhabited by writers of small histories, dictionaries, and temporary poems; whence any mean production is called *grubstreet.*" And in the definition of *Lexicographer* he is moved to sardonic self-portraiture: "A writer of dictionaries; a harmless drudge that busies himself in tracing the original, and detailing the signification of words."

Any bright person consulting any dictionary knows that he must not expect to find entirely "objective" definitions of political terms, which are always occasions of passion. Definitions have to be written by *someone.* Johnson's definitions of *Tory* and *Whig*, like anyone else's, are personal:

TORY. *n.s.* [A cant term derived, I suppose, from an Irish word signifying a savage.] One who adheres to the ancient constitution of the state, and the apostolical hierarchy of the Church of England; opposed to a Whig.

WHIG. . . . The name of a faction.

But what is easy to overlook is the mitigating quotation from Swift with which Johnson illustrates *Whig*: "Whoever has a true value for church and state should avoid the extremes of *Whig* for the sake of the former, and the extremes of *Tory* on the account of the latter." And Johnson's cool definition of *Republican* indicates that when he is in the mood he can exercise plenty of restraint on his instinctive outrage: "One who thinks a commonwealth without monarchy the best government."

Less judicious feelings attach to the definition of *Lich*:

A dead carcass; whence *lichwake*, the time or act of watching by the dead; *lichgate*, the gate through which the dead are carried to the grave;

Lichfield, the field of the dead, a city in Staffordshire, so named from martyred Christians. *Salve magna parens*. *Lichwake* is still retained in Scotland in the same sense.

The dynamics of this entry suggest what it means to "write" a dictionary. This entry alone would justify Sir James Murray's assertion that "In his hands [lexicography] became a department of literature."[4] The entry is shaped like a parabolic curve: it begins with sober literalism, quite the tone we expect in a dictionary definition. But by the time Johnson arrives at the phrase "to the grave" he heats up, and the image of "martyred Christians" triggers feelings of elegiac devotion which most appropriately assume the form of the touching ode-in-miniature (the words are lifted intact from Virgil), *"Salve magna parens"*—"Hail, great parent." After this passionate climax, we are released to return to the normal rhetorical mode of an "entry" with the dispassionate remark on Scottish usage. What Johnson has done in little here is what he is constantly doing: redeeming some received and often threadbare literary paradigm (here, "entry") by the technique of generating more than ordinary heat or light within it. And in making the *Dictionary* he is as much a recipient as in writing prayers or theatrical prologues: he is largely receiving his definitions from such earlier lexicographers as Bailey, Ainsworth, Skinner, Phillips, Martin, and Chambers, and then improving on them.[5] They have given Johnson what he is finishing off.

But the distinction of the definitions is not to be found in their whimsical or personal coloration. It is rather to be looked for in Johnson's serious attempts to improve on the definitions of his predecessors. His definition of *Net* is a good example. Nathan Bailey had defined it as "A device for catching fish, birds, etc." Yes, but what *is* it? A wooden or metal trap? A baited hook on a long string? Johnson anticipates and answers all the inquirer's questions: "*Net*: . . . A texture woven with large interstices or meshes, used commonly as a snare for animals." Similarly with *Mouse*, defined outrageously by Bailey as "An animal well known." If not a scientific definition, Johnson's has at least the merit of a homely "operational" clarity: "The smallest of all beasts; a little animal haunting houses and corn fields, destroyed by cats."

Much has been made of Johnson's more portentous-sounding definitions like *Cough*: "A convulsion of the lungs, vellicated by some sharp serosity." But as James H. Sledd and Gwin J. Kolb point out, here Johnson "compressed and simplified the description current in his time." *Cough* is defined in the dictionaries of both Chambers and Martin as "A disease affecting the lungs, occasioned by a sharp serous humor vellicating the fibrous coat thereof, and urging it to a discharge by spitting."[6] So anxious have some detractors been to catch Johnson in the act of making little fishes talk like whales that they have not always troubled to read closely. One modern anthology of English literature offers as "typically Johnsonian" a prolix definition of *Thunder*, a definition which actually is not Johnson's at all but Muschenbroek's and which Johnson carefully credits to him, just as he is careful to attribute all his quotations.[7] The fact is that generally Johnson's definitions are so clear, so conscious of the risk of misconstruction, and so succinctly worded that many—especially those explaining abstractions—have been borrowed literatim by the *O. E. D.* and subsequent modern dictionaries. Thus with the word *Requisite*: the phrase "required by the nature of things" used in the Funk and Wagnalls *Standard College Dictionary* (1963) is Johnson's. The same work appropriates Johnson's economical definition of *Midwife* ("A woman who assists women in childbirth") and simply Americanizes it, that is, adds a little jargon to pad it out and make it sound more social-scientific: "A woman whose occupation is the assisting of women in childbirth."

But stunning as Johnson's definitions are for unpretentiousness, economy, and point, they are still not his greatest achievement in the *Dictionary*. To appreciate what that is, we must turn to the copious illustrative quotations—there are some 114,000 of them—and consider their function and meaning. As early as the *Plan* he was indicating his ambition to make the *Dictionary* not just a philological resource but a virtual dictionary of quotations as well, and even better, a special kind of dictionary of quotations, one that might constitute an anthology of intelligence, wisdom, and piety:

> In citing authorities, on which the credit of every part of this work must depend, it will be proper to observe some obvious rules, such as of preferring writers of the first reputation to those of an inferior rank; of noting the quotations with accuracy; and of selecting, when it can be conveniently done, such sentences as, besides their immediate use [as indications of denotation and idiomatic usage], may give pleasure or instruction, by conveying some elegance of language, or some precept of prudence or piety.

Although Greek, Latin, Italian, French, and Portuguese dictionaries had used quotations to illustrate meanings, Johnson's was the first English dictionary to rely on them extensively, and his is the only dictionary ever to conceive for the quotations so complicated and so noble a role. Robert Browning is one of the many who have simply read the *Dictionary* through.

Johnson's gathering of these quotations during several years of reading specifically for the purpose is so far from what most of us can imagine ourselves doing adequately that if we think about it our heads reel. Pointing out that what is governing the *Dictionary* is the dominating presence of "a single master reader," W. K. Wimsatt invites us to consider what Johnson was doing:

Try to imagine Johnson at his task of single-handed reading for the *Dictionary*, and you will see, or feel, that the essential and operative principles in the enterprise were precisely his own great powers as a reader—his strength and tenacity, his initial familiarity with English usage, his comprehension of what his plan implied, and his continuing and cumulative capacity to remember what he had already done and what he had yet to do. Imagine yourself half-way through Johnson's program of reading for the *Dictionary*, arriving at [a] page of Bacon's *Natural History*. . . . Which of the words and passages on the page would you mark in black lead pencil for your amanuenses to copy? Which would you pass over? By what norms would you make your selection? How many minutes would you need to reach your decisions on one page?[8]

The most crucial of Wimsatt's questions is this: how would you remember which words you'd marked before? And how would you avoid finishing the job of reading and then discovering that you have no quotations illustrating, say, *To pump*, or *sixteen*? Johnson misses neither, and typically the quotations illustrating even these apparently "practical," neutral terms are selected to imply the imperatives and ironies of a world morally conceived: they become implicit "precepts of prudence or piety." Under *To pump* we find

> The folly of him, who *pumps* very laboriously in a ship, yet neglects to stop the leak.   *Decay of Piety.*

And under *sixteen,*

> I have been begging *sixteen* years in court.   *Shakespeare.*

and

> If men lived but twenty years, we should be satisfied if they died about *sixteen* or eighteen.   *Taylor.*

In the same way, the idea that prepositions like *above, about,* and *for* might offer occasions for prudential or moral or theological activity is not one that will occur naturally to the twentieth-century mind. But see what Johnson does. The following are among the quotations illustrating the various senses of *above*:

> Every one that passeth among them, that are numbered from twenty years old and *above*, shall give an offering unto the Lord.
> *Exodus,* 30:14.

> The Lord is high *above* all nations, and his glory *above* the heavens.   *Psalm* 113:4.

> The public power of all societies is *above* every soul contained in the same societies.   *Hooker,* b[ook] 1.

> There is no riches *above* a sound body, and no joy *above* the joy of the heart.   *Ecclesiasticus,* 30:16.

>   To her
> Thou didst resign thy manhood, and the place
> Wherein God set thee *above* her, made of thee,

> And for thee: whose perfection far excelled
> Hers, in all real dignity.
> *Milton's Paradise Lost*, b. x, l. 47.

It is an old and true distinction, that things may be *above* our reason, without being contrary to it. Of this kind are the power, the nature, and the universal presence of God, with innumerable other points.   *Swift.*

And to illustrate *about* Johnson finds these:

> Let not mercy and truth forsake thee. Bind them *about* thy neck; write them upon the table of thy heart.   *Proverbs,* 3:3.

> When Constantine had finished an house for the service of God at Jerusalem, the dedication he judged a matter not unworthy, *about* the solemn performance whereof the greatest part of the bishops in Christendom should meet together.   *Hooker,* b. v, # 12.

> Theft is always a sin, although the particular species of it, and the denomination of particular acts, doth suppose positive laws *about* dominion and property.
> *Stillingfleet's Defense of Discourses on Romish Idolatry.*

> They should always be heard, and kindly answered, when they ask after anything they would know, and desire to be informed *about—*

a mere lexicographer, someone not "writing" a dictionary, would have stopped there. Johnson goes on:

> —Curiosity should be as carefully cherished in children, as other appetites suppressed.   *Locke on Education,* # 108.

> Our blessed Lord was pleased to command the representation of His death and sacrifice on the cross should be made by breaking of bread and effusion of wine, to signify to us the nature and sacredness of the liturgy we are *about.*
> *Taylor's Worthy Communicant.*

> Good master, corporal, captain, for my old dame's sake, stand my friends: she hath nobody to do anything *about* her when I am gone, and she is old and cannot help herself.
> *Shakespeare's Henry IV,* p. ii.

And although among the quotations illustrating *for* we encounter a pious extract from Hooker, an allusion in Ralegh to Abraham's journey, an observation from Hammond's *Practical Catechism* on the wickedness of hypocritical or carnal hopes, and one of Locke's assertions of the indispensability of the empirical method, this possibly intimidating offering is shrewdly variegated with more alluring materials; for example, Suckling's

> Quit, quit, *for* shame; this will not move,
>   This cannot take her;
> If of herself she will not love,
>   Nothing can make her,

and Pope's reaction to the fake books in Timon's library:

> Lo, some are vellum, and the rest as good,
> *For* all his Lordship knows, but they are wood.

But even with *for*, the bulk of the quotations is such that no one can come away from them without a mind reinvigorated by contact with succinct moral formulations and images. To read an entry in the *Dictionary* is to undergo an intellectual and ethical overhaul. Johnson defines and at the same time does something else. We remember his conclusions about artistic unity and multiplicity in *Rambler* 139: "It is always a proof of extensive thought and accurate circumspection to promote various purposes by the same act."

To the end that various purposes may be promoted by the same act, the *Dictionary*, as Wimsatt has said, is "embellished by numerous aphorisms, anecdotes, thumbnail dramas, biographical glimpses, . . . miniature expressions of literary theory and of critical judgment. . . ."[9] But Johnson will not admit just anyone's gems. As Boswell observes, he was so careful to quote "no author whose writings had a tendency to hurt sound religion and morality" that he omitted Hobbes altogether ("I scorned, Sir, to quote him at all, because I did not like his principles"); and although he later came to value the sermons of Dr. Samuel Clarke for being "fullest on the propitiatory sacrifice," at the time of the *Dictionary* Johnson thought him heretical on the Trinity, and thus excluded him. Indeed, Johnson's concern for the wholesome tendency of his quotations laid him open to the charge that many of his writers, although of undeniable piety, were, as the critic Thomas Edwards said, "of no [literary] authority."[10] But as he explained to Mrs. Thrale, "I would not . . . send people to look for words in a book, that by such a casual seizure of the mind might chance to mislead it forever."

The sheer number of quotations is almost unimaginable. So is the ethical sensitivity controlling their selection and disposition. But equally remarkable is Johnson's achievement in even the tiniest matters of technique. For example, in illustrating *two-handed* the normal thing to do—that is, the easiest—would be to copy out the most famous passage where the word occurs, the "two-handed engine" passage in *Lycidas.* But Johnson is aware that no interpreter knows what that two-handed engine unambiguously means; consequently, he resists the temptation to use it and goes instead to *Paradise Lost,* where the term conveys a clear image:

> With huge *two-handed* sway,
> Brandished aloft, the horrid edge came down,
> Wide wasting.

Any one of us doing Johnson's job would doubtless often use the same quotation more than once to save work. Johnson does not. Illustrating *Glory,* he quotes from Matthew 6:29:

> Solomon, in all his *glory,* was not arrayed like one of these.

While reading and marking this passage, how natural, even how sensible, to make another slip at the same time for *To array,* with the meaning "To deck; to dress; to adorn the person," and to illustrate with the same passage. But Johnson can do better than that: when we turn to *Array* we find that he has come up with quite different quotations, from Job, *Paradise Lost,* and Dryden. Again, illustrating *Water,* he offers this quotation from *King Lear:*

> O let not women's weapons, *water*-drops,
> Stain my man's cheeks.

A superb opportunity to illustrate *Stain* as well. But turning to *Stain* (meaning "To blot; to spot; to maculate"), we find an entirely different passage from *King Lear*:

> Lend me a looking-glass;
> If that her breath will mist or *stain* the stone,
> Why then she lives.

A final example. As we have seen, Proverbs 3:3 is one of his illustrations of *About*:

> Let not mercy and truth forsake thee. Bind them *about* thy neck; write them upon the table of thy heart.

There is a powerful invitation here to use the same passage to illustrate *Upon*, and to use it again to illustrate *Table* (meaning "tablet"). But under *Upon* in this sense, he illustrates by citing *Macbeth*; and with *Table* he gives the impression of joyously showing off: disdaining to cite the Proverbs passage again, he provides other passages in exuberent excess, passages from Hooker, Shakespeare, Sir John Davies, Dryden, Bentley's *Sermons,* Ayliffe's *Parergon*, and Ayliffe again. He would be pleased to know that someone has been checking up on him and that his work has withstood a search for even those flaws whose exposure would bring him the least blame:

> He said, 'Dodsley first mentioned to me the scheme of an English Dictionary; but I had long thought of it.' BOSWELL. 'You did not know what you were undertaking.' JOHNSON. 'Yes, Sir, I knew very well what I was undertaking,—and very well how to do it,—and have done it very well.'

By July, 1754, he was all but finished. Still remaining were the introductory materials, and, bored and exhausted, he set to work on these: a brief "History of the English Language," an essentially frivolous document consisting largely of unanalyzed mere quotations arranged chronologically—the whole performance suggests impatient levity and even despair; and an almost equally uninterested "Grammar of the English Tongue." The history and grammar of the language were ceasing to interest him; what did interest him now was the whole act of writing a dictionary, and it is this subject to which he devotes his splendid Preface.

Much had changed since he wrote the *Plan*. Among the introductory materials, the most conspicuous omission is a dedication to Chesterfield. The Preface does not, like the *Plan*, take the form of "A Letter to a Noble Lord": rather, it assumes the form of a scholarly essay, but one of an especially rich and problematic sort. It is at once an apology and an exultation, the work of a mind conscious of having earned its independence, a mind proud of its achievement and yet borne down by the ironic awareness that it has been the victim of many kinds of literary hope too fondly indulged, as well as the crushing knowledge that it is now too late to please those—especially Tetty—who were alive to share his hopes when he began.

But the whole framework of the Preface is ironic, depending as it does on repeated contrasts between the pleasant clarities and simplicities of the job when first projected, and the sad obscurities, complexities, and frustrations experienced when the job was actually in hand. At first it all looked so clear:

When I took the first survey of my undertaking, I found our speech copious without order, and energetic without rule: wherever I turned my view there was perplexity to be disentangled and confusion to be regulated.

But even in trying to disentangle the perplexities of English spelling he found himself face to face with irregularities which he was obliged to register rather than reform, for "Every language has its anomalies, which, though inconvenient, and in themselves once unnecessary, must be tolerated among the imperfections of human things." Irrational perversions in orthography are not—as Chesterfield might want to put it—mitigable "errors": they are more like the stains of Original Sin, "spots of barbarity impressed so deep in the English language that criticism can never wash them away."

Thus, Johnson goes on, "Even in words of which the derivation is apparent, I have been often obliged to sacrifice uniformity to custom," writing, "in compliance with a numberless majority, *convey* and *inveigh, deceit* and *receipt, fancy* and *phantom.*" It is like the act of embracing the existing genres with all their limitations and defects because they are the only places where "a numberless majority"—rightly or wrongly—expect to find "writing."

In the *Plan* Johnson had alluded to the holy Richard Hooker, and now in the Preface he recovers him again to sanction his retention of the irrational received:

I have endeavored to proceed with a scholar's reverence for antiquity, and a grammarian's regard for the genius of our tongue. I have attempted few alterations, and among those few, perhaps the greater part is from the modern to the ancient practice; and I hope I may be allowed to recommend to those whose thoughts have been perhaps employed too anxiously on verbal singularities, not to disturb, upon narrow views or for minute propriety, the orthography of their fathers. It has been asserted that for the law to be *known* is of more importance than to be *right*. 'Change,' says Hooker, 'is not made without inconvenience, even from worse to better.' There is in constancy and stability a general and lasting advantage. . . .

It is an argument which will do just as well to sanction the use of traditional genres: the important thing about both inherited spellings and literary forms is that they are entirely conventional —they are *signs* only:

This recommendation of steadiness and uniformity does not proceed from an opinion that particular combinations of letters have much influence on human happiness; or that truth may not be successfully taught by modes of spelling fanciful and erroneous; I am not yet so lost in lexicography as to forget that *words are the daughters of earth, and that things are the sons of heaven*. Language is only the instrument of science, and words are but the signs of ideas: I wish, however, that the instrument might be less apt to decay, and that signs might be permanent, like the things which they denote.

But to "wish" for a reasonable world is not to imagine that one can have it, and it is certainly not to imagine that one can manufacture it by reforming spelling.

Johnson goes on to solicit sympathy for his difficulties in writing definitions. His method is to betake himself to the conventions of sincere confession. In his definitions, he says, "I cannot hope to satisfy those who are perhaps not inclined to be pleased, since I have not always been able to satisfy myself." His *perhaps* and *not always*, however, serve as signals that even this confession is not unattended with the irony appropriate to the very idea of a single man writing a whole dictionary. Sometimes this kind of irony drops away, yielding to other comic techniques: "Some words there are which I cannot explain because I do not understand them."

But there are countless impediments to satisfactory definition, and he is aware of them all: some words have no synonyms; the synonyms of those that have are never exactly synonymous; some words are too simple to be explained; some are mere expletives, which "have power and emphasis, though it be sometimes such as no other form of expression can convey"; in addition, English is maddeningly rich in loose, all-purpose verbs like *come, get, give, do, put, make, take*, "words [which] are hourly shifting their relations, and [which] can no more be ascertained in a dictionary than a grove, in the agitation of a storm, can be accurately delineated from its picture in the water." Indeed, he dwells with such anguish on the frustrations facing a definer that he begins to perceive that he may be stimulating the reader to the wrong reaction:

These complaints of difficulty will, by those that have never considered words beyond their popular use, be thought only the jargon of a man willing to magnify his labors and procure veneration to his studies by involution and obscurity. But every art is obscure to those that have not learned it; this uncertainty of terms and commixture of ideas is well known to those who have joined philosophy with grammar; . . .

And it is to bring some analytical clarity into the "commixture of ideas" that he has relied so heavily on illustrative quotations from the beginning: "The solution of all difficulties and the supply of all defects [in the definitions] must be sought in the examples subjoined to the various senses of each word, and ranged according to the time of their authors."

Ironic reversal is the psychic paradigm shaping Johnson's next little gesture of ironic autobiography. When he began reading for the dictionary, he naturally indulged high hopes:

When I first collected these authorities, I was desirous that every quotation should be useful to some other end than the illustration of a word; I therefore extracted from philosophers principles of science; from historians remarkable facts; from chemists complete processes; from divines striking exhortations; and from poets beautiful descriptions.

"Such"—sardonically—"is design, while it is yet at a distance from execution." What actually happened was that, while enthusiastically sniffing out all these beauties, he lost sight of his space limits and accumulated much too much material to use—quotation-hunting had become its own end, and, ironically again, "thus to the weariness of copying, I was condemned to add the vexation of expunging." And he has had to perform such "hasty truncation" to get his materials to fit his space that sometimes too much context has been excised, with the result that "the general tendency of the sentence may be changed: the divine may desert his tenets, or the philosopher his system."

At first he had resolved to do the job without using any quotations from living authors. But this resolution proved to be like all others—it failed when brought into contact with actuality: it had to be violated "when some performance of uncommon excellence excited my veneration; when my memory supplied me, from late books, with an example that was wanting; or when my heart, in the tenderness of friendship, solicited admission for a favorite name." Thus, despite his "design," he quotes from Samuel Richardson, David Garrick, and Charlotte Lennox. And he goes even further. Under *Important* he quotes a line from his own *Irene*, and under *Lacerate* and *Relax* he quotes from *The Vanity of*

Human Wishes. When in the Preface he contrived "reasons" for admitting now and then some contemporary favorite, he must have been smiling.

As he nears his conclusion he returns to develop the great presiding, Johnsonian theme, the theme of the ironic distance between human plans and performance, and here the *buts* and *yets*, as in the *Rambler*, bear a large burden of meaning. For example: "Thus have I labored . . . , but I have not always executed my own scheme, or satisfied my own expectations." Another passage dilates with humane affection on the noble fatuity animating his early resolutions about etymologies and definitions:

When first I engaged in this work, I resolved to leave neither words nor things unexamined, and pleased myself with a prospect of the hours which I should revel away in feasts of literature, the obscure recesses of Northern learning which I should enter and ransack, the treasures with which I expected every search into those neglected mines to reward my labor, and the triumph with which I should display my acquisitions to mankind.

If the image of Samuel Johnson as prince and conqueror dominates this part of the dream, the image of Samuel Johnson as universal Faustian inquirer and knower dominates the rest:

When I had thus inquired into the original of words, I resolved to show likewise my attention to things; to pierce deep into every science, to inquire the nature of every substance of which I inserted the name, to limit every idea by a definition strictly logical, and exhibit every production of art or nature in an accurate description, that my book might be in place of all other dictionaries whether appellative or technical.

The excess of these ambitions foreshadows the comically impossible requirements for the poet enunciated by Imlac in Chapter 10 of *Rasselas.* In addition to the five *everys,* the imagery of the whole passage is enough to notify us that an ironic reversal is imminent: he is going to please himself with a prospect, that is, a picturesque view of natural scenery beheld by an optimistic sentimentalist; he is going to revel at feasts like a hero of high Romance; he is going to conquer and sack Germanic Europe; he is going to enrich himself and astonish others by locating and working the undiscovered mines of El Dorado. Such grandiose and self-delusive hopes are clearly destined to destruction, and from the ensuing *but* we proceed precipitately downhill:

But these were the dreams of a poet doomed at last to wake a lexicographer. I soon found that it is too late to look for instruments when the work calls for execution, and that whatever abilities I had brought to my task, with those I must finally perform it.

He found, in short, that his earlier resolutions assumed an unreality like that associated with the naïve setting of pastoral, that "thus to pursue perfection was, like the first inhabitants of Arcadia, to chase the sun which, when they had reached the hill where he seemed to rest, was still beheld at the same distance from them."

The inevitability of failure is thus one of the themes on which he ends. Another, related to the first, surely, by the open-armed embrace of human imperfectability which accompanies it, is his old disinclination to play the role of dictator. His job has been to describe human unreason, not to try to reform it. As he says, anomalies are "not to be imputed to me, who do not form, but register the language; who do not teach men how they should think, but relate how they have hitherto expressed their thoughts." People without the experience of having written a dictionary— people like Chesterfield, actually—conceive it easy to arrest natural process and to fix the language; even Johnson himself was once so innocent:

Those who have been persuaded to think well of my design will require that it should fix our language and put a stop to those alterations which time and chance have hitherto been suffered to make in it without opposition. With this consequence I will confess that I flattered myself for awhile.

The "turn" to the requirements of actuality is enacted with the customary *but*:

But now [I] begin to fear that I have indulged expectation which neither reason nor experience can justify.

The hopes of the prescriptive lexicographer are, indeed, precisely as ridiculous (if still pathetic) as those of the alchemist:

When we see men grow old and die at a certain time one after another, from century to century—

(it is remarkable how suggestive this clause is, perhaps especially because it is dependent and incomplete, of Johnson's essential obsession and subject)

—we laugh at the elixir that promises to prolong life to a thousand years; and with equal justice may the lexicographer be derided who, being able to produce no example of a nation that has preserved their words and phrases from mutability, shall imagine that his dictionary can embalm his language and secure it from corruption and decay, that it is in his power to change sublunary nature, and clear the world at once from folly, vanity, and affectation.

If the image of the naïve aspirant lexicographer foreshadows Imlac, this image of the mad intermeddler into natural process points forward to the disordered astronomer in *Rasselas* who imagines that he is controlling the weather. It is surely an indication of Johnson's complexity of attitude in relation to his apparent rhetorical postures that it has been one clear intent of the *Rambler* exactly to help reduce—if not to "clear the world at once from"—"folly, vanity, and affectation."

Fatuous as such ambitions of stability seem, whole academies have been founded abroad to "fix" languages, and even Jonathan Swift once so far forgot himself as to go around "proposing" that no old word should be "suffered to become obsolete" and that an academy should be established to carry on this work. But, Johnson retorts, "What makes a word obsolete, more than general agreement to forbear it?" He has, of course, a running quarrel with Swift. Swift is, for Johnson, too much the theoretician of human nature, too willing to give it first the law and then the lash (although Johnson's general disapproval—characteristically—does not prevent his using plenty of Swift for his illustrative quotations in the *Dictionary*: there are 123 quotations from *Directions to Servants* alone). Johnson does not like academies just because they dictate and prescribe: he prefers even messiness to the inevitable pride and tyranny and self-righteousness engendered by academies in their members, and the hangdog dependence they engender in their creatures and followers. If an academy for purifying English ever were established, which God forbid, it should specialize in preventing translations of French books into an English resembling French:

If an academy should be established for the cultivation of our style (which I, who can never wish to see dependence multiplied, hope the spirit of English liberty will hinder or destroy), let them, instead of compiling grammars and dictionaries, endeavor with all their influence to stop the license of translators whose idleness and ignorance, if it be suffered to proceed, will reduce us to babble a dialect of France.

But just as our awareness that life is a death-sentence does nothing to prevent our making ourselves momentarily comfortable, the lexicographer while registering enormities is not obliged to withhold criticism of them:

If the changes that we fear be thus irresistible, what remains but to acquiesce with silence, as in the other insurmountable distresses of humanity?

Actually, something more than silence remains:

It remains that we retard what we cannot repel, that we palliate what we cannot cure. Life may be lengthened by care, though death cannot be ultimately defeated: tongues, like governments, have a natural tendency to degeneration; we have long preserved our constitution, let us make some struggles for our language.

We should pause here to notice how very "unoriginal," in one way, Johnson really is in both the *Plan* and the Preface. In both documents many of his positions are the commonplaces belonging to that common eighteenth-century genre, the discourse about lexicography. Much of his substance derives from the Preface to Ephraim Chambers's *Cyclopedia* (1728): Chambers like Johnson dwells on the "lowness" of lexicography; he is unwilling to believe that his work is going to "fix" the language; he recognizes the Johnsonian difficulties of making definitions; he insists that lexicography is a highly imperfect art; and he rejects the idea of an English Academy, pointing out that the present dictionary has been accomplished without one.[11] But as so often, Johnson's achievement is to redeem these commonplaces by making them appear vital, kinetic, dramatic, and genuinely debatable. What is not always perceived by those who know of Johnson's debt to his predecessors in both *Plan* and Preface is, as Sledd and Kolb say, "that no commonplace mind could give such strength and dignity to commonplaces, or even that a crowd of sleepy commonplaces, like dead metaphors, can jostle one another into embarrassing liveliness."[12] It all provides another example of Johnson's kind of "originality" or "creativeness": Johnson feels no need to erect a theory of art assuming that creation can occur without inherited technical materials to work on.

It is the final three paragraphs of the Preface that especially stick in the mind. The reason is perhaps suggested by Michael Joyce: "Johnson's writing is always at its noblest when he is dwelling on, and even exaggerating, the wretchedness of his condition."[13] While he is engaged in making the point that, because "The chief glory of every people arises from its authors," he will not think his work wasted if his labors—he is assuming that the quotations are his brightest achievement—"add celebrity to Bacon, to Hooker, to Milton, and to Boyle," he is soliciting our sympathy for the *Dictionary* by emphasizing that it has been "the labor of years," that "much of my life has been lost under the pressures of disease; much has been trifled away; and much has always been spent in provision for the day that was passing over me." He expects to be attacked by malice and folly and envy, but begs his enemies to realize that "the *English Dictionary* was written with little assistance of the learned, and without any patronage of the Great; not in the soft obscurities of retirement, or under the shelter of academic bowers, but amidst inconvenience and distraction, in sickness and in sorrow." And it is such Prayer-Book doublets as we have just heard that provide the scheme of the final sentence, written to sound like the last and feeblest utterance of an old man—Johnson was actually only forty-six—brought by the unremitting practice of virtue to the stasis of resignation: "I have protracted my work till most of those whom I wished to please have sunk into the grave, and success and miscarriage are empty sounds: I therefore dismiss it with frigid tranquillity, having little to fear or hope from censure or from praise." This sounds like "sincere" autobiography, even though the happy assonance of "frigid tranquillity" may suggest the sort of contrivance a man uses only when he is focusing more on the audience than on himself. But we realize how justified we are to suspect some duplicity when we remember a letter Johnson wrote to Thomas Warton (Feb. 1, 1755) just as he was finishing the *Dictionary*. In the letter the attitude toward both praise and censure is remarkably unlike the "frigid tranquillity" assumed officially at the end of the Preface:

I now begin to see land, after having wandered, in Mr. Warburton's phrase, in this vast sea of words. What reception I shall meet with upon the shore I know not, whether the sound of bells and acclamations of the people which Ariosto talks of in his last canto, or a general murmur of dislike. I know not whether I shall find upon the coast a Calypso that will court, or a Polypheme that will eat me.

And all the violence that attends his condemnation of those who would ravage the roof of Lichfield Cathedral is in the blunt and almost savage outburst that follows:

But if Polypheme comes at me, have at his eyes.

Faced with two rhetorics as distinct as these, what can we conclude but that the idea of artistic sincerity—together with related ideas about "authenticity"—stands in need of a new, even a Johnsonian, complication and refinement?

CHAPTER 8

"The Choice of Life"

The received version of the composition of *Rasselas* is given by Boswell:

Johnson wrote it that with the profits he might defray the expenses of his mother's funeral, and pay some little debts which she had left. He told Sir Joshua Reynolds that he composed it in the evenings of one week, sent it to the press in portions as it was written, and had never since read it over.

The traditional association of the composition of *Rasselas* with Johnson's mother's death in straitened circumstances has made it easy to read the work as in some way a response to her death, in some way a reflection of his feelings on that occasion. This association has encouraged some readers to look for, and to find, a heavy load of gloom in *Rasselas*, and to conclude that it constitutes little more than a series of dark variations on themes of mortality and loss. Thus W. P. Courtney and D. Nichol Smith, writing in 1915: "The circumstances in which *Rasselas* was composed would not inspire cheerfulness of feeling in its author, and Johnson was always predisposed to melancholy. A veil of sadness is cast over its pages."[1]

But actually *Rasselas* is a vastly (if subtly) comic performance, and the circumstances of its composition, when we scrutinize them closely, can help indicate Johnson's real relation to a literary theory of "self-expression." If we want to get a sense of the attitude Johnson chooses to reveal toward his mother's death, we must go not to *Rasselas* but to his last letters to her. In Johnson's eyes her situation is clearly too grave and pathetic to be in any way the occasion of a fictional theme. A week before her death he writes to her, characteristically allowing the rhetoric of the Prayer Book to shape his own as he does upon other emergent occasions:

Honored Madam,

The account which Miss gives me of your health pierces my heart. God comfort and preserve you and save you, for the sake of Jesus Christ.

I would have Miss read to you from time to time the Passion of our Saviour, and sometimes the sentences in the Communion Service beginning 'Come unto me, all ye that travail and are heavy laden, and I will give you rest.'

And again, consider Johnson's last letter to her:

Dear Honored Mother,

Neither your condition nor your character make it fit for me to say much. You have been the best mother, and I believe the best woman in the world. I thank you for your indulgence to me, and beg forgiveness of all that I have done ill, and all that I have omitted to do well. God grant you His Holy Spirit, and receive you to everlasting happiness, for Jesus Christ's sake. Amen. Lord Jesus receive your spirit. Amen.

I am, dear Mother, your dutiful son,
Sam: Johnson.

On this same day, Johnson writes another letter—a businesslike communication to his publisher telling him about a book he's starting called *The Choice of Life, or the History of* ———— *Prince of Abyssinia* and arranging the terms of sale and the date for the delivery of the manuscript. There is nothing in this letter but brisk efficiency: it is concerned only with format, length, sums of money, and the rights of the author.

At this moment, Johnson has three rhetorical jobs to perform: one is to comfort his mother; another is to persuade a publisher to accept his terms for a piece of writing; a third is to get started on a work, *The Choice of Life*, which will engage the reader by amusing him. The connection between these three rhetorical jobs is one of accidental occasion only. As a work, *Rasselas* is touched no more by the gravity of personal circumstance than the comic essays of the *Idler,* or indeed, than the merry satirical poem on the sillinesses of the young Sir John Lade. As a work of a unique "kind," *Rasselas* establishes its own thematic and technical imperatives from the outset: the whim of the author cannot seriously alter the mode of the work once it is begun. In producing the comic *Rasselas* on this occasion, Johnson is not being heartless: he is being literary.

If we want some verbal reflection of his grief for his mother it would be well to leave *Rasselas* alone and turn instead to *Idler* 41, written a week after her death. Here Johnson attains some "distance" and objectivity by choosing to write in the form of a letter to "Mr. Idler." He then works gradually, by means of general moral observations, to his personal subject:

Nothing is more evident than that the decays of age must terminate in death; yet there is no man, says Tully, who does not believe that he may yet live another year; and there is none who does not, upon the same principle, hope another year for his parent or his friend. But the fallacy will be in time detected; the last year, the last day must come. It has come and is past. The life which made my own pleasant is at an end, and the gates of death are shut upon my prospects.

Disguising his loss as that of "a friend" rather than a parent, he goes on to write a brief prose epitaph: "The blameless life, the artless tenderness, the pious simplicity, the modest resignation, the patient sickness, and the quiet death are remembered only to add value to the loss, to aggravate regret for what cannot be amended, to deepen sorrow for what cannot be realized." This survey of his mother's character brings him to the reflection that "Happiness is not found in self-contemplation; it is perceived only when it is reflected from another." And he concludes by asserting that on these occasions "philosophy"—that is, Stoicism—won't do; nothing short of Christian hope will work:

The precepts of Epicurus, who teaches us to endure what the laws of the universe make necessary, may silence but not content us. The dictates of Zeno, who commands us to look with indifference on external things, may dispose us to conceal our sorrow, but cannot assuage it. Real alleviation of the loss of friends, and rational tranquillity in the prospect of our own dissolution, can be received only from the promises of Him in whose hands are life and death, and from the assurance of another and better state, in which all tears will be wiped from the eyes, and the whole soul shall be filled with joy. Philosophy may infuse stubbornness, but religion only can give patience.

> I am, &c.

But at this moment Johnson needs more than patience. He needs money, and therefore he needs readers. Because he needs readers, he must select a genre for his new work which his readers will recognize as familiar and comfortable. The genre which Johnson chooses largely determines what *Rasselas* is like. Of course the writer's singularity colors the proceedings, but only in such ways as do not deform the paradigm out of all recognition.

The genre of *Rasselas* is the Oriental, or more accurately, the Near Eastern Tale, and as E. L. McAdam observes, it is "the first full-length Oriental Tale in English."[2] In Johnson's day the Oriental Tale was a form associated both with noble—if not, perhaps, quite attainable—moral idealism and also with fairly broad comedy. Addison's *Spectator* 159, on "The Visions of Mirzah," shows the way the genre harmonizes, or tries to harmonize, the elements of the noble-didactic and the farcical. The English speaker in

Addison's little allegory affects to be translating a Persian manuscript he's picked up on his travels. The Persian speaker, Mirzah,
recounts a rather clumsy and superficial allegorical vision of the
ironic conditions of human life.

He perceives before him a valley with a sinister river running
through it. Above the river stands the bridge "of life," dotted
with farcical trap-doors; and in speaking of the operation of these
trap-doors Mirzah glances at the contemporary infant-mortality
rate, although of course neither Addison, Mirzah, nor the reader
thinks of it as a "rate" amenable to amelioration but takes it as a
permanent condition of human existence:

[I] perceived there were innumerable trap-doors that lay concealed
in the bridge, which the passengers no sooner trod upon, but they
fell through them into the tide and immediately disappeared. These
hidden pitfalls were set very thick at the entrance of the bridge, so
that throngs of people no sooner broke through from the cloud [from
which they emerge], but many of them fell into them. They grew
thinner towards the middle, but multiplied and lay closer together
towards the end. . . .

Now notice the fusion of solemnity and almost Swiftian farce:

I passed some time in the contemplation of this wonderful structure.
. . . My heart was filled with a deep melancholy to see several
dropping unexpectedly in the midst of mirth and jollity, and catching
at everything that stood by them to save themselves. Some were looking
up towards the heavens in a thoughtful posture, and in the midst of a
speculation stumbled and fell out of sight. Multitudes were very busy
in the pursuit of bubbles that glittered in their eyes and danced before
them, but often when they thought themselves within the reach of
them, their footing failed and down they sunk.

At this point Addison feels appropriate a little standard Restoration
satire of generals and physicians as the prime agents of early
death:

I observed some with scimitars in their hands, and others with urinals,
who ran to and fro upon the bridge, thrusting several persons on

trap-doors which did not seem to lie in their way, and which they might have escaped had they not been thus forced upon them.

The interesting thing is that these broadly ironic and farcical details are accompanied by a rhetoric which moves off in a very different direction, a rhetoric of straight sentimental solemnity. For example:

I here fetched a deep sigh. Alas, said I, man was made in vain! How is he given away to misery and mortality! tortured in life, swallowed up in death!

But the Attendant Spirit who is exhibiting this allegorical spectacle to Mirzah quiets these complaints by disclosing a scene of beautiful islands, the regions of the blessed, toward which the multitudes crossing the bridge are unwittingly proceeding. "Are not those," he asks Mirzah, "habitations worth contending for?" And Mirzah, his farcical stage physicians with their prop urinals now forgotten, assures us that he "gazed with inexpressible pleasure on those happy islands."

When a reader of Johnson's time saw on a book-spine or title-page or in an advertisement a title containing a word like "Abyssinia" or "Persia" or "Arabia"—as in William Beckford's *Vathek: An Arabian Tale* (1786)—it was this sort of material and tone he expected, and the author with his wits about him was careful to provide him with just this mixture of the portentous and the ridiculous, all developed in a conventionally unbelievable and thus charming décor of palm trees, endless sands, and, if possible, broken monuments and *papier-mâché* pyramids. Shelley's "Ozymandias" reveals both by its setting and its portentous irony that it emanates from the tradition of the Oriental Tale. We can see that this tradition comes close to constituting an eighteenth-century version of Camp. This is what Johnson goes to work on to pay the expenses of his mother's funeral.

Misapprehensions about the comic tone of *Rasselas* are common today, largely, I suppose, because we have lost touch with the genre conventions that supply much of its meaning. In *The Sense of*

Humor (1954), Stephen Potter reprints the preposterous abstract
rationalizations and theorizings of the absurd Flying-Machine
Projector in Chapter 6 of *Rasselas* as an example of the "Uninten-
tionally Funny." And the 1964 Penguin re-issue of Potter's collection still presents this hilarious passage as if Johnson did not know
what he was about.[3] Such is the mythologizing power of literary
history to attach irrelevant or erroneous meanings to works whose
import would be quite clear if they were only read.

   Rasselas was not quite Johnson's first experience with the literary
Near East. We remember that when he was twenty-four he turned
a penny by translating and abridging Father Lobo's *A Voyage to
Abyssinia*, and he had adopted the Near Eastern mode for a couple
of the *Rambler* essays. It was probably by remembering the Lobo
book that he managed to fill the blank in his working title: Lobo
had mentioned an Abyssinian general named Rassela Christos.
Although Lobo's work is in a different genre from the Oriental
Tale—it is a travel book with anti-colonialist leanings—its procedure is not entirely dissimilar. The procedure is skepticism. We
recall Johnson asserting in his preface to Lobo that this traveler,
happily, has resisted the temptation to deck out and dramatize
the homely and rather dull truth that men and climates and
environments are pretty much the same everywhere—that is, pretty
boring—despite travel agents' insistence on exotic conditions and
mores elsewhere. Johnson's skepticism in the Lobo preface about
"romantic absurdities" and "incredible fictions," as well as his sense
that life is everywhere very similar and quite tiresome, reappears in
Rasselas.

   The Oriental Tale is a lucky fictional genre for Johnson to work
in, for by convention its fictions are too palpable for belief. The
Oriental Tale uses the scenic and exotic elements of Romanticism
in such a way that they are openly de-mystified and exposed. If
Coleridge's magic damsel with a dulcimer were somehow to make
an appearance in *Rasselas*, we should laugh. For Johnson, writing
about Abyssinia—and what, after all, could be funnier?—whether
in his twenty-fourth or his fiftieth year, and whether in the mode

of translating a travel book or composing a Near Eastern Tale, is an exercise in de-romanticization. He de-romanticizes because he conceives that it is beneficial to the reader.

Johnson was an extremely sensitive—indeed, neurotic—responder to literature. He is as delicate a sensor as Shelley announces himself to be. His responses are so sensitive that only a term like hyper-aesthesia seems adequate to describe them. The way Walter Pater exhorts us to react to experience is the way Johnson does react to his reading. When he was a boy, his reading of *Hamlet* scared him so badly that he had to drop the book and run out into the street to reassure himself of the essential benignity of the world. And forty years later, when he found himself editing Shakespeare, the impact upon him of the smothering scene in *Othello* was such that he could not restrain his profound personal horror from entering his editorial apparatus. He admits in a footnote: "I am glad that I have ended my revisal of this dreadful scene. It is not to be endured." Likewise with the end of *King Lear*. "I was many years ago so shocked by Cordelia's death," he says, "that I know not whether I ever endured to read again the last scenes of the play till I undertook to revise them as an editor."

Because he himself reacted to his reading so powerfully, all his life he was concerned about the affective operation of literature upon others. He was especially concerned about the impact of fiction upon the young, with their general bent toward "realistic" interpretations of their reading and their natural naïveté about the distance between literary rendering and actual substance. What he says in *Rambler* 4 is a measure of his concern.

Smollett's *Roderick Random* appeared in 1748; Fielding's *Tom Jones* in 1749. A year later, Johnson found himself thinking hard and deeply about the impact of works like these on young readers, and in *Rambler* 4 he records his conclusions. Writers of novels have a harder artistic job than writers of romances, he says, for they choose to represent what every reader can observe around him—real people, that is, rather than such incredibilities as knights, ladies, and dragons. "Other writings," he finds, "are safe, except from the malice of learning, but [novels] are in danger from every common reader." He goes on:

But the fear of not being approved as just copiers of human manners is not the most important concern that an author of this sort ought to have before him. These books are written chiefly to the young, the ignorant, and the idle, to whom they serve as lectures of conduct and introductions into life. They are the entertainment of minds unfurnished with ideas, and therefore easily susceptible of impressions; not fixed by principles, and therefore easily following the current of fancy; not informed by experience, and consequently open to every false suggestion and partial account.

The function of fiction, he continues, is "to initiate youth by mock encounters in the art of necessary defense" against the cunning, treachery, and fraud that lie in wait for virtue. Since their audience happens to be youth, novelists like Smollett and Fielding err in presenting a "realistic" blend of the virtuous and the vicious in their heroes. In its uncertainty and insecurity youth always imitates, and it will imitate anything authors—regardless of their artistic intention—set before it as a plausible simulacrum of the actual.

Johnson's worry about the effects of fiction upon the young is one of the springs of *Rasselas*. The work can be taken in part as a Johnsonian model for the reform of fiction exhibiting youthful heroes to youthful readers. It has not always been noticed that the first sentence of *Rasselas* establishes it as virtually a boy's book. This opening sentence addresses the reader directly, and when we take the trouble to deduce who he is from the characteristics Johnson carefully imputes to him, we perceive that he is a boy:

Ye who listen with credulity to the whispers of fancy, and pursue with eagerness the phantoms of hope; who expect that age will perform the promises of youth, and that the deficiencies of the present day will be supplied by the morrow,—attend to the history of Rasselas, Prince of Abyssinia.

Clearly the addressee, for all his assumed appreciation of Latinate diction, is someone who has not yet attained age, for he does not yet know by simple experience that age will not perform the promises of youth: he hasn't got there yet, and that is why the history of Rasselas is important for him to read. It is especially important for him to read at that stage in his development when he is beginning to make independent choices: as Johnson emphasizes in a letter to John Taylor, "The transition from the protection of others to our own conduct is a very awful point of human existence."

What Johnson is doing in this opening address is borrowing one of Aureng-Zebe's speeches in Dryden's play and adapting it for the use of young persons.[4] Aureng-Zebe makes the point this way:

> When I consider life, 'tis all a cheat;
> Yet, fooled with hope, men favor the deceit;
> Trust on, and think tomorrow will repay:
> Tomorrow's falser than the former day; . . .
> Strange cos'nage! None would live past years again,
> Yet all hope pleasure in what yet remain;
> And from the dregs of life think to receive
> What the first sprightly running could not give.

The mighty difference between Dryden's and Johnson's versions of this perception is that Johnson uses it, as always, as a goad to make the reader act. The reader is not, as in Dryden, expected to say, "How true!" or "How amusingly put"; he is expected to act, to do something moral and specific: "Attend to the history of Rasselas." And he is expected to attend for the sake of his own moral alteration toward redemption. We recall the rhetorical action of the end of the *Drury Lane Prologue.*

Johnson seems to imply that his book is addressed primarily to the young when he describes it, in a letter to Lucy Porter, as "a little story book." And although all his writings are distinguished in a loose age by their moral purity, there is something about the almost ostentatious purity of *Rasselas*—consider the long discussion of marriage which manages entirely to avoid the main point—that suggests also that Johnson is specifically addressing the young. In 1775 Mrs. Thrale met in Rouen an abbess who had heard about modern fiction and was naturally sensitive to its moral hazards. Mrs. Thrale reports: "I promised the abbess a French translation of Johnson's *Rasselas*. But may I read it? says she. Vestals might read it, Madame, replied I." Perhaps the abbess' question was motivated by her having been informed sometime—and her informant would have been accurate—that the Oriental Tale as genre was also a conventional arena for the disposition of pornographic materials.

Once we perceive who the reader of *Rasselas* is presumed to be, we can appreciate the tale's rhetorical proximity to a work from which it would seem to stand at some distance: Chesterfield's *Letters to His Son*. Although we easily remember Johnson's saying of Chesterfield's *Letters* that they "teach the morals of a whore and the manners of a dancing master," we recall less readily his less colorful observation: "Lord Chesterfield's *Letters to His Son*, I think, might be made a very pretty book. Take out the immorality, and it should be put into the hands of every young gentleman." It is into the hands of every young gentleman, and every young lady, too, that Johnson hopes *Rasselas* will fall. It is his version of a book of Advice to His Son, the son he never had. It is sad that while "Ozymandias" has been embraced by youth and while *Vathek* is newly popular among all sorts of drop-outs, *Rasselas* today finds its warmest admirers not among the fresh who might benefit from it but among the aging Imlacs of this world, who are past all help.

Like most eighteenth-century works, works written before the Romantic obsession with the mystique of organic unity, *Rasselas* is an accumulation of shining particles. The parts from which it is made are so memorable as parts that it is easy to neglect the whole action it embodies. We never forget the Flying-Machine Projector, or Imlac on the presumed obligations of the poet, or the Mad Astronomer who has confounded *post hoc* with *propter hoc* and who is cured simply by returning to social intercourse. But in treasuring delights like these we may lose our sense of what the whole structure is doing.

Rasselas takes place in that secular wasteland lying between *Paradise Lost* and *Paradise Regained.* The ironically "Happy" Valley has been left behind, and yet the search for the happiest choice of life is conducted, like the Grand Tour, in a way that manages to avoid reference to the eternal. We sense that we are close to a mock-*Paradise Lost* when we hear the naïve hero say at the end of Chapter 16: "I have here the world before me," which forces us to recall Milton's

> The world was all before them, where to choose
> Their place of rest, and Providence their guide.

The joke is that in *Rasselas* Providence is not their guide: they err and wander, guided only by the fallible Imlac. We sense again the proximity of *Paradise Lost* to the proceedings in *Rasselas* when Nekayah, in Chapter 23, becomes suspicious of Imlac's perpetual skepticism and imputes to him motives very like those which Eve, rationalizing her desire for the fruit, imputes to God: "Imlac favors not our search," says Nekayah, "lest we should in time find him mistaken." Self-expelled from the fertile but boring Happy Valley of uniform satisfactoriness, the young travelers set out on their distinctly secular quest prepared with all the wrong, rationalistic questions to ask. After a series of comical disappointments whose effects might have been salutary, these *ingenus* arrive finally at an uneasy "decision" to return to something like their starting point. They cannot return to the Happy Valley any more than Adam and Eve can return to Eden: it is forbidden by law, divine on the one hand, secular on the other. They could, however, return to Abyssinia wiser and therefore perhaps happier than they left it, but they do not, quite. The reason they do not is spoken over and over by the repeated action of ironic reversal which constitutes in little the action of *Rasselas* as a whole.

Typical of this repeated action out of which *Rasselas* is made is the shape of Chapter 6, "A Dissertation on the Art of Flying."

Here, meditating some means of escape from the Happy Valley, Rasselas meets an engineer whose projects have achieved remarkable success: the water system of the palace is his work, and he has succeeded even with an air-conditioning apparatus. He is now projecting a heavier-than-air flying machine to be propelled by the arm-power of the pilot. As he discourses enthusiastically and plausibly on the theory of flight, he manages to beat down all of Rasselas' instinctive, commonsense objections. Full of hope, the projector undertakes to build and test-fly his aircraft, and within a year all is ready:

On a morning appointed, the maker appeared, furnished for flight, on a little promontory: he waved his pinions awhile to gather air, then leaped from his stand, and in an instant dropped into the lake.

There are ironies within ironies:

His wings, which were of no use in the air, sustained him in the water, and the prince drew him to land half-dead with terror and vexation.

It is the sort of dénouement which reminds us of Voltaire's literary actions. The difference is that, as G. B. Hill has said, "Johnson is content with giving the artist a ducking. Voltaire would have crippled him for life at the very least; most likely would have killed him on the spot."[5] Johnson's simple humanity is of course operating to save the projector's life, but something else is making its contribution too, his disinclination to take a firm position even about enterprises which appear to promise only disaster. One never can tell, and besides being a projector is better than being an idle non-projector: he who hopes, mad as he is, is preferable to him who does nothing. As he says in *Adventurer* 99:

They who find themselves inclined to censure new undertakings only because they are new should consider that the folly of projection is very seldom the folly of a fool; it is commonly the ebullition of a capacious mind, crowded with variety of knowledge, and heated with intenseness of thought.

Close as Johnson's action is to many of Voltaire's, it does not

derive from *Candide,* a work which Johnson did not read until
Rasselas was finished.

This type-action of ironic reversal, imaged by a sudden drop
from high to low, derives from earlier English writing: from
Rochester's *Satire Against Mankind,* for example, where

> . . . the misguided foll'wer climbs with pain
> Mountains of whimsies, heaped in his own brain;
> Stumbling from thought to thought, falls headlong down
> Into doubt's boundless sea, where, like to drown,
> Books bear him up awhile, and make him try
> To swim with bladders of philosophy.

This type-action of dropping derives, too, from Gulliver's humiliation over the matter of the Struldbruggs, whose immortality he
admires extravagantly until he is informed about the facts of their
permanent nastiness and drops suddenly into a salutary disappointment. It derives from Pope's treatment of the naïve addressee in the
Essay on Man: after being exhorted ironically to

> teach Eternal Wisdom how to rule,

the listener is suddenly enjoined to

> drop into thyself, and be a fool!

It also derives from Addison's contriving that his naïve travelers
on the bridge of life shall drop all unwitting through the trap-
doors just when they suspect no evil, busied as they are in upward
"speculation." We can perceive this type-action informing even
some very outré works, things like Swift's poem "A Beautiful Young
Nymph Going to Bed." Here the whore, "Returning at the midnight hour," undresses, revealing a reality very different from
the more or less fine appearance which cosmetics and prosthetic
appliances have furnished. The opposition between *prop* and *drop*
here measures the usual distance between appearance and reality
disclosed by the type-action of dropping: Swift's heroine, after
removing her artificial hair, glass eye, fake eyebrows, and false
teeth,

> Pulls out the rags contrived to prop
> Her flabby dugs, and down they drop.

In arranging that the Flying-Machine Projector shall drop, Johnson is as usual taking his paradigm from the public repository. And that paradigm establishes the shape both for the whole of *Rasselas* and for the separate parts. We see this type-action repeated in the many "drops" into disappointed perception or ill-understood revelation which Rasselas and his sister undergo. And the fact that they do not satisfactorily understand even such revelations as are vouchsafed them is one of the main points of *Rasselas*: the travelers keep pressing on for more because they refuse to learn, which is to say that they refuse to abandon the rationalistic, theoretical hopes on which their false visions of life have been built. They refuse to learn, with Imlac, simply to play life by ear. And yet neither is wholly "right" or "wrong."

Chapter 18 is another good example of the repeated action of comic reversal. Here Rasselas encounters a Stoic philosopher to whom he listens "with the veneration due to the instructions of a superior being." Imlac warns as usual against a hasty embrace of this as of other pre-concerted theories of life. And very soon the trap-door drops. When Rasselas next visits the philosopher to get more Stoicism, he finds all changed: he discovers that the philosopher's daughter has suddenly died, and that his mentor has broken down just like any frailer, non-philosophic man. Rasselas says to him: "Have you then forgot the precepts . . . which you so powerfully enforced?" The Stoic answers: "What comfort . . . can truth and reason afford me? Of what effect are they now, but to tell me that my daughter will not be restored?" As the episode ends, we are given one of Johnson's most delightful gestures of wry complicity in this whole farce of the gulf between principle and practice. It is a gesture accomplished through so conventional a device as a bit of alliteration: "[Rasselas] . . . went away, convinced of the emptiness of rhetorical sound, and the inefficacy of polished periods and studied sentences." That studied sentence itself commits

Johnson to both sides of the vision at once: he is erecting a gorgeous ideal which he undermines with a grace deriving only from that ideal. This single sentence suggests with what complicated feelings of serious comedy Johnson senses his own involvement in the half-admirable folly which he is at pains to expose: as A. R. Humphreys has seen, the irony in *Rasselas* "never indicates on Johnson's part any self-congratulation on superior wisdom."[6]

Like the action which results in the discomfiture of the Flying-Machine Projector, the action in the exposure of the poor Stoic derives less from Johnson's insides than from common external tradition. We can sense the public availability of this motif of the Stoic Exposed from its appearance in Fielding's *Joseph Andrews* (1742), a book Johnson maintained he had never read. Chapter viii of Book IV depicts Parson Adams exhorting Joseph to Stoicism. His exhortation is rudely violated by the arrival of news that his youngest son has just drowned. Adams has been going on in this vein:

When any accident threatens us, we are not to despair, nor, when it overtakes us, to grieve; we must submit in all things to the will of Providence, and not set our affections so much on anything here, as not to be able to quit it without reluctance. . . . No Christian ought so to set his heart on any person or thing in this world, but that, whenever it shall be required or taken from him in any manner by Divine Providence, he may be able peaceably, quietly, and contentedly to resign it.

The trap is now ready for springing:

At which words one came hastily in and acquainted Mr. Adams that his youngest son was drowned. He stood silent a moment, and soon began to stamp about the room and deplore his loss with the bitterest agony.

Joseph tries to comfort him the way Rasselas tries to comfort his Stoical philosopher, that is, by pressing the arguments he's just received from his master:

Joseph . . . recovered himself sufficiently to endeavor to comfort the parson; in which attempt he used many arguments that he had at several times remembered out of [Adams's] own discourses . . . but [Adams] was not at leisure now to hearken to his advice. 'Child, child,' said he, 'do not go about impossibilities. Had it been any other of my children, I could have borne it with patience; but my little prattler, the darling and comfort of my old age . . . My poor Jacky, shall I never see thee more?' cries the parson.—'Yes, surely,' says Joseph, 'and in a better place; you will meet again, never to part more.'

Fielding then interjects: "I believe the parson did not hear these words, for he paid little regard to them, but went on lamenting, whilst the tears trickled down into his bosom." Johnson's kind of originality is that which catches such motifs out of the air and turns them to his own local ends.

The type-action established in *Rasselas* of a rise to illusion or hope or grandiosity or self-sufficiency followed by a drop or a deflation or an exposure complicates the famous tenth chapter, in which Imlac, uttering opinions plausibly like Johnson's own, discourses on the nature of poetry and the proper business of the poet. As Imlac conceives of him, the poet is distinguished from other people by the universality of his knowledge both of separate objects and of the species to which they belong: "The business of the poet," he asserts, "is . . . to remark general properties and large appearances; he does not number the streaks of the tulip, or describe the different shades in the verdure of the forest." Nor is this all. "He must be acquainted likewise with all the modes of [human] life . . . . He must consider right and wrong in their abstracted and invariable state; he must disregard present laws and opinions, and rise to general and transcendental truths which will always be the same." And if he does all this he will not look to a contemporary audience: "He must, therefore, content himself with the slow progress of his name, contemn the applause of his own time, and commit his claims to the justice of posterity." As we listen to Imlac going on and on, we begin to realize that these are the notions less of a poet than of a failed poet. The chapter ends with his weighty prescription: "He must know many languages and many sciences; and, that his style may be worthy of his thoughts, must by incessant practice familiarize to himself every delicacy of speech and grace of harmony." Ho, hum. There is no doubt that Johnson himself is committed *en principe* to all these pompous requirements, just as he is really committed to most of his Dick Minim's critical commonplaces. But the positioning of these requirements within the established dynamics of *Rasselas* gives them the sort of comic overtones which turn any show of excess toward farce. It is the language of Imlac's discourse that helps tip us off: the sly exposure is accomplished by words like *all, incessant,* and *every.*

And yet at the same time Imlac *is* Johnson rather than a mere objective target of gentle ridicule. But he is Johnson in the very special, complex way in which, in Dryden's *Essay of Dramatic Poesy,* "Neander" is Dryden, that is, articulates the views that Dryden's mature consideration can be conceived probably to approve. But look what Dryden the author does with Neander-Dryden just after Neander has finished his impressive peroration:

Neander was pursuing this discourse so eagerly that Eugenius had called to him twice or thrice ere he took notice that the barge stood still and they were at the foot of Somerset Stairs, where they had appointed it to land.

So eagerly suggests the reason for Dryden's smile; so does *ere he took notice.*

The beginning of Johnson's next chapter indicates what he has derived from Dryden's *Essay.* The opening of Chapter 11 serves to place these all-but-impossible ideal requirements for the poet, requirements unmodified in any way by the conditions of actual life as it must be lived, in their proper human context:

Imlac now felt the enthusiastic fit, and was proceeding to aggrandize his own profession, when [Rasselas] cried out, 'Enough! thou hast convinced me that no human being can ever be a poet. . . .'

'To be a poet,' said Imlac, 'is indeed very difficult.'

'So difficult,' returned the prince, 'that I will at present hear no more of his labors. . . .'

By thus reminding ourselves of the context in which Imlac's remarks on poetry take place we can recover some sense of just how complicated Johnson is as a critic and theorist of literature. He is certainly not a magisterial "Dr." Johnson dignifying his stuffy prejudices by couching them in a bullying style: he is poor, bored, frightened, impatient, self-conscious, inconsistent Samuel Johnson, much more like the rest of us than we may have imagined.

In considering T. S. Eliot's achievement in criticism, Richard Poirier has noticed our natural desire to simplify what is lively, complex, and natural into a notable, memorizable, and indeed teachable body of dicta. Eliot's essential critical principles, Poirier observes, have been severely vulgarized by being detached from a most subtle rhetorical context. And he goes on to say:

Johnson has been similarly vulgarized and for much the same reason. Recollected, Eliot [read Johnson as well] is a poet-critic of provoking decisiveness; re-read, he becomes again so full of intelligent nuance that we are forced to see why frailer minds like our own have wanted to impose decisiveness upon him.[7]

We have too often imposed decisiveness on Johnson ("[The poet] does not number the streaks of the tulip!") just because our need to recall and exhibit his critical opinions has little use for his own nuance and complexity. Like most good critical intelligences, Johnson does not "hold" views—he entertains them or experiences them or tries them on as appropriate spectacles for scrutinizing the work at hand. It is just this in him, by the way, that Boswell finds puzzling.

Rasselas's treatment of Imlac's grandiosity reflects Johnson's own perception of the ultimate vanity of the life of writing. The delusions of grandeur and authority which an auctorial consciousness easily generates are to be disciplined by a constant return to the condition and business of actual humanity. This necessary return is what is enacted in the humiliation of the Flying-Machine

Projector, the exposure of the plausible Stoic, and the puncturing of Imlac's pomposities. The theme of great expectations impossible to realize is the substance of *Rasselas*. And even if a great expectation momentarily appears to have been realized, what is achieved is certain to bespeak, as Imlac says, "the insufficiency of human enjoyments." The travelers' encounter with the Great Pyramid is a case in point.

Imlac's interpretation of the meaning of the Great Pyramid brings us close to the heart of *Rasselas*, and even more important for our purposes, it brings us near the center of Johnson's whole theory of writing. The Pyramid, Imlac says, testifies to the power of boredom as the central distinguishing human fact. Which is another way of saying, as Johnson does in *Rambler* 41, that man differs from animals in having an "exuberance of understanding" to which the objects of the present moment are always inadequate. And as he finds in *Rambler* 85, "The old peripatetic principle that *Nature abhors a vacuum* may be properly applied to the intellect, which will embrace anything, however absurd or criminal, rather than be wholly without an object." It is Johnson's understanding of this principle that lies behind his frequent expressions of sympathy for ne'er-do-wells, backsliders, and even petty criminals. Mrs. Thrale was once tut-tutting about someone who was "profligate and wild," who "followed the girls, or sat still at the gaming-table." Johnson retorted: "Why, life must be filled up . . . , and the man who is not capable of intellectual pleasures must content himself with such as his senses can afford." There is a rare absence of irony in Johnson's presentation of Imlac's conclusions on the Great Pyramid: to the word *incessantly*, as Imlac uses it now, Johnson is fully committed. The Pyramid, Imlac says,

seems to have been erected only in compliance with that hunger of imagination which preys incessantly upon life, and must always be appeased by some employment. Those who have already all that they can enjoy must enlarge their desires. He that has built for use till use is supplied must begin to build for vanity, and extend his plan to the utmost power of human performance, that he may not be soon reduced to form another wish.

I consider [the Pyramid] as a monument to the insufficiency of human enjoyments.

Works of literature are like the Pyramids in being quarried and assembled from existing materials, and, as the *Lives of the Poets* will imply, the motive that urges the writer to project and execute a piece of writing is the same motive—attended with the same ironic consequences—as that impelling a Pharaoh to "build for vanity." Some of the ironic consequences of writings being like Pyramids are explored in *Rambler* 106:

An assurance of unfading laurels and immortal reputation is the settled reciprocation of civility between amicable writers. To raise *monuments more durable than brass, and more conspicuous than pyramids* has been long the common boast of literature; but among the innumerable architects that erect columns to themselves, far the greater part, either for want of durable materials or of art to dispose them, see their edifices perish as they are towering to completion, and those few that for awhile attract the eye of mankind are generally weak in the foundation, and soon sink by the saps of time.

And the same pathetic motive that causes pyramids and writing also causes reading. It is the "hunger of imagination" that urges a reader to encounter literature in the first place and, on rare occasions testifying to the consummate skill of the author, actually to "read books through." Such occasions were rare for Johnson, who once said, "I have read few books through; they are generally so repulsive that I cannot."[8]

Johnson's capacity for boredom was profound. As Mrs. Thrale noticed,

The vacuity of life had at some early period of his life struck so forcibly on [his] mind . . . that it became by repeated impression his favorite hypothesis, and the general tenor of his reasonings generally ended there, wherever they might begin.

So extraordinary was his capacity for being bored that he disliked reading even more than writing. Once discussing with Boswell rates of payment for book reviews in journals like the *Monthly Review* and the *Critical Review*, he tells him that the author is paid by the printer's sheet, which makes sixteen pages of printed text:

BOSWELL. 'Pray, Sir, by a sheet of review is it meant that it shall be all of the writer's own composition? or are extracts made from the book reviewed deducted?' JOHNSON. 'No, Sir, it is a sheet, no matter of what.' BOSWELL. 'I think that it is not reasonable.' JOHNSON. 'Yes, Sir, it is. A man will more easily write a sheet all his own than read an octavo volume to get extracts.'

"All pleasure," he says in the *Preface to Shakespeare*, "consists in variety." The reason Homer is the greatest writer of narrative and Shakespeare the greatest writer of drama is ultimately and simply that, being the most varied, they are the least boring. The imagination of the reader is incessantly being gnawed by hunger, and this continuous pressure of appetite, which is contented not at all by run-of-the-mill writing, is appeased finally by Homer and Shakespeare and Milton, almost alone. As Johnson says of Shakespeare,

every man finds his mind more strongly seized by the tragedies of Shakespeare than of any other writer; others please us by particular speeches, but he always makes us anxious for the event, and has per-haps excelled all but Homer in securing the first purpose of a writer, by exciting restless and unquenchable curiosity, and compelling him that reads his work to read it through.

Notice the language: the mind is not entertained or amused but *seized*; where others please us, he makes us *anxious for the event*; even the normally bored are *compelled* to read the work through.

Just as countless particular physical laws derive from the General Theory of Relativity, so in Johnson countless particular critical responses derive from the General Theory of Boredom. For as he says and understands, "What is nearest us touches us most," and the opposite is equally true. Thus the conceits of Metaphysical poetry can gratify the curiosity and assuage the boredom of only those few readers who share the perverse, local bent of mind that can see the separation of lovers as usefully resembling the separated points of a draughtsman's compass. The technical and nautical language of Dryden's *Annus Mirabilis* can awake an echo only in the bosoms of those professionally acquainted with it before the reading of the poem. The boredom of life drives us to literature, and we are frustrated and embittered when we encounter there, after all our pains, things that are "unaffecting" or "remote," to use two of Johnson's favorite terms of disvalue. His whole central premise that literature must disclose "general nature" rather than mirror odd local details reposes on his general theory of boredom: the greatest good of the greatest number—that is, the deepest satisfaction of the universal hunger of imagination—can be achieved only if the writer uses his work to transmit to the largest possible audience "general and transcendental truths, which will always be the same." "The only end of writing," as he says while finding Soame Jenyns's book insufficient, "is to enable the readers better to enjoy life, or better to endure it." The likelihood of readers shutting books or even throwing them away in boredom and frustration is an ever-present probability underlying many a Johnsonian critical observation. Thus in the *Life of Dryden*:

The reader may be weary though the critic may commend. Works of imagination excel by their allurement and delight; by their power of attracting and detaining the attention. That book is good in vain which the reader throws away. He only is the master who keeps the mind in pleasing captivity; whose pages are perused with eagerness, and in hope of new pleasure are perused again; and whose conclusion is perceived with an eye of sorrow, such as the traveler casts upon departing day.

If enjoyment be defined—as Johnson does define it—as the temporary alleviation of boredom, the writer hoping to perform this operation must first be aware how bored his readers are in their essential human nature. He must then know which things from the public stock of actions and themes are most likely to alleviate boredom. It is not easy for a writer, unless he is extraordinarily gifted, to know what is boring and what isn't. The road to this knowledge is a profound understanding of human nature in general. Matthew Prior, Johnson tells us, lacked this understanding, with the result that his long poem *Solomon* is deficient in "that without which all other [merits] are of small avail, the power of engaging attention and alluring curiosity." He goes on:

Tediousness is the most fatal of all faults; negligences or errors are single and local, but tediousness pervades the whole: other faults are censured and forgotten, but the power of tediousness propagates itself. He that is weary the first hour is more weary the second; . . .

And ironically it is the very process of writing that prevents an author's perceiving how tedious he is becoming. The process goes like this: the author is so bored that he decides to write; as he writes, the hunger of his imagination is gradually appeased as he forces himself to make decisions, to turn over alternative phrasings in his mind, to locate synonyms in his memory (or in his dictionary), to decide where he shall next direct his attention. *His* mind, at least, is momentarily full with all these distractions of choice. As Johnson puts it,

[Tediousness,] this pernicious failure, is that which an author is least able to discover. We are seldom tiresome to ourselves; and the act of composition fills and delights the mind with change of language and succession of images: every couplet when produced is new, and novelty is the great source of pleasure.

Likewise, all writing is produced with great labor, and, Johnson asks, "Who is willing to think that he has been laboring in vain?" The author thus is supplied with numerous efficient motives for concealing from himself the quantum of tediousness that he may sometimes suspect in what he is writing.

Taking Imlac's interpretation of the Pyramid as the center of *Rasselas*, we can agree with M. J. C. Hodgart that the book constitutes "a serious study, almost the first in literature, of that scourge

of modern man—*taedium vitae*. It is not quite the first"—Burton's
Anatomy of Melancholy is that.[9] But we remember that Burton's
is the only book that, as Boswell reports, "ever took [Johnson] out
of bed two hours sooner than he wished to rise." The young
people's earnest quest for "The Choice of Life" in *Rasselas* makes
them perhaps the earliest fictional characters to ask the questions
posed by the society lady in *The Waste Land*, questions which have
become central in twentieth-century writing:

> 'What shall I do now? What shall I do?
> I shall rush out as I am, and walk the street
> With my hair down, so. What shall we do tomorrow?
> What shall we ever do?'

It is boredom that has driven the Prince and his sister out of
the Happy Valley in the first place, and it is boredom of a new
but equally wearing sort that drives them back to Abyssinia again.
Johnson knows that he is approaching the end of *Rasselas* because
he is reaching his contracted word-length; but the young travelers
know they are reaching the end because they begin to perceive that
the whole action they have been playing out, the illusioned inquiry
into the correct choice of life, can end only in more of the disappointment and frustration, the false expectation and real disgust,
which they have repeatedly courted. They finally decide that enough
is enough and that they should abandon their quest. The final
chapter, "The Conclusion, in Which Nothing is Concluded," will
strike us as the most comic of all. A premise of the whole quest has
been that those occupied in it are capable of learning from what
they encounter. Without this assumption, the whole excursion of
inquiry becomes a palpable waste of time. But the last chapter
reveals that even this assumption has been more shaky than we
have imagined.

What the travelers have been shown over and over again is the
vanity of human wishes, the psychological impossibility of gratifying human desires. They have been shown this by a series of specific

exempla exposing the unsatisfactoriness of various choices of life: the life of solitary devotion, for example, the life of learning, and the life of political power. Now confined to their quarters by the flooding of the Nile, they have ample time for speculation, and Johnson allows them each one more choice. The wishes they make are ironic not only because they can't possibly be fulfilled: they are ironic in a new and more important way. Each wish betrays the secret lust for power over others which, among decent, cultivated people like these, cloaks itself in proclaimed motives of beneficent intention. Perhaps it is because the travelers have not noticed this ambition for power in themselves that their inquiries have all come to nothing.

Pekuah, Nekayah's maid, chooses, she says, to enter a convent. "She was weary," Johnson writes, "of expectation and disgust, and would gladly be fixed in some unvariable state"—as if the hunger of the imagination could be appeased by mechanical claustration. But the important thing about Pekuah's wish is that, in her fantasy of convent life, she naturally assumes that she will be top dog— in her case, prioress.

Nekayah's final choice of life is similar to Pekuah's. It takes a more secular but no less self-aggrandizing turn. She proposes to found a women's college because she has decided that, "of all sublunary things, knowledge [is] the best." Or at least a regard for learning is her announced motive; her actual motive Johnson ironically tucks away in the tiny dependent clause *in which she would preside*:

She desired first to learn all sciences, and then proposed to found a college of learned women, in which she would preside, that, by conversing with the old and educating the young, she might divide her time between the acquisition and communication of wisdom, and raise up for the next age models of prudence, and patterns of piety.

Uh huh. Accustomed by Johnson to attend to the most minute features of syntactical emphasis, we perceive that Nekayah is less concerned with either wisdom, prudence, or piety than excited by the heady image of domination, exercised through the very modern technique of academic administration.

Rasselas regales himself with a different but related fantasy. Where Nekayah wants to domineer in a women's college, Rasselas wants to run a little kingdom, of which he will, of course, be king. Just as Nekayah conceals her secret lust for domination beneath a professed admiration for learning, Rasselas conceals his beneath a proclaimed devotion to justice. "The prince," says Johnson, "desired a little kingdom, in which he might administer justice in his own person, and see all the parts of government with his own eyes; ./. ." But his problem is the insatiable hunger of his very human imagination, for despite his announced wish to have only a "little" kingdom, "he could never fix the limits of his dominion, and was always adding to the number of his subjects."

Even here Johnson is not being all that original: wishes of exactly this sort are a well established eighteenth-century satiric convention. We can compare Gulliver's wishes when he encounters the Struldbruggs, the famous Immortals of Luggnagg, and permits himself to rise to an *O altitudo* speculating on the happiness that would be his if he could live forever. After his first wish, which is openly a wish for riches serving as a sort of enabling act for the wishes that follow, he seems as adept as Rasselas and his companions at contriving wishes which cloak self-regard and the will to power beneath apparent motives of beneficence and public service:

I would from my earliest youth apply myself to the study of arts and sciences, by which I should arrive in time *to excel all others* in learning . . . . I would carefully record every action and event of consequence that happened in the public, impartially draw the characters of the several successions of princes and great ministers of state, with my own observations on every point. I would exactly set down the several changes in customs, languages, fashions, dress, diet, and diversions. By all which acquirements I should be a living treasury of knowledge and wisdom, and *certainly become the oracle of the nation* [my emphases].

Close as he may come to embracing the image of the objective archivist or historian, Gulliver's impulse to self-advantage is such that he can attain only to a fantasy of political power. Even Johnson's Dick Minim, sad as he is, has yet enough strength to hanker after domination. In *Idler* 60 and 61, his ambition of founding a British Academy of Criticism is clearly attended by the idea that he will not be the lowest or newest member. He is, after all, already presiding "four nights a week in a Critical Society selected by himself, where he is heard without contradiction...."

The final wishes of both Imlac and the now-recovered astronomer establish the commonsense norm against which the wishes of their young friends are seen to be both vain and corrupt: "Imlac and the astronomer were contented to be driven along the stream of life, without directing their course to any particular port." Quietism is not being recommended; contentment is.

But Johnson does not dismiss his young people in a state of total folly: he is finally willing to grant that their prolonged wandering in the real world has brought them some of the benefits of awareness. "Of these wishes that they had formed," he says, "they well knew that none could be obtained." But we are not certain that it is not the prospect of practical rather than psychological impediments that produces this knowledge. Johnson dismisses them in so subtle a state of suspension that, for an instant, they almost violate the genre of which they are an element and come to resemble real people. But his last sentence restores them to the world of Oriental Tale where they belong: "They deliberated awhile what was to be done, and resolved, when the inundation should cease, to return to Abyssinia."

Johnson's whole version of experience in *Rasselas* suggests one reason he is so ready to recognize and confess the domination of genre in writing. What he implies throughout this naïve quest for the right choice of life is that others have been on the quest before, others have asked the same questions, encountered the same perplexities, and experienced the same repeated descents from the ideal. Miranda and Prospero are two who have been there before, acting out in one memorable moment the roles of Nekayah and Imlac:

Miranda:	O brave new world
That has such people in't!	
Prospero:	'Tis new to thee.

What Johnson is implying is that the modes of common and accidental life are satisfactory so long as we don't over-invest in them. In the same way, the common genres, received from the long experience of writers and their readers, are satisfactory so long as we recognize them for what they are: customs and usages, mere codes within which meaning can take place. Emphasizing the genres results in a supreme convenience: their recognition and acceptance relieves the writer of the idle self-torment of trying to devise a wholly new form for everything he writes, a form which finally, after all the agonies of choice, will convey in itself little to the reader to whom it is unprecedented. That is, the genres free him from choices that are meaningless. As Johnson says in *Rambler* 1, wishing for some conventional way to execute the first paper in a periodical series, "Judgment [is] wearied with the perplexity of being forced upon choice, where there [is] no motive to preference." Meaningless choices, no matter how great an illusion of importance and self-sufficiency they supply to the chooser, are finally only distracting. As he argues in *Idler* 85, the anthologies and compilations "poured lately from the press have been seldom made at any great expense of time or inquiry, and therefore only serve to distract choice without supplying any real want." And while people are busy "choosing" they must neglect doing something more useful; as he says in *Idler* 94, "The continual multiplication of books not only distracts choice but disappoints inquiry."

Human nature is too problematical and irrational to make self-conscious "choosing" much more than a delusive and wasteful exercise. It is the nature of man, Johnson says in *Rambler* 184, "to close tedious deliberations with hasty resolves, and after long

consultations with reason to refer the question to caprice. . . ."
Economy of time is the guiding principle of the experienced, for,
as Geoffrey Tillotson perceives,

In *Rasselas*, perhaps uniquely, time is seen as a prime condition
governing human life—indeed as *the* prime condition, for the worth
of human life is to be measured, as Johnson sees it, by how time has
been used.[10]

Thus Johnson in *Rambler* 19:

After a great part of life spent in inquiries which can never be resolved,
the rest must often pass in repenting the unnecessary delay, and can be
useful to few other purposes than to warn others against the same folly,
and to show that, of two states of life equally consistent with religion
and virtue, he who chooses earliest chooses best.

The implicit recommendation in *Rasselas* of a wise economy of
effort is an expression of that sense of economy underlying Johnson's acceptance of genres. His adherence to the genre system has
the empirical wisdom of Parson Adams's injunction: "Do not go
about impossibilities." He once wrote to the virtual boy James
Boswell, "Life is not long, and too much of it must not pass in
idle deliberation how it shall be spent; deliberation, which those
who begin it by prudence, and continue it with subtlety, must, after
long expense of thought, conclude by chance." And in a letter to
Mrs. Thrale, although he is talking about literal traveling, what
he says illuminates the meaning both of the young people's ad-
ventures in *Rasselas* and of the actual, homely facts of literary
composition and transmission. "The use of traveling," he writes,
"is to regulate imagination by reality, and instead of thinking how
things may be, to see them as they are." It is a lesson boys need to
learn early, especially if they want to write.

CHAPTER 9

The Irony of Literary Careers

Johnson's *Lives of the Poets* belongs to an age distinguished for its historical and judicial prose. It could not have been executed at all except in that literary context. When we look at the general literary output of Johnson's time, we will probably not conclude that great poems make up a large part of its production. Nor would we want to say, despite the novels of Smollett and Sterne and the comedies of Goldsmith and Sheridan, that it is the fiction or the drama of the age that give it its special literary identity. Its special identity arises rather from its extraordinary production of works of intellectual, critical, and polemic prose. Although we perceive a waxing and waning of fads like graveyard poems, ballad imitations, odes strutting on tiptoe, and picaresque, sentimental, Shandean, and Gothic novels, the stream of unforgettable discursive prose is constant. It is what establishes the norm.

There is hardly a year without its masterpiece. We have Hume's *Philosophical Essays Concerning Human Understanding* in 1748; Johnson's *Rambler* from 1750 to 1752; Hume's *History of England* from 1754 to 1762; William Robertson's *History of Scotland* in 1759; Blackstone's *Commentaries on the Laws of England* from 1765 to 1769; the first of Sir Joshua Reynolds's *Discourses on Art* in 1769; Adam Smith's *Wealth of Nations* in 1776; Gibbon's *History of the Decline and Fall of the Roman Empire* from 1776 to 1788; the histories of music by Sir John Hawkins and Charles Burney in 1776; Robertson's *History of America* in 1777; Hume's *Dialogues Concerning Natural Religion* in 1779; Johnson's *Lives of the Poets* from 1779 to 1781; Boswell's *Journal of a Tour to the Hebrides* in 1785; Gilbert White's *Natural History of Selborne* in 1789; Burke's *Reflections on the Revolution in France* in 1790; and finally Boswell's *Life of Johnson* in 1791. In focusing on the *Lives of the Poets* we must be mindful of its firm location within this context of prose enlisted for purposes essentially legal, historical, skeptical, and ethical. Which is to say that the thematic obsessions of the *Lives of the Poets* are those of the other prose works that surround it, and which lend it a method and a special vision. Like these other works, it is concerned with the nature and, more importantly, the limits of human achievement. It assumes what its surrounding works assume: the continuity and dignity of the uniquely human—man's will, conscience, and rage for order, ironically menaced by man's ever-present impulse to delusion, triviality, incompetence, vanity, sloth, and plain stupidity.

The usual way of "dealing with" the *Lives of the Poets* is to attend to a very few of the Lives—those of Cowley, Milton, Dryden, Addison, Pope, Gray—or even to neglect everything but the set pieces of criticism, like the workout on the Metaphysical Poets in the *Life of Cowley*, or the treatments of *Lycidas* and *Paradise Lost*. As Eliot has said, speaking of the neglect of Johnson's writings in general, "As for the *Lives of the Poets*, few educated persons have read more than half a dozen of them, and of these half-dozen, what is remembered is chiefly the passages with which everyone disagrees."[1] What attention has been brought to the various Lives has largely been directed to the question, What is *in* them? They have been regarded more as inert receptacles ("critical biographies") for sound or erroneous or even comical doctrine than as artistic things in themselves.

Everyone would agree that the *Lives* is Johnson's greatest piece of writing. But it would be harder to specify exactly in what its greatness consists. The sheer magnitude of it, for one thing, is impressive: 52 separate Lives, 378,000 words—the equivalent of five modern novels—produced from Johnson's 68th to his 72nd year in an environment when writing at 70 was like one of our contemporaries writing at 105. Impressive too is the fineness of the taste in the *Lives*. For perceiving the inferiority of Gray's odes and Shenstone's elegies—works most people were praising—Johnson earns marks as high as Francis Jeffrey for observing of Wordsworth's *Excursion* that "This will never do." Time has indicated that it has not done, any more than Gray's odes or Shenstone's elegies have. Anna Seward was so far wrong as to assert: "From the publication of the *Lives of the Poets* I date the downfall of just poetic taste in this kingdom." As evidence of Johnson's faulty taste she offers this: "I heard him pronounce [James] Beattie's charming *Minstrel* a dull, heavy, uninteresting fragment whose second book he could never prevail upon himself to look into." Johnson was right. And as conclusive proof of his aesthetic obtuseness she tells us that "[William] Mason's *English Garden* he calls a very miserable piece of labored insignificance."[2] He was right again. Just as right as he was in the *Dictionary* to sense that *vastidity* and *vaulty* are jargon rather than English. They have not done, either.

The *Lives* is impressive also in its sheer bravery. It must be the most honest critical work ever written. What other critic could earn the right to say of anything, as Johnson says of Congreve's romance *Incognita*, "I would rather praise it than read it"? Boswell says: "Johnson said he expected to be attacked on account of his *Lives of the Poets*. 'However,' said he, 'I would rather be attacked than unnoticed. For the worst thing you can do to an author is to be silent as to his works.'" And Johnson was attacked. Horace Walpole, furious at Johnson's dismissal of his friend Gray's odes, concluded that "Prejudice, and bigotry, and pride, and presumption, and arrogance, and pedantry are the hags that brew his ink." Even the pacific William Cowper, annoyed by Johnson's lack of enthusiasm about Milton's non-epic achievement, was moved to write a friend: "O! I could thresh his old jacket, till I made his pension jingle in his pocket." I don't want to suggest that risking the rage of Walpole or Cowper constitutes bravery, but I do want to suggest that one thing that attracts us to the *Lives* and holds us to it once we are in contact is its very quality of courage verging even on impudence or folly, a quality we find elsewhere in Johnson's behavior. Boswell writes:

One day, at Mr. Beauclerk's house in the country, when two large dogs were fighting, he went up to them and beat them till they separated; and at another time, when told of the danger there was that a gun might burst if charged with many balls, he put in six or seven and fired it off against a wall. Mr. Langton told me that when they were swimming together near Oxford, he cautioned Dr. Johnson against a pool which was reckoned particularly dangerous; upon which Johnson swam directly into it. . . . In the playhouse at Lichfield, as Mr. Garrick informed me, Johnson for a moment having quitted a chair which was placed for him between the side-scenes, a gentleman took possession of it, and when Johnson on his return civilly demanded his seat, rudely refused to give it up; upon which Johnson laid hold of it, and tossed him and the chair into the pit.

A critic accustomed to soliciting risks like these is not likely either to misrepresent his own critical responses or to be at all impressed by what other people say they think.

Poor Boswell, with his customary lack of sophistication about the complicated and sometimes disingenuous springs of literary work, testifies that he

was somewhat disappointed in finding that the edition of the English poets, for which [Johnson] was to write Prefaces and Lives, was not an undertaking directed by him; but that he was to furnish a Preface and Life to any poet the booksellers pleased. I asked him if he would do this to any dunce's work, if they should ask him. JOHNSON. 'Yes, Sir; and *say* he was a dunce.'

The publishers did let Johnson add a few poets of his own choosing, pre-eminently Sir Richard Blackmore and Isaac Watts, who had recommended themselves to Johnson by versifying Christian materials. Of his choice of Watts he explained, "I wish to distinguish Watts, a man who never wrote but for a good purpose." The limits of the project were these: no poet who wrote before the Restoration was to be included, nor any living poet. The series of Lives begins thus with Cowley, who died in 1667, and ends with Gray, who died in 1771. In effect, Johnson is writing a critical interpretation of modern poetry, that is, of "The New Poetry": in interpreting a new poetry to readers perhaps sighing for the old, his role is not all that different from F. R. Leavis's in *New Bearings in English Poetry* or Cleanth Brooks's in *Modern Poetry and the Tradition.*

The signing of the contract between Johnson and the publishers, always a moment of satisfaction for the publisher but of ritual anxiety for an author like Johnson, took place on Easter Eve, 1777. We can suspect that this date was no accident, for Johnson managed to finish the whole project by Easter, 1781, and throughout the progress of the writing he seems to set his sequential deadlines for groups of the Lives at Easter time. Just as for most modern academics the working year runs from September to June (or, for some who write, from June to September), the literary year for Johnson runs from Easter to Easter. Thus he had the Lives of Waller, Denham, and Butler ready for Easter, 1778. Addison, Prior, and Rowe were done by the self-imposed deadline of Easter, 1779. Granville, Sheffield, Collins, and Pitt were done by Easter, 1780. He had behaved the same way with the *Rambler* and the *Idler*: he brought the *Rambler* to a close on March 14, 1752—Easter fell on March 29 that year; and he concluded the *Idler* on Holy Saturday, 1760, writing:

As the last *Idler* is published in that solemn week which the Christian world has always set apart for the examination of the conscience, the review of life, the extinction of earthly desires, and the renovation of holy purposes, I hope that my readers are already disposed to view every incident with seriousness, and improve it by meditation;

He is working up to the theme of redeeming the time:

and that when they see this series of trifles brought to a conclusion, they will consider that by outliving the *Idler* they have passed weeks, months, and years which are now no longer in their power; that an end must in time be put to everything great as to everything little; that to life must come its last hour, and to this system of being its last day, the hour at which probation ceases and repentance will be vain; the day in which every work of the hand and imagination of the heart shall be brought to judgment, and an everlasting futurity shall be determined by the past.

When we see Johnson setting Easter as his deadline for the *Lives* as for other projects, we perceive that this project has a distinct quality of religious obligation about it. It becomes part of his customary Easter self-examinations and meditations on his own and on general human frailty. It takes the tincture of his own private devotions. So seriously did he regard Easter Week that, as Boswell says, "He would not even look at a proof-sheet of his 'Life of Waller' on Good-Friday." We remember his memorandum when the project was finished: "Last week I published *The Lives of the Poets*, written, I hope, in such a manner as may tend to the promotion of piety." Hence the savaging of the smart-aleck clergyman Swift; hence the reprehension of the mingling of Pagan and Christian in *Lycidas*.

We catch the tone of a religious humility teetering right on the brink of irony when he writes to Boswell at the outset of the project: "I am engaged to write little lives, and little prefaces, to a little edition of the English poets." Again, while working on the first of the Lives, Cowley, in November, 1777, he writes Mrs. Thrale in the same vein: "It will be proper for me to work pretty diligently now for some time. I hope to get through, though so many weeks have passed. Little lives and little criticisms may serve."

In writing the *Lives* he is doing many things at once: he is gratifying his Sovereign, who we remember had "expressed a desire to have the literary biography of this country ably executed, and proposed to Dr. Johnson to undertake it"; he is also making money; he is also promoting piety. For another thing, he is consciously testing his own powers, which in his sixty-ninth year he suspects to be failing slightly. For the man who said on his deathbed, "I will be conquered, I will not capitulate," the project of the *Lives* is in one sense a test and an exercise of the powers required to resist intellectual dissolution. He seems to imply as much in this memorandum of 1778, written, characteristically, the day after Easter:

I have written a little of the *Lives of the Poets*, I think with all my usual vigor. I have made sermons perhaps as readily as formerly. My memory is less faithful in retaining names and, I am afraid, in retaining occurrences. Of this vacillation and vagrancy of mind I impute a great part to a fortuitous and unsettled life, and therefore purpose to spend my time with more method.

And when he comes to consider Waller's Sacred Poems, "the work of Waller's declining life," he writes as one conscious of a competition to resist senility:

That natural jealousy which makes every man unwilling to allow much excellence in another always produces a disposition to believe that the mind grows old with the body, and that he whom we are now forced to confess superior is hastening daily to a level with ourselves. By delighting to think this of the living we learn to think it of the dead; and [Elijah] Fenton, with all his kindness for Waller, has the luck to mark the exact time when his genius passed the zenith, which he places at his fifty-fifth year.

But Johnson will resist such assumptions by both argument and example:

This is to allot the mind but a small portion. Intellectual decay is doubtless not uncommon; but it seems not to be universal. Newton was, in his eighty-fifth year, improving his *Chronology* a few days before his death; and Waller appears not, in my opinion, to have lost at eighty-two any part of his poetical power.

Another of Johnson's motives in the *Lives*, perceived by Mrs. Thrale, was his desire to show off and to astonish his audience. He knew more about literature and literary history than any living person, and he was delighted to have the opportunity to do exactly what he could do best. Mrs. Thrale writes: "Mr. Johnson's knowledge of literary history was extensive and surprising: he knew every adventure of every book you could name almost, and was exceedingly pleased with the opportunity which writing the Poets' Lives gave him to display it." To see the "majestic teacher of moral and religious wisdom" playing the peacock will not, by this time, surprise us.

Despite all the motives urging him to proceed in the writing with decent speed and even some pleasure, as usual he had trouble, and for the usual reason—he disliked writing so much. Of the *Lives* he confesses: "I wrote [them] in my usual way, dilatorily and hastily, unwilling to work, and working with vigor and haste." The main reason he hated to write is that one must be alone to write, and when one is alone with the mind undistracted by the constantly varying dynamics of conversation and personal intercourse, one must encounter only oneself. And when Johnson encounters himself he is brought face to face with the terrifying gulf between capacity and accomplishment. Those ill-invested talents generate nightmare images: time advances and judgment approaches with ever-accelerating urgency. We must expect to find the *Lives* touched very often by Johnson's unflagging awareness of the inexorable advance of Christian time.

But for all their undeniable personality, the individual lives are constructed in a highly formalized, conventionalized way. They must be, for Johnson is virtually filling in the same paradigm fifty-two times. To treat the same things in the same order in each Life is to save time for both writer and reader: the writer—like

Imlac being "driven along the stream of life"—liberates himself from the obligation to make needless decisions, and the reader quickly learns where to look in a given Life for what he wants. As Johnson once told Joseph Baretti, justifying and at the same time patronizing monastic life, "Men will submit to any rule, by which they may be exempted from the tyranny of caprice and of chance." The "rule" which the *Lives* establishes is a tripartite form: the first element is a biography; the second is a "character" (sketch), after the seventeenth-century model; the third is a critical essay which considers the poet's works in chronological order. As usual, Johnson is not making up this form: he is taking it from the public armory, going this time to Fontenelle and imitating the *notices biographiques* in his *Recueil de plus belles pièces des Poètes Français* (1692).[3] By adopting Fontenelle's tripartite division of his brief essays—life, character, criticism—Johnson both saves time and, more important, secures the reader within a world of the apparently familiar.

Johnson also pays his respects to the familiar by re-presenting some of his own earlier published materials: the *Life of Savage*, of course, first published thirty-seven years earlier; the *Life of Roscommon*, published thirty-five years earlier; the essay on Pope's Epitaphs, a piece of writing twenty-five years old; and the character sketch of William Collins, an essay eighteen years old. As he proceeds with the writing, he has recourse occasionally to the 1753 *Lives of the Poets* compiled by Robert Shiels and Theophilus Cibber, a work consisting of 202 Lives of poets from Chaucer to John Banks. Johnson borrows from it for his Lives of Hammond, Rowe, Fenton, Smith, Pitt, Philips, and Thomson. The irony is that much of what he is taking he is rather repossessing than pilfering, for it was Johnson who, much earlier, had given Shiels the materials for the Lives of these authors.[4]

But writing requires thematic paradigms as well as structural ones. I think we must take the *Life of Savage*, published first in 1744, to be the immediate thematic original of the subsequent Lives. The *Life of Savage* is not the formal paradigm—what in the later Lives become Parts I and III are here fused, and Part II, the "character," comes at the end—but it does establish a model for the theme of the *Lives*, which proves to be the vanity of literary wishes and the irony of literary hopes.

In trying to answer the question, What is *The Lives of the English Poets*, we can begin by disabusing ourselves of the notion that it is primarily a series of biographies, even if not "objective" ones. The title itself is not Johnson's: it appeared first on the pirated Dublin edition and was adopted as presumably more descriptive than the original title by G. B. Hill for his influential edition of 1905. The original title was not *Lives* but *Prefaces*: the whole title is *Prefaces, Biographical and Critical, to the Works of the English Poets*. Bate points to some erroneous assumptions arising from the Victorian instinct for seeing biographical meaning everywhere:

[The *'Lives'*] were not written as an experiment in biographical criticism. Commissioned primarily to write 'a concise account of the *life* of each author,' [Johnson] . . . almost instinctively stretched these biographical prefaces into a form of literary criticism. They are biography turning into criticism, not criticism withdrawing into biography.[5]

And as we shall see, they are even more than mere criticism. The great prevailing error in the common view of Johnson's *Prefaces* is to take them for biographies, and to collect and bring to bear as a tool of exegesis and appraisal all Johnson's theory of biography. It seems to me that exactly the wrong way of proceeding is that of John Butt, who indicates his method thus: "I shall first survey Johnson's views on how biographies should be written, and I shall then consider how far he succeeded in writing Lives that illustrate his theories."[6] It is better to try to see what the Lives really are.

The designation of these works as Prefaces invites us to recall Johnson's sense of what a Preface is. James Northcote quotes him as saying,

There are two things . . . which I am confident I can do very well: one is an introduction to any literary work, stating what it is to contain, and how it should be executed in the most perfect manner; the other is a conclusion showing, from various causes, why the execution has not been equal to what the author promised to himself and to the public.

The theme of a Preface, thus, is ironic disappointment: its focus is necessarily on the comic and touching distance between human schemes and human accomplishments. By its very characteristics as genre a Preface is—it must be—about the frailty of man. As we have seen, Johnson's own Preface to the *Dictionary* is a good example, full of the imagery of noble-comic illusion followed by grim disappointment, of the fugitive delights of "design, while it is yet at a distance from execution," of "the dreams of a poet doomed at last to wake a lexicographer." We will never read the *Lives of the Poets* accurately if, taking each as biography or even as literary criticism, we allow ourselves to forget Johnson's stunning analysis of the pathology of literary hopes in *Rambler* 106:

No place affords a more striking conviction of the vanity of human hopes than a public library. For who can see the wall crowded on every side by mighty volumes, the works of laborious meditation and accurate inquiry, now scarcely known but by the catalog, and preserved only to increase the pomp of learning, without considering how many hours have been wasted in vain endeavors, how often imagination has anticipated the praises of futurity, how many statues have risen to the eye of vanity, how many ideal converts have elevated zeal, how often wit has exulted in the eternal infamy of his antagonists, and dogmatism has delighted in the gradual advances of his authority, the immutability of his decrees, and the perpetuity of his power.

All his life Johnson remembered his early teacher Tom Browne. He published, says Johnson, "a spelling-book, and dedicated it to the Universe; but I fear no copy of it can now be had." A Life of even Tom Browne would have its uses as a gripping and instructive ironic moral fable: as he says in *Idler* 102, virtually establishing at this early moment the necessary sardonic emphases of the later Lives,

Nothing detains the reader's attention more powerfully than deep involutions of distress or sudden vicissitudes of fortune, and these might be abundantly afforded by memoirs of the sons of literature. They are entangled by contracts which they know not how to fulfill, and obliged to write on subjects which they do not understand. Every publication is a new period of time from which some increase or declension of fame is to be reckoned. The gradations of a hero's life are from battle to battle, and of an author's from book to book.

Johnson is warning us: the *Prefaces, Biographical and Critical,* while remotely biography and less remotely literary criticism, are going to be essentially moral fables, and some are going to turn in the direction of the mock-heroic. Sometimes they will move toward sermon or moral exemplum, sometimes toward satire, comedy, or farce.

Indeed, everyone has noticed Johnson's carelessness about the purely biographical elements in the *Lives:* we can assume that he is not very interested in such matters. Verifying dates and facts bores him. When engaged in mere biographical narration, he is quite willing to cut corners, to borrow from others, to rest content with vagueness or with minor error. Edmund Blunden, in a parody *Life of Wordsworth* published with the subtitle "If Dr. Johnson Had Lived Rather Longer," catches exactly the Johnsonian tone of airy biographical negligence:

This writer was born in Sockermouth, in the north of England, about the year 1770. His father, an attorney, died shortly after, and left but slender means for the education of several children. Such instruction as could be had in the village grammar school the boy William obtained, and that he exhibited a respectable degree of application and ability his subsequent appearance on the books of St. John's College, Cambridge, may be held to prove.

. . .

About the year 1792 his republican morbidity drove him over the English Channel, where he masqueraded in the assumed name of Vaudracour among some French officers. Where there is looseness of politics, irregularity of conduct towards the female sex quickly prevails.

Vaudracour's chief victim, of whom we know only the name Julia, contrived to extort from him the legal acknowledgement of the paternity of their children, and if it be necessary to remark that Vaudracour extricated himself from the situation by a sudden flight to his own country, he at least continued to contribute to the maintenance of this miserable family, by quarterly remittances, until he mislaid the postal direction of Julia.[7]

Johnson's carelessness with the purely biographical element, so happily suggested by Blunden, indicates that his attention is elsewhere. In the year the final volume of the *Lives* was published, he suggests in conversation the sort of actions and motifs his attention has been fixed on during the past four years. Speaking of Walter Harte and his massive *History of Gustavus Adolphus* (1759), he says: "Poor man! He left London the day of the publication of his book, that he might be out of the way of the great praise he was to receive; and he was ashamed to return, when he found how ill his book had succeeded."

A persistent challenge in reading Johnson is distinguishing his topics from his subjects. The topic of the *Dictionary* is the discrimination of meanings in the English language; the subject—we deduce it from the energy lavished on the didactic illustrative quotations—is moral virtue. The topic of the *Prefaces, Biographical and Critical*, is the careers of recent poets and the relative value of their writings; the subject is the pathos of hope and the irony of all human and especially all literary careers. Robert Burns was an acute enough reader to sense an important part of what the *Lives* is about:

There is not among all the martyrologies that ever were penned so rueful a narrative as Johnson's *Lives of the Poets.*—In the comparative view of wretches, the criterion is not what they are doomed to suffer, but how they are formed to bear.

Johnson's decision to include the *Life of Savage* in the collection was essentially an act of sentimental commemoration. But it was an act that carried deep thematic consequences for the rest of the

Lives. By a sort of automatic parallelism, they tended to take on the tone of affectionate irony obviously appropriate to Savage's farcical, touching career. Johnson's achievement in the *Lives* as a whole is to convince us that this tone is only slightly less obviously appropriate to all literary careers. It is important to understand that Johnson's darkly comic view of the general life of writing is not one necessitated by the accidents of failure and frustration in the careers—many of them notably trivial—he happens to be assigned to write about. He is not, that is, deploring the state of things in the Restoration and his own time. He would treat with similar moral penetration any writing career, from Chaucer's to Joyce's.

Richard Savage was a literary Micawber. As we read Johnson's account of him, we experience two alternating reactions: we are moved by his instinctive sympathy for the feckless Savage's "complicated virtue," we are perhaps surprised that he can contrive so powerful an environmental defense of such an irresponsible, self-deluded, and self-destructive charlatan. Pointing to Savage's social circumstances as an explanation of his behavior, Johnson says,

> Those are no proper judges of his conduct who have slumbered away their time on the down of plenty; nor will any wise man easily presume to say, 'Had I been in Savage's condition, I should have lived or written better than Savage.'

Thus one of our reactions is to be touched by the warmth and sweet unreason of Johnson's identification with his hero. But our other reaction is to laugh, for throughout Johnson is at pains to emphasize the comic dimension of Savage's behavior. This he does without for a moment letting us forget that Savage is a victim—a victim of his relatives and even more a victim of his own passion and grandiosity. It is a complicated comedy we are given, a comedy which never stops implying that the narrator of it is, by his humanity, deeply implicated in it, just as we are.

First of all Savage is disowned by his wicked mother. With his aristocrat's lack of any professional preparation, what remains for him but to undertake a literary career?

All his assiduity and tenderness were without effect, for he could neither soften her heart nor open her hand, and was reduced to the utmost miseries of want while he was endeavoring to awaken the affection of a mother. He was therefore obliged to seek some other means of support; and, having no profession, became by necessity an author.

As Johnson proceeds to recount Savage's career, it becomes clear that his writing *con amore* this time—the whole *Life of Savage*, all 30,000 words of it, was finished in thirty-six hours—is in part the result of his perceiving himself in Savage and his own literary career in that of his luckless friend. We sense that we are in the presence of that kind of "autobiography disguised as biography" of which André Maurois speaks.[8] Is it Savage or Johnson who is the subject in the following?

Accidentally meeting two gentlemen, his acquaintances, . . . he went in with them to a neighboring coffee-house, and sat drinking till it was late, it being in no time of Mr. Savage's life any part of his character to be the first of the company that desired to separate.

Likewise, we feel that Johnson is fully aware of his complicity with Savage when he dwells upon "the insurmountable obstinacy of his spirit"; when he points out that compassion was his "distinguishing quality"; when he admires his almost impertinent assumption of his own free will; and when he points to the gulf between his noble principles and his comically ignoble practice:

These [noble] reflections . . . were . . . like many other maxims treasured up in his mind rather for show than use, and operated very little upon his conduct, however elegantly he might sometimes explain, or however forcibly he might inculcate them.

We think of Johnson earnestly exhorting himself and others to a total command of mind and body, and then having constant occasion to reprove himself for late rising. "If a jack is seen, a spit will be presumed."

As Johnson proceeds to juxtapose Savage's moral and literary ambitions with his constantly aborting schemes, he manages to incarnate Savage as a typical eighteenth-century anti-hero. He enrolls him in a large representative company of actual and fictive type-characters, all of them amiably inept men occupied in self-delusion and gentle self-destruction. Their perversion of their own admirable designs is caused in large part by their admirable energy. This company includes Lemuel Gulliver, Parson Adams, the Vicar of Wakefield, Uncle Toby, Bennet Langton, and James Boswell himself. It is characteristic of the eighteenth-century anti-hero that his life, as Sir John Hawkins says of Savage's, will be "a succession of disappointments." And it is characteristic of the conventional eighteenth-century depiction of the anti-hero that it will focus on these disappointments for purposes which are moral-comical rather than melodramatic. The anti-hero becomes a type of eighteenth-century man in general, diminished within an empirical world, with sufficient Lockean knowledge of his own mind to sense the conventionality of what goes on there and with sufficient Newtonian awareness of the universe to measure his own tininess within it.

The *Life of Savage* is conducted so that it becomes a virtual eighteenth-century type-comedy of the dynamics of hopes and "schemes." Savage is always scheming a recovery of his fortunes, and his schemes are always exploded either by his own grandiosity and ineptitude or by common ill luck. Typical is Johnson's account of Savage's lust for the Laureateship, left vacant by the death of Laurence Eusden in 1730. Savage's propensity to having his hopes frustrated is almost epic in size: it is so powerful that some of it appears to come off even on the King:

[Savage] exerted all the interest which his wit, or his birth, or his misfortunes could procure, to obtain, upon the death of Eusden, the place of Poet Laureate, and prosecuted his application with so much diligence that the King publicly declared it his intention to bestow it upon him; but such was the fate of Savage that even the King, when he intended his advantage, was disappointed in his schemes. . . . The Lord Chamberlain . . . either did not know the King's design, or did

not approve it, or thought the nomination of the Laureate an encroach-
ment upon his rights, and therefore bestowed the Laurel upon Colley
Cibber.

It is like the comedy of James Boswell soliciting his commission
in the Guards, or Parson Adams trustingly bearing to a London
publisher his quite unpublishable sermons. And Savage's comic
resilience is as striking as his comic energy. Here, too, he is like
Boswell or Adams. As Johnson points out, not even the "neglect
and contempt" which repeated failure and constant poverty brought
him ever depressed him; for, as Johnson writes,

he always preserved a steady confidence in his own capacity, and
believed nothing above his reach which he should at any time earnestly
endeavor to attain. He formed schemes . . . with regard to knowledge
and to fortune, and flattered himself with advances to be made in
science, as with riches, to be enjoyed in some distant period of his
life.

And all this scheming does him credit, for it testifies to the "lively
fancy" that marks him as an author. Johnson is aware that writers
are especially subject to self-delusion by schemes just because they
must work in solitude and are distinguished by thoughtfulness and
by liveliness of fancy. As he says in *Rambler* 41,

It is . . . much more common for the solitary and the thoughtful
to amuse themselves with schemes of the future than reviews of the
past. For the future is pliant and ductile, and will be easily molded by
a strong fancy into any form.

The life of writing offers very special temptations to live on self-
delusive hope. Johnson indicates why in *Rambler* 2:

Perhaps no class of the human species requires more to be cautioned
against this anticipation of happiness than those that aspire to the
name of authors. A man of lively fancy no sooner finds a hint moving
in his mind, than he makes momentous excursions to the press and
to the world, and with a little encouragement from flattery pushes
forward into future ages and prognosticates the honors to be paid him
when envy is extinct and faction forgotten. . . .

One long-standing scheme of Savage's was an elaborate sub-scription edition of his works. Needless to say, it never got off the ground:

This project of printing his works was frequently revived; and, as his proposals grew obsolete, new ones were printed with fresher dates. To form schemes for the publication was one of his favorite amusements; nor was he ever more at ease than when, with any friend who readily fell in with his schemes, he was adjusting the print, forming the advertisements, and regulating the dispersion of the new edition, which he really intended some time to publish. . . .

Like Rasselas and his sister, Savage is also susceptible to the scheme of pastoral felicity. A number of his friends and sympathizers, including Alexander Pope, accumulated a fund to support him at Swansea, well away from the temptations which London offered to grandiose expenditure. Johnson is perhaps nowhere more comic in the whole of the *Lives of the Poets* than in his account of Savage's pastoral hopes:

As he was ready to entertain himself with future pleasures, he had planned out a scheme of life for the country, of which he had no knowledge but from pastorals and songs. He imagined that he should be transported to scenes of flowery felicity, like those which one poet has reflected to another; and he projected a perpetual round of innocent pleasures, of which he suspected no interruption from pride, or ignorance, or brutality.

With these expectations he was so enchanted that when he was once gently reproached by a friend for submitting to live upon a subscription, and advised rather by a resolute exertion of his abilities to support himself, he could not bear to debar himself from the happiness which was to be found in the calm of a cottage, or lose the opportunity of listening without intermission to the melody of the nightingale, which he believed was be heard from every bramble, and which he did not fail to mention as a very important part of the happiness of a country life.

The opening of Johnson's next paragraph puts all this into its proper context:

While this scheme was ripening, his friends directed him to take a lodging in the liberties of the Fleet, that he might be secure from his creditors. . . .

The *Life of Savage* stands thus as Johnson's archetypal Portrait of the Artist. "We are perpetually moralists, but we are geometricians only by chance": we are perpetually men, but writers only by accident. Despite his livelier powers of fancy, essentially the life of the writer will body forth the life of man in general. Writers' frustrations and disappointments will be the normal human ones, differing only in being somewhat brisker, as well as being articulated more formally and published more permanently.

It is the pre-eminence of delusion and energetic self-destruction in human affairs that is the great theme of the *Lives*. Each Life is a study less of a literary man and his works than of the symptoms and effects of a uniquely human ailment. Being men, writers are useful examples of the "unnumbered suppliants" who "crowd preferment's gate" in *The Vanity of Human Wishes*:

> They mount, they shine, evaporate, and fall.

Very like this action is the dynamics of ultimate literary failure among writers who begin in success. As he puts it in *Rambler* 21,

There is a general succession of events in which contraries are produced by periodical vicissitudes: labor and care are rewarded with success, success produces confidence, confidence relaxes industry, and negligence ruins that reputation which accuracy had raised.

It is not a bad description of, say, Hemingway's career. "The pride of wit and knowledge," he writes in *Rambler* 6, "is often mortified by finding that they confer no security against the common errors which mislead the weakest and meanest of mankind." The reason why literary careers are likely to resemble tragi-comedies runs deeper than the peculiar kind of vanity, the special delusion of power, and the extraordinary capacity for making pleasing images of the future that attend the life of writing. As Arieh Sachs declares,

The soul and the will are infinite, the objectifications of will in the temporal flow of life finite, and that is why life is inherently unsatisfactory—not merely because of some contingent misery or special misfortune.[9]

While busy for four years attending to the ironies in the lives and pretensions of the literary Great and Little, in his off hours Johnson was reading one of his favorite works, Suetonius' *Lives of the Caesars*. In the fall of 1777, when starting to work, he was reading Suetonius' Lives of Galba, Otho, and Vitellius. And from his recurring references to Suetonius' *Life of Caligula* we can deduce that he had it by heart. What Suetonius offers, among other things, is an exhibition of triumphant auctorial control: the most outrageous events, the most outlandish human actions, are retailed with a cool detachment which avoids cynicism only by the speaker's awareness that being human, he is deeply implicated in the follies he is depicting.

Suetonius' cool treatment of the irony of hope is the sort of thing that Johnson is clearly unable to resist imitating. The auspicious accession of Caligula, the monster-to-be, is rendered this way:

Caligula's accession seemed to the Roman people—one might almost say, to the world—like a dream come true. . . . When he escorted Tiberius's catafalque from Misenum to Rome he was, of course, dressed in mourning, but a dense crowd greeted him uproariously with altars, sacrifices, torches, and such endearments as 'star,' 'chicken,' 'baby,' and 'pet.'

But the enthusiastic populace soon wakened from this dream of hope to find itself saddled with a moral monster adept at Sick Humor:

Often [Caligula] would send for men whom he had secretly killed, as though they were still alive, and remark offhandedly a few days later that they must have committed suicide.

. . .

During gladiatorial shows he would have the canopies removed during the hottest time of the day and forbid anyone to leave; . . . or stage comic duels between respectable householders who happened to be physically disabled in some way or other.

. . .

Caligula made parents attend their sons' executions, and when one father excused himself on grounds of ill-health, provided a litter for him.

. . .

Once, while presiding appropriately robed at the sacrificial altar, he swung his mallet, as if at the victim, but instead felled the assistant priest.

If Suetonius' *Life of Caligula* exposes the irony of hope, the *Life of Galba* offers Johnson a model for the career of the archetypal loser, like "Poor Shenstone," "Poor Prior," or even "Poor Collins." Fearful of disaster, Galba rushes to the altars at Tusculum,

having sent outriders ahead to prepare sacrifices; but when he arrived, [he] found only warm ashes on the altar and an old black-cloaked fellow offering incense in a glass bowl, and wine in an earthenware cup—whereas decency called for a white-robed boy with a chalice and thurible of precious metal. It was noticed too that while he was sacrificing on the kalends of January his garland fell off, and that the sacred chickens flew away when he went to read the auspices.

Poor Galba! But his successor Vitellius is even less fortunate. Suetonius depicts his difficulties with a positively Johnsonian humor:

As soon as news reached Germany of Galba's murder, Vitellius put his affairs in order, splitting the army into two divisions, one of which stayed with him. He sent the other against Otho, and it was at once granted a lucky augury: an eagle, swooping down from the right hand, hovered over the standards and flew slowly ahead of the advancing columns. However, when he marched off with the second division, several equestrian statues raised in his honor collapsed because the horses' legs were weakly made.

It is all a little like the comic downfall of the Flying-Machine Projector. Deep in Suetonius as he was during the period of the *Lives*, Johnson instinctively added a mock-heroic dimension to certain important passages. His treatment of the death of Pope is a good example. Like Vitellius, Pope indulged the vice of gluttony. Suetonius says that

Vitellius paid no attention to place or time in satisfying his remarkable appetite. While a sacrifice was in progress, he thought nothing of snatching lumps of meat or cake off the altar . . . and bolting them down.

Pope, says Johnson,

was too indulgent to his appetite: . . . at the intervals of the table, [he] amused himself with biscuits and dry conserves. If he sat down to a variety of dishes, he would oppress his stomach with repletion, and though he seemed angry when a dram was offered him, did not forbear to drink it. . . . The death of great men is not always proportioned to the luster of their lives. Hannibal, says Juvenal, did not perish by a javelin or a sword: the slaughters of Cannae were revenged by a ring. The death of Pope was imputed by some of his friends to a silver saucepan, in which it was his delight to heat potted lampreys.

If we turn to the *Life of Dryden* we can appreciate how little interested in mere biographical fact Johnson is. Although highly skeptical of its authenticity, calling it "a wild story . . . by a writer of I know not what credit," Johnson carefully includes an anonymous account of Dryden's funeral which tells us nothing about Dryden but which depicts his funeral in quite the mode of ghoulish farce. We are told how, through a series of ludicrous misapprehensions, the arrangements degenerated from the quiet private service desired by Dryden's widow, Lady Elizabeth, into a scandalously delayed, "tumultuary," and "confused" brouhaha. The cause of it all was the drunken young Lord Jefferies, one of Dryden's less stable admirers, who, discovering that a relatively modest private funeral had been arranged, interrupted the proceedings by announcing that he would give Dryden a grandiose service more appropriate for the greatest poet of the age. He waited upon the prostrate Lady Elizabeth with this scheme. When she refused his offer,

he fell on his knees, vowing never to rise till his request was granted. The rest of the company, by his desire, kneeled also; she, being naturally of a timorous disposition, and then under a sudden surprise, fainted away. As soon as she recovered her speech she cried, 'No, no!' 'Enough, gentlemen,' replied he, 'my lady is very good, she says, "Go, go!"' She repeated her former words with all her strength; but alas, in vain; her feeble voice was lost in their acclamations of joy; and Lord Jefferies ordered the hearsemen to carry the corpse to Russell's, an undertaker in Cheapside, and leave it there till he sent orders for the embalmment, which, he added, should be after the royal manner.

When Russell, "after three days' expectance of orders for embalmment," asked Lord Jefferies what he was to do, Jefferies, now sober, "turned it off with an ill-natured jest, saying those who observed the orders of a drunken frolic deserved no better; that he remembered nothing at all of it; and that he might do what he pleased with the corpse." Things were now moving swiftly:

The season was very hot, the deceased had lived high and fast, and, being corpulent and abounding with gross humors, grew very offensive.

Dr. Samuel Garth finally intervened and had the corpse removed to the premises of the College of Physicians. At the same time he proposed a funeral by subscription, followed by interment at Westminster Abbey. Three weeks after Dryden's death the great day arrived:

Dr. Garth pronounced a fine Latin oration over the corpse at the college; but the audience being numerous and the room large, it was requisite that the orator should be elevated that he might be heard; but, as it unluckily happened, there was nothing at hand but an old beer barrel, which the Doctor with much good-nature mounted; and, in the midst of his oration, beating time to the accent with his foot, the head broke in and his feet sunk to the bottom, which occasioned the malicious report of his enemies that he was turned Tub-Preacher.

Finally, the procession began to move from the College to the Abbey,

—but good God! in what disorder. . . . At last the corpse arrived at the Abbey, which was all unlighted. No organ played, no anthem sung; only two of the singing boys preceded the corpse, who sung an ode of Horace, with each a small candle in their hand. The butchers and other mob broke in like a deluge, so that only about eight or ten gentlemen could get admission, and those forced to cut the way with their drawn swords.

But we are not finished yet:

The coffin, in this disorder, was let down into Chaucer's grave, with as much confusion and as little ceremony as was possible, everyone glad to save themselves from the gentlemen's swords or the clubs of the mob.

As a result of these miscarriages, Dryden's son tried to challenge Lord Jefferies, "which his lordship hearing, left the town; and Mr. Charles [Dryden] could never have the satisfaction to meet him, though he sought it to his death with the utmost application."

This example will indicate that the *Lives* is much more than the series of critical biographies it has been taken for. One thing that makes the various Lives operate as something other than critical biographies is that their audience—Burns is typical—expected to read them with a simultaneous awareness of the genres of satire and elegy.

One of Johnson's achievements in the *Lives*, indeed, was to devise a special way of representing authorship which became a virtual tradition in succeeding centuries. Rachel Trickett is right in observing that "Isaac D'Israeli's catalog of literary misfortunes, *The Calamities of Authors* [1812–1813], . . . has something more than a purely scholarly or antiquarian interest because it was written with this [Augustan elegiac] tradition in mind, under the shadow of Johnson's *Lives*."[10] A few items from D'Israeli's index will suggest how much he has picked up from attending to Johnson's method and focus:

Barnes, Joshua, his pathetic letter descriptive of his literary calamities
Bayne, Alexander, dies of intense application
Carey, Henry, author of several of our national poems, of the words and the air of 'God Save the King' . . . etc., his miserable end
Cotgrave, Randle, falls blind in the labor of his *Dictionary*
Drake, Dr. John, a political writer, his miserable life
Drayton's national work, the *Polyolbion,* ill received, and the author greatly dejected
Howell, nearly lost his life by excessive study
Hume, his literary life how mortified with disappointments
Logan, . . . dies broken-hearted
Macdiarmid, John, died of over-study and exhaustion
Ockley, Simon, exults in prison for the leisure it affords for study
Prynne, seldom dined
Ritson, Joseph, the late poetical antiquary, carried criticism to insanity
Ritson, Isaac, a young Scotch writer, perishes by attempting to exist by the efforts of his pen
Walpole, Horace, his literary mortifications . . .

And the tradition passed from Johnson to D'Israeli—and to Gissing, in *New Grub Street*—still has abundant life in it: witness Edmund Wilson's edition of Fitzgerald's *The Crack-Up,* or John Malcolm Brinnin's *Dylan Thomas in America.*

Very few of the Lives could be accurately described even minimally as critical biographies. The *Life of Cowley* would be better described as a moral essay on the plausibility and folly of literary fads. But it would be best described as a treatise on the uniformity of human nature and on the ever-present temptation in writers to evade the consequences of their common humanity. Cowley's pastoral delusion, his imagining that happiness will attend his rural solitude at Chertsey, is presented as a biographical objectification of the Metaphysical Poets' liability to folly. Much irony in the *Life of Cowley* stems from the unsuspected distinction of Cowley's *Essays,* a part of his output he would have considered clearly inferior to his poems. For these essays Johnson reserves the highest praise, praise he has been unable to award to the poems:

No author ever kept his verse and his prose at a greater distance from each other. [In the *Essays*] his thoughts are natural, and his style has a smooth and placid equability, which has never yet obtained its due commendation. Nothing is far-sought or hard-labored; but all is easy without feebleness, and familiar without grossness.

Irony is everywhere in the *Lives*, but it is not always so gentle as in the treatment of Cowley. When Johnson comes to treat of Thomas Otway's death, the irony grows overtly farcical, and we perceive a resemblance to Suetonius' ironic way with outrageous details:

Having been compelled by his necessities to contract debts . . . he retired to a public house on Tower Hill, where he is said to have died of want; or, as it is related by one of his biographers, by swallowing, after a long fast, a piece of bread which charity had supplied.

Johnson tells the story in his own way, with an economy and pace which intensify the horror:

He went out, as is reported, almost naked in the rage of hunger, and, finding a gentleman in a neighboring coffee-house, asked him for a shilling: the gentleman gave him a guinea; and Otway going away bought a roll, and was choked with the first mouthful.

Another ironic death is Edmund Smith's. In the paragraph dealing with it Johnson manages to weave into subtle union most of his recurring moral themes: the folly of expecting rural retirement to produce a tendency to virtue or happiness; the collision between the noble acceptance of literary obligation and the foolish facts of literary hopes; and the liability of those of forceful character to the more vigorous forms of self-destruction, like the military captain in *The Vanity of Human Wishes* whose very courage and impulse to act—his "restless fire"—are what destroy him. Smith, Johnson writes, settled on the sensible scheme of writing a play about the career of Lady Jane Grey:

Having formed his plan and collected materials, he declared that a few months would complete his design; and, that he might pursue his work with less frequent avocations, he was . . . invited by Mr. George Ducket to his house at Hartham, in Wiltshire. Here he found such opportunities of indulgence as did not much forward his studies, and particularly some strong ale, too delicious to be resisted. He ate and drank till he found himself plethoric; and then resolving to ease himself by evacuation, he wrote to an apothecary in the neighborhood a prescription of a purge so forcible that the apothecary thought it his duty to delay it till he had given notice of its danger. Smith, not pleased with the contradiction of a shopman and boastful of his own knowledge, treated the notice with rude contempt, and swallowed his own medicine, which in July, 1710, brought him to the grave. He was buried at Hartham.

This is the most rhetorically important, and thus the most interesting, paragraph in the *Life of Smith*. It is a comment on the way Johnson has been read that E. L. McAdam, Jr., discussing the *Life of Smith* in his recent *Johnson and Boswell: A Survey of Their Writings*, passes over it in silence.

Ironies are embedded so deeply in the *Lives* that they become the virtual substance. Ironically, Sir John Denham's hopes for happiness in old age are blasted by lunacy. Ironically, Dryden's hopes for the Laureateship are blasted by the Revolution. Ironically, Ambrose Philips, "having purchased an annuity of four hundred pounds . . . now certainly hoped to pass some years of life in plenty and tranquillity; but his hope deceived him: he was struck with a palsy. . . ."

Writers are conveniently representative of general humanity too in mistaking their nature and talents and expending whole careers on enterprises for which they have no bent. In the *Lives* Johnson is busy fleshing out Swift's conclusion in *The Beasts' Confession to the Priest*:

> Creatures of every kind but ours
> Well comprehend their nat'ral powers;
> While we, whom Reason ought to sway,
> Mistake our talents every day.

Thus Matthew Prior, with his undoubted talent for elegant light verse, must aspire to the pompous heroics of *Solomon*, a poem, as Johnson says, "to which he entrusted the protection of his name, and which he expected succeeding ages to regard with veneration." The poem is actually so bad that Johnson, as we recall, uses it as the quintessential model of the tedious, and indeed erects his whole theory of literary boredom upon it. Nicholas Rowe is another who ironically mistakes his talents: after a laborious lifetime earning a literary identity as a dramatist, he dies unaware that his translation of Lucan is the only thing of his that is any good. Waller is another comic and pathetic case: his folly was in expending his life and, as Johnson says, "growing illustrious in his own opinion" in writing poems whose titles speak volumes: "On a Braid of Divers Colors Woven by Four Ladies," for example, or "On a Tree Cut in Paper."

One of the most memorable ironies takes place in the *Life of Gray*. Gray labored for years at the British Museum to amass the learning he needed to write his Pindaric and Scandinavian odes: in them he invested all his awareness and all his care. And, as Johnson shows, the odes remain monuments of incoherence and insecure taste, while the local, unpretentious, conventional *Elegy*, by locating and realizing "sentiments to which every bosom returns an echo," has triumphed over time.

The irony in the *Lives* develops in countless ways. One of Johnson's methods is to display in full the pompous Latin epitaphs inscribed on the tombs and monuments of minor and temporary poets: this mode of ironic elegy is the treatment he accords the pretensions of Ambrose Philips, the Earl of Dorset, John Philips, and Matthew Prior—he displays Prior's epitaph in such a way that it occupies three pages. Another of his methods is to explode hypocrisy by swift jabs penetrating into actual if concealed human motives. For example: "[Pope's] scorn of the Great is repeated too often to be real: no man thinks much of that which he despises." Another method—we see it in the treatment of Ambrose Philips—is to dwell on injudicious because excessive praise of a poet, in the process revealing critical praise itself as a destructive weapon wielded, ironically, by friends rather than enemies: "Philips became ridiculous, without his own fault, by the absurd admiration of his friends, who decorated him with honorary garlands which the first breath of contradiction blasted."

And yet for all these ironies either overtly or covertly comical, Johnson's view of his dead poets is softened by an elegiac twilight. While he was writing the *Lives* he was engaged in outliving his friends: they were languishing and dying while he was at work. John Taylor's final illness was growing worse, and Garrick died, prompting Johnson to write to Elizabeth Aston just after having sent to the printer the Life of poor John Philips:

Futurity is uncertain. Poor David had doubtless many futurities in his head, which death has intercepted, a death, I believe, totally unexpected; he did not in his last hour seem to think his life in danger.

As he was finishing the *Lives*, in 1780, he had before him the monitory spectacle of Henry Thrale destroying himself by mad, compulsive eating. The folly of Thrale's bondage to his alimentary canal moves Johnson to write John Taylor after Thrale's death: "I have just lost one friend by his disobedience to his physician; let me not lose another."

We can appreciate Johnson's urge toward general elegy in the *Lives* by noticing how careful he is to react to the deaths of his friends in the texts of the *Lives* themselves; if no relevant occasion for elegy presents itself in a Life he is writing, he contrives one. Thus in the *Life of Edmund Smith* he manages to memorialize his early benefactor Gilbert Walmesley and to use his memory of Walmesley as a means for commemorating Dr. Robert James and—with due irony—Garrick as well:

At [Walmesley's] table I enjoyed many cheerful and instructive hours, with companions such as are not often found: with one who has lengthened, and one who has gladdened life; with Dr. James, whose skill in physic will be long remembered; and with David Garrick, whom I hoped to have gratified with this character of our common friend. But what are the hopes of man! I am disappointed by that stroke of death which has eclipsed the gaiety of nations and impoverished the public stock of harmless pleasure.

The elegiac action here is almost as formal and calculated as that undertaken in Yeats's *In Memory of Major Robert Gregory*:

> I'll name the friends that cannot sup with us . . .
> All, all are in my thoughts tonight being dead.

Again, in the *Life of Thomas Parnell*, Johnson manages to perform an elegiac gesture in the direction of Oliver Goldsmith, dead three years before Johnson began the *Lives*. He begins:

> The Life of Dr. Parnell is a task which I should very willingly decline, since it has been lately written by Goldsmith, a man of such variety of powers and such felicity of performance that he always seemed to do best that which he was doing. . . .
> What such an author has told, who would tell again? I have made an abstract from his larger narrative; and have this gratification from my attempt, that it gives me an opportunity of paying tribute to the memory of Goldsmith.

And he goes on to quote a Homeric formulaic tag which translates: "[Tribute] is the due of the dead."

In addition to this elegiac tendency in the *Lives*, there is even something like the practice of epitaph itself, as we see in Johnson's ritual urge to name and mark his poets' early teachers. As he says near the beginning of the *Life of Addison*, "Not to name the school or the masters of men illustrious for literature is a kind of historical fraud, by which honest fame is injuriously diminished." Not to name them is as indecent as to leave a Christian grave unmarked.

In the career of every writer there is one moment when it will seem appropriate for him to look back and assess what he has done in relation to a tradition, to consider what his career has meant as one of countless similar careers. This moment, which necessarily comes late, is generally attended by intimations of mortality adding both urgency and irony to a writer's consciousness of what he has been doing. *Under Ben Bulben* marks this moment in Yeats's career; *East Coker* in Eliot's. Notice the self-consciousness about technique here in Eliot's poem:

> That was a way of putting it—not very satisfactory:
> A periphrastic study in a worn-out poetical fashion,
> Leaving one still with the intolerable wrestle
> With words and meanings. . . .

And then immediately a turn to the ironies of aging:

> It was not (to start again) what one had expected.
> What was to be the value of the long looked forward to,
> Long hoped for calm, the autumnal serenity
> And the wisdom of age? Had they deceived us
> Or deceived themselves, the quiet-voiced elders,
> Bequeathing us merely a receipt for deceit?
> The serenity only a deliberate hebetude,
> The wisdom only the knowledge of dead secrets. . . .

And finally the full confrontation of the speaker's own circumstances:

> O dark dark dark. They all go into the dark,
> The vacant interstellar spaces, the vacant into the vacant,
> The captains, merchant bankers, eminent men of letters, . . .

At a certain age, to write about literature at all is inevitably to confront the question of the relation of art to human mortality and limitation. This is what Johnson's *Lives of the Poets* is about.

Which is to say that one of the reasons the *Lives* turns in the direction of both elegy and epitaph is that it reflects Johnson's consciousness that he is bringing to a close his own life of writing. As he wrote Mrs. Thrale in 1776 about the death of her nine-year-old son Harry, "He is gone, and we are going." Mrs. Thrale herself, a bright reader, sensed the quantum of elegy and perceived the autobiographical thrust in the *Lives*. Just after reading it, she writes to Johnson about the decline of John Perkins, one of the purchasers of Thrale's brewery:

Perkins is ill, not ill but broken somehow; and looking like a man that would not live two years: . . .

She then turns to address Johnson affectionately, connecting him both with the ailing Perkins and with the whole company of dead poets, and rendering her point with the kind of terrible irony available from her recent reading of the *Lives*:

Dear Heart! how shocking it is, that if the ship does with hard fighting weather the storm, it is at last almost sure to sink in the harbor. But so all the poets' lives say, and though Perkins has very little poet's stuff in him, I trow—yet he will die, just like the best of them.

And there are touching and instructive letters from Johnson to Mrs. Thrale while he is at work. While trying hard to discriminate the artistic virtues of Sir Richard Blackmore, the failed epic poet whose *Creation, A Philosophical Poem* Johnson insisted on adding to the collection because of its usefulness as doctrine, he writes Mrs. Thrale:

I wish the work was over, and I was at liberty. And what would I do if I was at liberty? Would I go to see Mrs. Aston and Mrs. Porter, and see the old places, and sigh to find that my old friends are gone?

Better perhaps to be miserably busy and hag-ridden by deadlines than hag-ridden by an unencumbered mind and thus by retrospective shame:

Would I recall plans of life which I never brought into practice, and hopes of excellence which I once presumed, and never have attained? Would I compare what I now am with what I once expected to have been? Is it reasonable to wish for suggestions of shame, and opportunities of sorrow? I will end my letter and go to Blackmore's Life. . . .

Johnson's literary environment offered no paradigm for open autobiography or confession. We can find some buried autobiography in the *Rambler* and the *Idler*, to be sure; but one of our losses is, as Boswell reports, the "two quarto volumes containing a full, fair, and most particular account of his own life, from his earliest recollection," which he kept secretly and burnt just before his death. Boswell in a pert mood once acknowledged to Johnson that he had been tempted simply to carry these volumes off and never come back. "Upon my inquiring how this would have affected him, 'Sir,' said he, 'I believe I should have gone mad.'" In the absence of a public literary convention for intimate disclosure, Johnson's understanding of the ultimate irony of his own career, his sense of his own defeat by time, took refuge in the genre of "critical biography." But we must not mistake what he is doing. There is abundant autobiographical meaning in the *Lives* but it is not really so singular and personal as it might appear. To the very end he remains faithful to his root conception of writing as an elucidation of general human nature. The *Lives of the Poets* is finally rhetorical: it is the way it is because it is what its writer thinks the reader needs to remind him of that central humanity in himself—a central humanity which much in life tempts him to forget but which, if he is wise, he will be ceaselessly engaged in reviving and reanimating. It is as if Johnson were writing the *Lives* to illustrate his own observation about Shakespeare's characters: "In the writings of other poets a character is too often an individual; in those of Shakespeare it is commonly a species." For all the variety of satiric or compassionate detail with which Johnson discriminates his characters as they play out their literary careers, they are all given enough in common to merge into something like a species. Johnson's species in the *Lives* is the writer as representative man, obliged by his frailty to imitate and to adhere to genres and conventions which he has not devised; tormented by the hunger of imagination only to be always defeated of his hopes; and finally carried away by the very stream of time which it has been his ironic ambition to shape, and by shaping, to arrest.

Notes

Preface

1. *Publishers' Weekly*, March 17, 1969, p. 28.

2. "The Manner of Proceeding in Certain Eighteenth- and Early Nineteenth-Century Poems," *Augustan Studies* (London, 1961), pp. 111–146.

I—"A Life Radically Wretched"

Throughout this chapter I am deeply indebted to James L. Clifford's *Young Samuel Johnson* (London, 1955; reprinted [Mercury Books] 1962); and to Donald J. Greene's *The Politics of Samuel Johnson* (New Haven, 1960).

1. *Young Samuel Johnson* (1962), p. 62.

2. Quoted by James L. Clifford, *Hester Lynch Piozzi* (*Mrs. Thrale*) (2nd. ed., Oxford, 1968), p. 56.

3. *Young Samuel Johnson,* p. 91.

4. *Partisan Review,* XXXI (Fall, 1964), p. 525.

5. *Politics of Samuel Johnson,* p. 61.

6. "To Criticize the Critic," *Encounter,* XXXIII (November, 1969), p. 76.

7. *A B C of Reading* (London, 1934), p. 13.

8. *Politics of Samuel Johnson,* p. 306.

9. See Katharine Balderston's essay "Johnson's Vile Melancholy" in F. W. Hilles, ed., *The Age of Johnson: Essays Presented to Chauncey Brewster Tinker* (New Haven, 1949), pp. 3–14.

2—*The Facts of Writing and the Johnsonian Senses of Literature*

1. *James Joyce's Ulysses* (London, 1930; reprinted [Peregrine Books] 1963), p. 213, n. 1.

2. *Visible Words: A Study of Inscriptions in and as Books and Works of Art* (Cambridge, 1969), p. 2.

3. *Anatomy of Criticism* (Princeton, 1957), p. 97.

4. Review of John Wilson Croker's edition of Boswell's *Life of Johnson* in the *Edinburgh Review,* September, 1831. I have altered the order of Macaulay's strictures.

5. *Samuel Johnson* (London, 1955), p. vii.

6. *Johnson: Prose and Poetry* (London, 1957), p. 9.

7. *Spectator,* February 14, 1970, p. 210.

8. "The Double Tradition of Dr. Johnson," *ELH: A Journal of English Literary History,* XVIII (June, 1951), pp. 90–106.

9. " 'Pictures to the Mind': Johnson and Imagery," in *Johnson, Boswell, and Their Circle: Essays Presented to Lawrence Fitzroy Powell* (Oxford, 1965), p. 156.

10. *Johnson Agonistes and Other Essays* (Cambridge, 1946), p. 8.

11. Marshall Waingrow, ed., *The Correspondence and Other Papers of James Boswell relating to the Making of the Life of Johnson* (New York, 1969), p. 249.

12. E. L. McAdam, Jr., *Dr. Johnson and the English Law* (Syracuse, 1951), pp. 162–63.

13. *Samuel Johnson's Literary Criticism* (Minneapolis, 1952), p. 48.

14. Introduction to Johnson's *Lives of the Poets* (Everyman edition, 2 vols.: London, 1925), p. ix. Reprinted unchanged in 1946.

15. *Samuel Johnson: A Layman's Faith* (Madison, 1964), p. 196.

16. Waingrow, ed., *Correspondence,* p. 31.

3—*The Force of Genre*

1. First published in *Accent* (Spring, 1946); rewritten as part of *The Gates of Horn: A Study of Five French Realists* (New York, 1963).

2. *Ibid.,* pp. 22–3.

3. Review of James W. Mavor, Jr., *Voyage to Atlantis,* in *New York Review of Books,* May 22, 1969, p. 39. See also M. I. Finley, "Digging the Trojans," *New York Review of Books,* August 3, 1967, pp. 32–4.

4. See Leonard Cottrell, *The Bull of Minos* (London, 1953), p. 72.

5. *Samuel Johnson and His Times* (London, 1962), p. 29.

6. *Samuel Johnson's Parliamentary Reporting* (Berkeley and Los Angeles, 1953), p. 109.

7. *Samuel Johnson the Moralist* (Cambridge, Mass., 1961), p. ix.

8. In *Lectures on the English Comic Writers* (1819).

9. *Samuel Johnson and His Times,* p. 91.

10. (New York, 1955), pp. 93–4.

11. *Encounter,* XXVI (January, 1966), p. 36.

12. *James Boswell: The Earlier Years* (London, 1966), p. 129.

4—*The Sacrament of Authorship*

1. *The Life of the Drama* (London, 1965), p. 111.

2. *Hugh Dormer's Diaries* (London, 1947), pp. 131–2.

3. *The Prose Style of Samuel Johnson* (New Haven, 1941), p. 123.

4. In *Movie-Going and Other Poems* (New York, 1962).

5—*Writing as Imitation*

1. Franz Mautner and Henry Hatfield, trans. and eds., [*Georg Christoph*] *Lichtenberg: Aphorisms and Letters* (London, 1969), p. 26.

2. *The Well-Tempered Critic* (Bloomington, 1963), pp. 81–2.

3. *Art and Illusion* (rev. ed., New York, 1961), p. 376.

4. Waingrow, ed., *Correspondence,* p. 235.

5. James H. Sledd and Gwin J. Kolb, *Dr. Johnson's Dictionary: Essays in the Biography of a Book* (Chicago, 1955), p. 103.

6. *Times Literary Supplement,* March 22, 1963, p. 208.

7. *Listener,* December 18, 1969, p. 866.

8. *Samuel Johnson in Grub Street* (Providence, 1957), p. 47.

9. *The Language of the Book of Common Prayer* (London, 1965), p. 34.

10. *Johnsonian and Other Essays and Reviews* (Oxford, 1953), pp. 180–1.

11. *Samuel Johnson and His Times*, p. 108.

12. *Yale Edition of the Works of Samuel Johnson* (New Haven, 1958–), III, xxxii.

13. *Validity in Interpretation* (New Haven, 1967), p. 104.

14. *Listener*, December 25, 1969, p. 890.

15. Nigel Nicolson, ed. (New York, 1967), II, 447–8.

16. *Anatomy of Criticism*, pp. 96–7.

17. *Validity in Interpretation*, p. 105.

18. Allen Tate, ed., *T. S. Eliot: The Man and His Work* (London, 1967), pp. 118–9.

19. *Anatomy of Criticism*, p. 247.

6—*"The Anxious Employment of a Periodical Writer"*

1. *Samuel Johnson the Moralist*, pp. 33–4.

2. *The Achievement of Samuel Johnson* (New York, 1955), p. 103.

3. *Ibid.*, p. 72.

4. James L. Clifford, "Some Problems of Johnson's Obscure Middle Years," in *Johnson, Boswell, and Their Circle*, p. 107. Clifford is alluding to the research of Professor R. W. Wiles.

5. *Ibid.*, pp. 107–8.

6. *Doctor Johnson and His World* (London, 1968), p. 30.

7. Violet Bonham Carter, *Winston Churchill as I Knew Him* (London, 1967), pp. 78–9.

7—*Writing a Dictionary*

In this chapter I depend heavily on Sledd and Kolb's expert *Dr. Johnson's Dictionary: Essays in the Biography of a Book*, as well as on Clifford's *Young Samuel Johnson*.

1. "The Naked Science of Language, 1747–1786," in Howard Anderson and John S. Shea, eds., *Studies in Criticism and Aesthetics, 1660–1800: Essays in Honor of Samuel Holt Monk* (Minneapolis, 1967), pp. 268–9; p. 274.

2. "Dr. Johnson and the Literature of Experience," in Magdi Wahba, ed., *Johnsonian Studies* (Cairo, 1962), p. 19.

3. *Samuel Johnson: Selected Writings* (Baltimore, 1968), p. 246 n.

4. *The Evolution of English Lexicography* (Oxford, 1900), p. 42.

5. Sledd and Kolb, *Dr. Johnson's Dictionary*, p. 4.

6. *Ibid.*, p. 36.

7. *Ibid.*, p. 210, n. 74.

8. "Johnson's Dictionary," in Frederick W. Hilles, ed., *New Light on Dr. Johnson* (New Haven, 1959), pp. 69–71.

9. *Ibid.*, p. 79.

10. Sledd and Kolb, *Dr. Johnson's Dictionary*, p. 135.

11. *Ibid.*, pp. 19–25.

12. *Ibid.*, p. 181.

13. *Samuel Johnson*, p. 81.

8—"The Choice of Life"

1. *A Bibliography of Samuel Johnson* (Oxford, 1915), p. 86.

2. *Johnson and Boswell: A Survey of Their Writings* (Boston, 1969), p. 50.

3. S. T. Fisher, "Johnson on Flying," in *Times Literary Supplement*, November 4, 1965, p. 988.

4. Joseph Wood Krutch, *Samuel Johnson* (New York, 1944), pp. 174–5.

5. *Rasselas* (Oxford, 1887), p. 165.

6. "Johnson," in Boris Ford, ed., *From Dryden to Johnson* (Baltimore, 1963), pp. 412–13.

7. "T. S. Eliot and the Literature of Waste," *New Republic,* May 20, 1967, p. 23.

8. Waingrow, ed., *Correspondence*, p. 251

9. *Samuel Johnson and His Times*, p. 56.

10. "Time in *Rasselas*," in Magdi Wahba, ed., *Bicentenary Essays on Rasselas* (Cairo, 1959), p. 97.

9—The Irony of Literary Careers

1. "Johnson as Critic and Poet" (1944), *On Poetry and Poets* (London, 1957), p. 162.

2. Waingrow, ed., *Correspondence*, p. 192.

3. George Watson, *The Literary Critics* (Baltimore, 1962), p. 95.

4. William R. Keast, "Johnson and 'Cibber's' *Lives of the Poets, 1753*," in *Eighteenth-Century English Literature: Essays in Honor of Alan Dugald McKillop* (Chicago, 1963), pp. 89–101.

5. *Achievement of Samuel Johnson*, p. 185.

6. *Biography in the Hands of Walton, Johnson, and Boswell* (Los Angeles, 1966), p. 19.

7. *Times Literary Supplement*, May 20, 1955, p. 276.

8. S. C. Roberts, trans., *Aspects of Biography* (Cambridge, 1929), p. 111.

9. *Passionate Intelligence: Imagination and Reason in the Work of Samuel Johnson* (Baltimore, 1967), p. 3.

10. *The Honest Muse: A Study in Augustan Verse* (Oxford, 1967), pp. 244–5.

Sources

I. Johnson's Writings

1. EDITIONS

The Works of Samuel Johnson, LL.D. (11 vols., Oxford, 1825).

The Yale Edition of the Works of Samuel Johnson, Allen T. Hazen and John H. Middendorf, eds. (New Haven, 1958–   ). In progress.

      I. *Diaries, Prayers, and Annals,* E. L. McAdam, Jr., ed., with Donald and Mary Hyde.

      II. *The Idler and The Adventurer,* W. J. Bate, John M. Bullitt, and L. F. Powell, eds.

      III, IV, V. *The Rambler,* W. J. Bate and Albrecht B. Strauss, eds.

      VI. *Poems,* E. L. McAdam, Jr., ed., with George Milne.

      VII, VIII. *Johnson on Shakespeare,* Arthur Sherbo, ed., Introduction by Bertrand H. Bronson.

Rasselas, George Birkbeck Hill, ed. (Oxford, 1887).

Lives of the English Poets, George Birkbeck Hill, ed. (3 vols., Oxford, 1905).

Journey to the Western Islands of Scotland, R. W. Chapman, ed. (Oxford, 1924).

Samuel Johnson's Prefaces and Dedications, Allen T. Hazen, ed. (New Haven, 1937).

The Poems of Samuel Johnson, D. Nichol Smith and E. L. McAdam, Jr., eds. (Oxford, 1941).

The Letters of Samuel Johnson, with Mrs. Thrale's Genuine Letters to Him, R. W. Chapman, ed. (3 vols., Oxford, 1952).

A Dictionary of the English Language (1755), (facsimile, 2 vols., New York, 1967).

2. CONVENIENT READING TEXTS AND VOLUMES OF SELECTIONS

Lives of the English Poets (2 vols., London: Everyman, 1946).

Johnson: Prose and Poetry, Mona Wilson, ed. (London: Nonesuch, 1957).

Rasselas, Poems, and Selected Prose, B. H. Bronson, ed. (New York: Rinehart, 1958).

Selected Writings, Patrick Cruttwell, ed. (Baltimore: Penguin, 1968).

II. Other Works

Addison, Joseph and Sir Richard Steele, *The Spectator,* Donald F. Bond, ed. (5 vols., Oxford, 1965).

Anon., *Dr. Samuel Johnson and His Birthplace* (Lichfield, 1933).

Balderston, Katharine, "Johnson's Vile Melancholy," in *'The Age of Johnson: Essays Presented to Chauncey Brewster Tinker,'* F. W. Hilles, ed. (New Haven, 1949).

Bate, W. J., *The Achievement of Samuel Johnson* (New York, 1955).

Bentley, Eric, *The Life of the Drama* (London, 1965).

Bloom, Edward A., *Samuel Johnson in Grub Street* (Providence, 1957).

Boothby, Sir Brooke, in Hill, ed., *Johnsonian Miscellanies.*

Boswell, James, *The Correspondence and Other Papers of James Boswell relating to the Making of the Life of Johnson,* Marshall Waingrow, ed. (New York, 1969).

——— *The Journal of a Tour to the Hebrides,* Frederick A. Pottle and Charles H. Bennett, eds. (New York, 1936).

——— *The Life of Samuel Johnson, LL.D.,* George Birkbeck Hill, ed., rev. by L. F. Powell (6 vols., Oxford, 1934–50).

———— *The Private Papers of James Boswell,* Geoffrey Scott and Frederick A. Pottle, eds. (18 vols., New York, 1928–34).

Bowles, William, in Boswell's *Life.*

Bronson, Bertrand, *Johnson Agonistes and Other Essays* (Cambridge, 1946).

Brook, Stella, *The Language of the Book of Common Prayer* (London, 1965).

Browne, E. Martin, "T. S. Eliot in the Theatre: The Director's Memories," in *T. S. Eliot: The Man and His Work,* Allen Tate, ed. (London, 1967).

Burney, Frances, in Hill, ed., *Johnsonian Miscellanies.*

Burns, Robert, *Letters of Robert Burns,* J. DeLancey Ferguson, ed. (2 vols., Oxford, 1931).

Butt, John, *Biography in the Hands of Walton, Johnson, and Boswell* (Los Angeles, 1966).

Campbell, George, *The Philosophy of Rhetoric* (London, 1776).

Carter, Violet Bonham, *Winston Churchill as I Knew Him* (London, 1967).

Chapman, R. W., *Johnsonian and Other Essays and Reviews* (Oxford, 1953).

Chesterfield, Fourth Earl of, *Miscellaneous Works of the Late Philip Dormer Stanhope, Earl of Chesterfield* (2nd ed., 4 vols., London, 1777).

Clifford, James L., *Hester Lynch Piozzi (Mrs. Thrale)* (2nd ed., Oxford, 1968).

———— "Some Problems of Johnson's Obscure Middle Years," in *Johnson, Boswell, and Their Circle: Essays Presented to Lawrence Fitzroy Powell,* Mary Lascelles and others, eds. (Oxford, 1965).

———— *Young Samuel Johnson* (London, 1955; 1962).

Cottrell, Leonard, *The Bull of Minos* (London, 1953).

Courtney, William Prideaux and David Nichol Smith, *A Bibliography of Samuel Johnson* (Oxford, 1915).

Cowper, William, *The Correspondence of William Cowper,* T. Wright, ed. (4 vols., London, 1904).

Croker, J. W., ed., *Johnsoniana, or Supplement to Boswell* (London, 1836).

D'Israeli, Isaac, *Miscellanies of Literature* (London, 1840).

Dormer, Hugh, *Hugh Dormer's Diaries* (London, 1947).

Dryden, John, *Of Dramatic Poesy and Other Critical Essays,* George Watson, ed. (2 vols., London, 1962).

Eliot, T. S., *On Poetry and Poets* (London, 1957).

Elledge, Scott, "The Naked Science of Language, 1747–1786," in *Studies in Criticism and Aesthetics, 1660–1800: Essays in Honor of Samuel Holt Monk*, Howard Anderson and John S. Shea, eds. (Minneapolis, 1967).

Frye, Northrop, *Anatomy of Criticism* (Princeton, 1957).

—— *The Well-Tempered Critic* (Bloomington, 1963).

Gilbert, Stuart, *James Joyce's Ulysses* (London, 1930; 1963).

Gombrich, E. H., *Art and Illusion* (rev. ed., New York, 1961).

Greene, Donald J., " 'Pictures to the Mind': Johnson and Imagery," in *Johnson, Boswell, and Their Circle: Essays Presented to Lawrence Fitzroy Powell* (Oxford, 1965).

—— *The Politics of Samuel Johnson* (New Haven, 1960).

Hagstrum, Jean, *Samuel Johnson's Literary Criticism* (Minneapolis, 1952).

Halliday, F. E., *Dr. Johnson and His World* (London, 1968).

Hawkins, Sir John, *The Life of Samuel Johnson, LL.D.* (1787), Bertram H. Davis, ed. and abridg. (New York, 1962).

Hazlitt, William, *Lectures on the English Comic Writers* (London, 1819).

Hill, George Birkbeck, ed., *Johnsonian Miscellanies* (2 vols., Oxford, 1897).

Hirsch, E. D., *Validity in Interpretation* (New Haven, 1967).

Hobbes, Thomas, *Leviathan,* M. Oakeshott, ed. (Oxford, 1947).

Hodgart, M. J. C., *Samuel Johnson and His Times* (London, 1962).

Hollander, John, *Movie-Going and Other Poems* (New York, 1962).

Hoover, Benjamin B., *Samuel Johnson's Parliamentary Reporting* (Berkeley and Los Angeles, 1953).

Horne, George, Bishop of Norwich, in Croker, ed., *Johnsoniana.*

Humphreys, A. R., "Johnson," in *From Dryden to Johnson,* Boris Ford, ed. (Baltimore, 1963).

Joyce, Michael, *Samuel Johnson* (London, 1855).

Keast, William R., "Johnson and 'Cibber's' *Lives of the Poets,* 1753," in *Eighteenth-Century English Literature: Essays in Honor of Alan Dugald McKillop,* Carroll Camden, ed. (Chicago, 1963).

Krutch, Joseph Wood, *Samuel Johnson* (New York, 1944).

Levin, Harry, *The Gates of Horn: A Study of Five French Realists* (New York, 1963).

Lichtenberg, Georg Christoph, *Lichtenberg: Aphorisms and Letters,* Franz Mautner and Henry Hatfield, trans. and eds. (London, 1969).

Macaulay, Thomas Babington, "Johnson," in *Critical and Historical Essays,* F. C. Montague, ed. (3 vols., London, 1903).

Maurois, André, *Aspects of Biography*, S. C. Roberts, trans. (Cambridge, 1929).

McAdam, Jr., E. L., *Dr. Johnson and the English Law* (Syracuse, 1951).

———— *Johnson and Boswell: A Survey of Their Writings* (Boston, 1969).

Murphy, Arthur, in Hill, ed., *Johnsonian Miscellanies.*

Murray, Sir James, *The Evolution of English Lexicography* (Oxford, 1900).

Nelson, Robert, *A Companion for the Festivals and Fasts of the Church of England, with Collects and Prayers for Each Solemnity* (1703) (London, 1845).

Nichols, John, in Hill, ed., *Johnsonian Miscellanies.*

Nicolson, Harold, *Diaries and Letters*, Nigel Nicolson, ed. (3 vols., New York, 1966–68).

Northcote, James, in Croker, ed., *Johnsoniana.*

Parker, the Rev. Mr., in Hill, ed., *Johnsonian Miscellanies.*

Pottle, Frederick A., *James Boswell: The Earlier Years* (London, 1966).

Pound, Ezra, *A B C of Reading* (London, 1934).

Quinlan, Maurice, *Samuel Johnson: A Layman's Faith* (Madison, 1964).

Reynolds, Frances, in Hill, ed., *Johnsonian Miscellanies.*

Reynolds, Sir Joshua, *Discourses on Art*, R. R. Wark, ed. (San Marino, Calif., 1959).

———— *Portraits by Sir Joshua Reynolds*, Frederick W. Hilles, ed. (New York, 1952).

Sachs, Arieh, *Passionate Intelligence: Imagination and Reason in the Work of Samuel Johnson* (Baltimore, 1967).

Sledd, James H. and Gwin J. Kolb, *Dr. Johnson's Dictionary: Essays in the Biography of a Book* (Chicago, 1955).

Smith, Adam, in Hill, ed., *Johnsonian Miscellanies.*

Smollett, Tobias, *Letters of Tobias Smollett*, E. S. Noyes, ed. (Cambridge, Mass., 1926).

Sparrow, John, *Visible Words: A Study of Inscriptions in and as Books and Works of Art* (Cambridge, 1969).

Suetonius, *The Twelve Caesars*, Robert Graves, trans. (London, 1962).

Swift, Jonathan, "A Proposal for Correcting, Improving, and Ascertaining the English Tongue," in *The Prose Works of Jonathan Swift*, Herbert Davis, ed. (13 vols., Oxford, 1957–59).

Thrale, Hester Lynch, *Anecdotes of the Late Samuel Johnson, LL.D.* (1786), S. C. Roberts, ed. (Cambridge, 1932).

———— *The French Journals of Mrs. Thrale and Dr. Johnson,* Moses Tyson and Henry Guppy, eds. (Manchester, 1932).

———— *Thraliana*, Katherine Balderston, ed. (2nd ed., 2 vols., Oxford, 1951).

Tillotson, Geoffrey, *Augustan Studies* (London, 1961).

———— "Time in *Rasselas*," in *Bicentenary Essays on Rasselas,* Magdi Wahba, ed. (Cairo, 1959).

Trickett, Rachel, *The Honest Muse: A Study in Augustan Verse* (Oxford, 1967).

Tyers, Thomas, in Hill, ed., *Johnsonian Miscellanies.*

Voitle, Robert, *Samuel Johnson the Moralist* (Cambridge, Mass., 1961).

Voltaire, *Lettres Philosophiques*, G. Lanson, ed. (2 vols., Paris, 1924).

Walpole, Horace, *Horace Walpole's Correspondence with William Mason,* W. S. Lewis, Grover Cronin, Jr., and Charles H. Bennett, eds. (2 vols., New Haven, 1955).

Watson, George, *The Literary Critics* (Baltimore, 1962).

Watt, Ian, "Dr. Johnson and the Literature of Experience," in *Johnsonian Studies,* Magdi Wahba, ed. (Cairo, 1962).

Wimsatt, W. K., "Johnson's Dictionary," in *New Light on Dr. Johnson*, Frederick W. Hilles, ed. (New Haven, 1959).

———— *The Prose Style of Samuel Johnson* (New Haven, 1941).

Index